TIME and FREE WILL

280
175
―――
105

TIME
and FREE WILL

AN ESSAY ON THE IMMEDIATE DATA OF CONSCIOUSNESS

Henri Bergson

HARPER TORCHBOOKS The Academy Library

Harper & Row, Publishers
New York and Evanston

HARPER TORCHBOOKS / *The Academy Library*

Advisory Editor in the Humanities and Social Sciences: Benjamin Nelson.

TIME AND FREE WILL:

An Essay on the Immediate Data of Consciousness

Authorized Translation by F. L. POGSON

Originally published by
Swan Sonnenschein & Co., Ltd., London,
and The Macmillan Company, New York,
in 1910, and reprinted by arrangement
with the latter.

First HARPER TORCHBOOK edition published 1960

Printed in the United States of America

TRANSLATOR'S PREFACE

HENRI LOUIS BERGSON was born in Paris, October 18, 1859. He entered the École normale in 1878, and was admitted agrégé de philosophie in 1881 and docteur ès lettres in 1889. After holding professorships in various provincial and Parisian lycées, he became maître de conférences at the École normale supérieure in 1897, and since 1900 has been professor at the Collège de France. In 1901 he became a member of the Institute on his election to the Académie des Sciences morales et politiques.

A full list of Professor Bergson's works is given in the appended bibliography. In making the following translation of his *Essai sur les données immédiates de la conscience* I have had the great advantage of his co-operation at every stage, and the aid which he has given has been most generous and untiring. The book itself was worked out and written during the years 1883 to 1887 and was originally published in 1889. The foot-notes in the French edition contain a certain number of references to French translations of English works. In the present translation I am responsible for citing these references from the original English. This will account for the fact that editions are sometimes referred to which have appeared subsequently to 1889. I have also added fairly extensive marginal summaries and a full index.

In France the *Essai* is already in its seventh edition. Indeed, one of the most striking facts about Professor Bergson's works is the extent to which they have appealed not only to the professional philosophers, but also to the ordinary cultivated public. The method which he pursues is not the conceptual and abstract method which has been the dominant tradition in philosophy. For him reality is not to be reached by any elaborate construction of thought : it is given in immediate experience as a flux, a continuous process of becoming, to be grasped by intuition, by sympathetic insight. Concepts break up the continuous flow of reality into parts external to one another, they further the interests of language and social life and are useful primarily for practical purposes. But they give us nothing of the life and movement of reality ; rather, by substituting for this an artificial reconstruction, a patchwork of dead fragments, they lead to the difficulties which have always beset the intellectualist philosophy, and which on its premises are insoluble. Instead of attempting a solution in the intellectualist sense, Professor Bergson calls upon his readers to put these broken fragments of reality behind them, to immerse themselves in the living stream of things and to find their difficulties swept away in its resistless flow.

In the present volume Professor Bergson first deals with the intensity of conscious states. He shows that quantitative differences are applicable only to magnitudes, that is, in the last resort, to space, and that intensity in itself is purely qualitative. Passing then from the consideration of separate conscious states to their multiplicity, he finds that there are two forms of multiplicity : quantitative or discrete multiplicity involves the intuition of space, but the multiplicity of conscious states is wholly qualitative. This unfolding multiplicity constitutes duration, which is a succession without distinction, an interpenetration of elements so heterogeneous that former states can never recur. The idea of a homogeneous and measurable time is shown to be an artificial concept, formed by the intrusion of the idea of space into the realm of pure duration. Indeed, the whole of Professor Bergson's philosophy centres round his conception of *real concrete duration* and the specific *feeling* of duration which our consciousness has when it does away with convention and habit and gets back to its natural attitude. At the root of most errors in philosophy he finds a confusion between this *concrete duration* and the *abstract time* which mathematics, physics, and even language and common sense, substitute for it. Applying these results to the problem of free will, he shows that the difficulties arise from taking up one's stand *after* the act has been performed, and applying the conceptual method to it. From the point of view of the living, developing self these difficulties are shown to be illusory, and freedom, though not definable in abstract or conceptual terms, is declared to be one of the clearest facts established by observation.

It is no doubt misleading to attempt to sum up a system of philosophy in a sentence, but perhaps some part of the spirit of Professor Bergson's philosophy may be gathered from the motto which, with his permission, I have prefixed to this translation :—" If a man were to inquire of Nature the reason of her creative activity, and if she were willing to give ear and answer, she would say—' Ask me not, but understand in silence, even as I am silent and am not wont to speak.' "

F. L. POGSON.

OXFORD,
June, 1910.

AUTHOR'S PREFACE

WE necessarily express ourselves by means of words and we usually think in terms of space. That is to say, language requires us to establish between our ideas the same sharp and precise distinctions, the same discontinuity, as between material objects. This assimilation of thought to things is useful in practical life and necessary in most of the sciences. But it may be asked whether the insurmountable difficulties presented by certain philosophical problems do not arise from our placing side by side in space phenomena which do not occupy space, and whether, by merely getting rid of the clumsy symbols round which we are fighting, we might not bring the fight to an end. When an illegitimate translation of the unextended into the extended, of quality into quantity, has introduced contradiction into the very heart of the question, contradiction must, of course, recur in the answer.

The problem which I have chosen is one which is common to metaphysics and psychology, the problem of free will. What I attempt to prove is that all discussion between the determinists and their opponents implies a previous confusion of duration with extensity, of succession with simultaneity, of quality with quantity : this confusion once dispelled, we may perhaps witness the disappearance of the objections raised against free will, of the definitions given of it, and, in a certain sense, of the problem of free will itself. To prove this is the object of the third part of the present volume : the first two chapters, which treat of the conceptions of intensity and duration, have been written as an introduction to the third.

H. BERGSON.

February, 1888.

CONTENTS

CHAPTER I

THE INTENSITY OF PSYCHIC STATES

Quantitative differences applicable to magnitudes but not to intensities, 1–4 ; Attempt to estimate intensities by objective causes or atomic movements, 4–7 ; Different kinds of intensities, 7 ; Deep-seated psychic states : desire, 8, hope, 9, joy and sorrow, 10 ; Aesthetic feelings, 11–18 : grace, 12, beauty, 14–18, music, poetry, art, 15–18 ; Moral feelings, pity, 19 ; Conscious states involving physical symptoms, 20 : muscular effort, 21–26, attention and muscular tension, 27–28 ; Violent emotions, 29–31 : rage, 29, fear, 30 ; Affective sensations, 32–39 : pleasure and pain, 33–39, disgust, 36 ; Representative sensations, 39–60 : and external causes, 42, sensation of sound, 43, intensity, pitch and muscular effort, 45–6, sensations of heat and cold, 46–7, sensations of pressure and weight, 47–50, sensation of light, 50–60, photometric experiments, 52–60, Delbœuf's experiments, 56–60 ; Psychophysics, 60–72 : Weber and Fechner, 61–65, Delbœuf, 67–70, the mistake of regarding sensations as magnitudes, 70–72 ; Intensity in (1) representative, (2) affective states, intensity and multiplicity, 72–74.

pp. 1–74

CHAPTER II

THE MULTIPLICITY OF CONSCIOUS STATES
THE IDEA OF DURATION

Number and its units, 75–77, number and accompanying intuition of space, 78–85 ; Two kinds of multiplicity, of

material objects and conscious states, 85–87, impenetrability of matter, 88–89, homogeneous time and pure
duration, 90–91 ; Space and its contents, 92, empirical
theories of space, 93–94, intuition of empty homogeneous
medium peculiar to man, 95–97, time as homogeneous
medium reducible to space, 98–99 ; Duration, succession
and space, 100–104, pure duration, 105–106 ; Is duration
measurable ? 107–110 ; Is motion measurable ? 111–
112 ; Paradox of the Eleatics, 113–115 ; Duration and
simultaneity, 115–116 ; Velocity and simultaneity, 117–
119 ; Space alone homogeneous, duration and succession belong to conscious mind, 120–121 ; Two kinds of
multiplicity, qualitative and quantitative, 121–123, superficial psychic states invested with discontinuity of their
external causes, 124–126, these eliminated, real duration
is felt as a quality, 127–128 ; The two aspects of the self,
on the surface well-defined conscious states, deeper down
states which interpenetrate and form organic whole,
129–139, solidifying influence of language on sensation,
129–132, analysis distorts the feelings, 132–134, deeper
conscious states forming a part of ourselves, 134–136 ;
Problems soluble only by recourse to the concrete and
living self, 137–139.

pp. 75–139

CHAPTER III

THE ORGANIZATION OF CONSCIOUS STATES
FREE WILL

Dynamism and mechanism, 140–142 ; Two kinds of determinism, 142 ; Physical determinism, 143–155 : and
molecular theory of matter, 143, and conservation of
energy, 144, if conservation universal, physiological and
nervous phenomena necessitated, but perhaps not conscious states, 145–148, but is principle of conversation
universal ? 149, it may not apply to living beings and
conscious states, 150–154, idea of its universality depends
on confusion between concrete duration and abstract
time, 154–155 ; Psychological determinism, 155–163 :

implies associationist conception of mind, 155–158, this involves defective conception of self, 159–163 ; The free act : freedom as expressing the fundamental self, 165–170 ; Real duration and contingency, 172–182 : could our act have been different ? 172–175, geometrical representation of process of coming to a decision, 175–178, the fallacies to which it leads determinists and libertarians, 179–183 ; Real duration and prediction, 183–198 : conditions of Paul's prediction of Peter's action (1) being Peter (2) knowing already his final act, 184–189, the three fallacies involved, 190–192, astronomical prediction depends on hypothetical acceleration of movements, 193–195, duration cannot be thus accelerated, 196–198 ; Real duration and causality, 199–221 : the law " same antecedents, same consequents," 199–201, causality as regular succession, 202–203, causality as prefiguring : two kinds (1) prefiguring as mathematical pre-existence ; implies non-duration, but we *endure* and therefore may be free, 204–210, (2) prefiguring as having idea of future act to be realized by effort; does not involve determinism, 211–214, determinism results from confusing these two senses, 215–218 ; Freedom real but indefinable, 219–221.

pp. 140 221

CONCLUSION

States of self perceived through forms borrowed from external world, 223 ; Intensity as quality, 225 ; Duration as qualitative multiplicity, 226 ; No duration in the external world, 227 ; Extensity and duration must be separated, 229 ; Only the fundamental self free, 231 ; Kant's mistaken idea of time as homogeneous, 232, hence he put the self which is free outside both space and time, 233 ; Duration is heterogeneous, relation of psychic state to act is unique, and act is free, 235–240. *pp.* 222–240

BIBLIOGRAPHY 241

INDEX 251

Καὶ εἴ τις δὲ τὴν φύσιν ἔροιτο τίνος ἕνεκα ποιεῖ, εἰ τοῦ ἐρωτῶντος ἐθέλοι ἐπαίειν καὶ λέγειν, εἴποι ἄν· "ἐχρῆν μὲν μὴ ἐρωτᾶν, ἀλλὰ συνιέναι καὶ αὐτὸν σιωπῇ, ὥσπερ ἐγὼ σιωπῶ καὶ οὐκ εἴθισμαι λέγειν."

PLOTINUS.

TIME and FREE WILL

CHAPTER I

THE INTENSITY OF PSYCHIC STATES

IT is usually admitted that states of consciousness, sensations, feelings, passions, efforts, are capable of growth and diminution ; we are

Can there be quantitative differences in conscious states ? even told that a sensation can be said to be twice, thrice, four times as intense as another sensation of the same kind. This latter thesis, which is maintained by psychophysicists, we shall examine later ; but even the opponents of psychophysics do not see any harm in speaking of one sensation as being more intense than another, of one effort as being greater than another, and in thus setting up differences of quantity between purely internal states. Common sense, moreover, has not the slightest hesitation in giving its verdict on this point ; people say they are more or less warm, or more or less sad, and this distinction of more and less, even when it is carried over to the region of subjective facts and unextended objects, surprises nobody. But this involves a very obscure point and a much more important problem than is usually supposed.

When we assert that one number is greater than

1

another number or one body greater than another
body, we know very well what we mean.

Such differ-
ences applica-
ble to magni-
tudes but not
to intensities.
For in both cases we allude to unequal
spaces, as shall be shown in detail a
little further on, and we call that space
the greater which contains the other. But how
can a more intense sensation contain one of less
intensity ?   Shall we say that the first implies the
second, that we reach the sensation of higher
intensity only on condition of having first passed
through the less intense stages of the same sensation, and that in a certain sense we are concerned,
here also, with the relation of container to contained ?   This conception of intensive magnitude
seems, indeed, to be that of common sense, but we
cannot advance it as a philosophical explanation
without becoming involved in a vicious circle.
For it is beyond doubt that, in the natural series of
numbers, the later number exceeds the earlier,
but the very possibility of arranging the numbers
in ascending order arises from their having to
each other relations of container and contained,
so that we feel ourselves able to explain precisely
in what sense one is greater than the other. The
question, then, is how we succeed in forming a
series of this kind with intensities, which cannot
be superposed on each other, and by what sign
we recognize that the members of this series increase, for example, instead of diminishing : but
this always comes back to the inquiry, why an
intensity can be assimilated to a magnitude.

It is only to evade the difficulty to distinguish, as is usually done, between two species of quantity, the first <u>extensive and measurable</u>, the

Alleged distinc-
tion between
two kinds of
quantity : ex-
tensive and
intensive mag-
nitude.

second <u>intensive and not admitting of measure</u>, but of which it can neverthe- less be said that it is greater or less than another intensity. For it is recognized thereby that there is something common to these two forms of magnitude, since they are both termed magnitudes and declared to be equally capable of increase and diminution. But, from the point of view of magnitude, what can there be in common between the extensive and the intensive, the extended and the unextended ? If, in the first case, we call that which contains the other the greater quantity, why go on speak- ing of quantity and magnitude when there is no longer a container or a contained ? If a quantity can increase and diminish, if we perceive in it, so to speak, the *less* inside the *more*, is not such a quantity on this very account divisible, and thereby extended ? Is it not then a contradiction to speak of an inex- tensive quantity ? But yet common sense agrees with the philosophers in setting up a pure inten- sity as a magnitude, just as if it were something extended. And not only do we use the same word, but whether we think of a greater intensity or a greater extensity, we experience in both cases an analogous impression ; the terms " greater " and " less " call up in both cases the same idea.

If we now ask ourselves in what does this idea
consist, our consciousness still offers us the image
of a container and a contained. We picture to
ourselves, for example, a greater intensity of effort
as a greater length of thread rolled up, or as a
spring which, in unwinding, will occupy a greater
space. In the idea of intensity, and even in the
word which expresses it, we shall find the image
of a present contraction and consequently a future
expansion, the image of something virtually
extended, and, if we may say so, of a compressed
space. We are thus led to believe that we
translate the intensive into the extensive, and
that we compare two intensities, or at least
express the comparison, by the confused intuition
of a relation between two extensities. But it is
just the nature of this operation which it is difficult to determine.

The solution which occurs immediately to the
mind, once it has entered upon this path, consists
in defining the intensity of a sensation,
Attempt to dis- or of any state whatever of the ego, by
tinguish inten-
sities by objec- the number and magnitude of the objective causes.
But we judge of tive, and therefore measurable, causes
intensity with-
out knowing which have given rise to it. Doubtless,
magnitude or
nature of the a more intense sensation of light is the
cause
one which has been obtained, or is
obtainable, by means of a larger number of luminous sources, provided they be at the same distance and identical with one another. But, in
the immense majority of cases, we decide about

the intensity of the effect without even knowing
the nature of the cause, much less its magnitude :
indeed, it is the very intensity of the effect which
often leads us to venture an hypothesis as to the
number and nature of the causes, and thus to
revise the judgment of our senses, which at first
represented them as insignificant.   And it is no use
arguing that we are then comparing the actual
state of the ego with some previous state in which
the cause was perceived in its entirety at the same
time as its effect was experienced.   No doubt
this is our procedure in a fairly large number of
cases ; but we cannot then explain the differences
of intensity which we recognize between deep-
seated psychic phenomena, the cause of which is
within us and not outside.   On the other hand,
we are never so bold in judging the intensity of a
psychic state as when the subjective aspect of
the phenomenon is the only one to strike us, or
when the external cause to which we refer it does
not easily admit of measurement.   Thus it seems
evident that we experience a more intense pain
at the pulling out of a tooth than of a hair ; the
artist knows without the possibility of doubt that
the picture of a master affords him more intense
pleasure than the signboard of a shop ; and there
is not the slightest need ever to have heard of
forces of cohesion to assert that we expend less
effort in bending a steel blade than a bar of iron.
Thus the comparison of two intensities is usually
made without the least appreciation of the

number of causes, their mode of action or their extent.

There is still room, it is true, for an hypothesis of the same nature, but more subtle. We know that mechanical, and especially kinetic,

Attempt to distinguish intensities by atomic movements.

theories aim at explaining the visible and sensible properties of bodies by

But it is the sensation which is given in consciousness, and not the movement.

well defined movements of their ultimate parts, and many of us foresee the time when the intensive differences of qualities, that is to say, of our sensations, will be reduced to extensive differences between the changes taking place behind them. May it not be maintained that, without knowing these theories, we have a vague surmise of them, that behind the more intense sound we guess the presence of ampler vibrations which are propagated in the disturbed medium, and that it is with a reference to this mathematical relation, precise in itself though confusedly perceived, that we assert the higher intensity of a particular sound ? Without even going so far, could it not be laid down that every state of consciousness corresponds to a certain disturbance of the molecules and atoms of the cerebral substance, and that the intensity of a sensation measures the amplitude, the complication or the extent of these molecular movements ? This last hypothesis is at least as probable as the other, but it no more solves the problem. For, quite possibly, the intensity of a sensation bears witness to a more or less considerable work accomplished in our organism ; but it is the sensation which is given to us in consciousness, and not this mechanical work. Indeed, it is by the intensity of the sensation that we judge of the greater or less amount of work accomplished : intensity then remains, at least apparently, a property of sensation. And still the same question recurs : why do we say of a higher intensity that it is greater ? Why do we think of a greater quantity or a greater space ?

Perhaps the difficulty of the problem lies chiefly in the fact that we call by the same name, and picture to ourselves in the same way, intensities which are very different in nature, e.g. the intensity of a feeling and that of a sensation or an effort. The effort is accompanied by a muscular sensation, and the sensations themselves are connected with certain physical conditions which probably count for something in the estimate of their intensity : we have here to do with phenomena which take place on the surface of consciousness, and which are always connected, as we shall see further on, with the perception of a movement or of an external object. But certain states of the soul seem to us, rightly or wrongly, to be self-sufficient, such as deep joy cr sorrow, a reflective passion or an aesthetic emotion. Pure intensity ought to be more easily

Different kinds of intensities. (1) deep-seated psychic states (2) muscular effort. Intensity is more easily definable in the former case.

definable in these simple cases, where no extensive
element seems to be involved.   We shall see, in
fact, that it is reducible here to a certain quality
or shade which spreads over a more or less considerable mass of psychic states, or, if the expression be preferred, to the larger or smaller number
of simple states which make up the fundamental
emotion.

For example, an obscure desire gradually becomes a deep passion.   Now, you will see that
Take, for ex- the feeble intensity of this desire con-
ample, the
progress of a sisted at first in its appearing to be
desire.   isolated and, as it were, foreign to the
remainder of your inner life.   But little by little
it permeates a larger number of psychic elements,
tingeing them, so to speak, with its own colour :
and lo! your outlook on the whole of your
surroundings seems now to have changed radically.   How do you become aware of a deep
passion, once it has taken hold of you, if
not by perceiving that the same objects no
longer impress you in the same manner ?   All
your sensations and all your ideas seem to brighten
up : it is like childhood back again.   We experience something of the kind in certain dreams, in
which we do not imagine anything out of the
ordinary, and yet through which there resounds
an indescribable note of originality.   The fact is
that, the further we penetrate into the depths
of consciousness, the less right we have to treat
psychic phenomena as things which are set side

by side. When it is said that an object occupies a large space in the soul or even that it fills it entirely, we ought to understand by this simply that its image has altered the shade of a thousand perceptions or memories, and that in this sense it pervades them, although it does not itself come into view. But this wholly dynamic way of looking at things is repugnant to the reflective consciousness, because the latter delights in clean cut distinctions, which are easily expressed in words, and in things with well-defined outlines, like those which are perceived in space. It will assume then that, everything else remaining identical, such and such a desire has gone up a scale of magnitudes, as though it were permissible still to speak of magnitude where there is neither multiplicity nor space ! But just as consciousness (as will be shown later on) concentrates on a given point of the organism the increasing number of muscular contractions which take place on the surface of the body, thus converting them into one single feeling of effort, of growing intensity, so it will hypostatize under the form of a growing desire the gradual alterations which take place in the confused heap of co-existing psychic states. But that is a change of quality rather than of magnitude.

What makes hope such an intense pleasure is the fact that the future, which we dispose of to our liking, appears to us at the same time under a multitude of forms, equally attractive and equally possible. Even if the most coveted of these becomes realized, it will be necessary to give up the others, and we shall have lost a great deal. The idea of the future, pregnant with an infinity of possibilities, is thus more fruitful than the future itself, and this is why we find more charm in hope than in possession, in dreams than in reality.

Let us try to discover the nature of an increasing intensity of joy or sorrow in the exceptional cases where no physical symptom intervenes. Neither inner joy nor passion is an isolated inner state which at first occupies a corner of the soul and gradually spreads. At its lowest level it is very like a turning of our states of consciousness towards the future. Then, as if their weight were diminished by this attraction, our ideas and sensations succeed one another with greater rapidity ; our movements no longer cost us the same effort. Finally, in cases of extreme joy, our perceptions and memories become tinged with an indefinable quality, as with a kind of heat or light, so novel that now and then, as we stare at our own self, we wonder how it can really exist. Thus there are several characteristic forms of purely inward joy, all of which are successive stages corresponding to qualitative alterations in the whole of our psychic states. But the number of states which are concerned with each of these alterations is more or less considerable, and, without explicitly counting them, we know very

The emotions of joy and sorrow. Their successive stages correspond to qualitative changes in the whole of our psychic states.

well whether, for example, our joy pervades all
the impressions which we receive in the course of
the day or whether any escape from its influence.
We thus set up points of division in the interval
which separates two successive forms of joy, and
this gradual transition from one to the other makes
them appear in their turn as different intensities
of one and the same feeling, which is thus supposed to change in magnitude. It could be easily
shown that the different degrees of sorrow also
correspond to qualitative changes. Sorrow begins
by being nothing more than a facing towards the
past, an impoverishment of our sensations and
ideas, as if each of them were now contained
entirely in the little which it gives out, as if the
future were in some way stopped up. And it
ends with an impression of crushing failure, the
effect of which is that we aspire to nothingness,
while every new misfortune, by making us understand better the uselessness of the struggle,
causes us a bitter pleasure.

The aesthetic feelings offer us a still more
striking example of this progressive stepping in
of new elements, which can be detected
in the fundamental emotion and which
seem to increase its magnitude, although
in reality they do nothing more than
alter its nature. Let us consider the simplest
of them, the feeling of grace. At first it is only
the perception of a certain ease, a certain facility
in the outward movements. And as those move-

The aesthetic
feelings. Their
increasing in-
tensities·are
really differ-
ent feelings.

ments are easy which prepare the way for others, we are led to find a superior ease in the movements which can be foreseen, in the present attitudes in which future attitudes are pointed out and, as it were, prefigured. If jerky movements are wanting in grace, the reason is that each of them is self-sufficient and does not announce those which are to follow. If curves are more graceful than broken lines, the reason is that, while a curved line changes its direction at every moment, every new direction is indicated in the preceding one. Thus the perception of ease in motion passes over into the pleasure of mastering the flow of time and of holding the future in the present. A third element comes in when the graceful movements submit to a rhythm and are accompanied by music. For the rhythm and measure, by allowing us to foresee to a still greater extent the movements of the dancer, make us believe that we now control them. As we guess almost the exact attitude which the dancer is going to take, he seems to obey us when he really takes it : the regularity of the rhythm establishes a kind of communication between him and us, and the periodic returns of the measure are like so many invisible threads by means of which we set in motion this imaginary puppet. Indeed, if it stops for an instant, our hand in its impatience cannot refrain from making a movement, as though to push it, as though to replace it in the midst of this movement, the rhythm of which has taken complete possession

of our thought and will.   Thus a kind of physical
sympathy enters into the feeling of grace.   Now,
in analysing the charm of this sympathy, you will
find that it pleases you through its affinity with
moral sympathy, the idea of which it subtly suggests.   This last element, in which the others are
merged after having in a measure ushered it in,
explains the irresistible attractiveness of grace.
We could hardly make out why it affords us such
pleasure if it were nothing but a saving of effort,
as Spencer maintains.[1] But the truth is that
in anything which we call very graceful we imagine
ourselves able to detect, besides the lightness
which is a sign of mobility, some suggestion of a
possible movement towards ourselves, of a virtual
and even nascent sympathy.   It is this mobile
sympathy, always ready to offer itself, which is
just the essence of higher grace.   Thus the increasing intensities of aesthetic feeling are here
resolved into as many different feelings, each one
of which, already heralded by its predecessor,
becomes perceptible in it and then completely
eclipses it.   It is this qualitative progress which
we interpret as a change of magnitude, because
we like simple thoughts and because our language
is ill-suited to render the subtleties of psychological
analysis.
     To understand how the feeling of the beautiful
itself admits of degrees, we should have to submit

---

[1] *Essays,* (Library Edition, 1891), Vol. ii, p. 381

it to a minute analysis. Perhaps the difficulty

The feeling of
beauty : art
puts to sleep
our active
and resistant
powers and
makes us re-
sponsive to
suggestion.

which we experience in defining it is largely owing to the fact that we look upon the beauties of nature as anterior to those of art : the processes of art are thus supposed to be nothing more than means by which the artist expresses the beautiful, and the essence of the beautiful remains unexplained. But we might ask ourselves whether nature is beautiful otherwise than through meeting by chance certain processes of our art, and whether, in a certain sense, art is not prior to nature. Without even going so far, it seems more in conformity with the rules of a sound method to study the beautiful first in the works in which it has been produced by a conscious effort, and then to pass on by imperceptible steps from art to nature, which may be looked upon as an artist in its own way. By placing ourselves at this point of view, we shall perceive that the object of art is to put to sleep the active or rather resistant powers of our personality, and thus to bring us into a state of perfect responsiveness, in which we realize the idea that is suggested to us and sympathize with the feeling that is expressed. In the processes of art we shall find, in a weakened form, a refined and in some measure spiritualized version of the processes commonly used to induce the state of hypnosis. Thus, in music, the rhythm and measure suspend the normal flow of our sensations and ideas by causing our attention to swing to and

fro between fixed points, and they take hold of us
with such force that even the faintest imitation
of a groan will suffice to fill us with the utmost
sadness. If musical sounds affect us more power-
fully than the sounds of nature, the reason is that
nature confines itself to *expressing* feelings, whereas music *suggests* them to us. Whence indeed
comes the charm of poetry ? The poet is he with
whom feelings develop into images, and the images
themselves into words which translate them while
obeying the laws of rhythm. In seeing these
images pass before our eyes we in our turn experience the feeling which was, so to speak, their
emotional equivalent : but we should never realize
these images so strongly without the regular movements of the rhythm by which our soul is lulled
into self-forgetfulness, and, as in a dream, thinks
and sees with the poet. The plastic arts obtain
an effect of the same kind by the fixity which
they suddenly impose upon life, and which a
physical contagion carries over to the attention of
the spectator. While the works of ancient sculpture express faint emotions which play upon them
like a passing breath, the pale immobility of the
stone causes the feeling expressed or the movement just begun to appear as if they were fixed for
ever, absorbing our thought and our will in their
own eternity. We find in architecture, in the
very midst of this startling immobility, certain
effects analogous to those of rhythm. The sym-
metry of form, the indefinite repetition of the same

architectural motive, causes our faculty of perception to oscillate between the same and the same again, and gets rid of those customary incessant changes which in ordinary life bring us back without ceasing to the consciousness of our personality : even the faint suggestion of an idea will then be enough to make the idea fill the whole of our mind. Thus art aims at impressing feelings on us rather than expressing them ; it suggests them to us, and willingly dispenses with the imitation of nature when it finds some more efficacious means. Nature, like art, proceeds by suggestion, but does not command the resources of rhythm. It supplies the deficiency by the long comradeship, based on influences received in common by nature and by ourselves, of which the effect is that the slightest indication by nature of a feeling arouses sympathy in our minds, just as a mere gesture on the part of the hypnotist is enough to force the intended suggestion upon a subject accustomed to his control. And this sympathy is shown in particular when nature displays to us beings of *normal* proportions, so that our attention is distributed equally over all the parts of the figure without being fixed on any one of them : our perceptive faculty then finds itself lulled and soothed by this harmony, and nothing hinders any longer the free play of sympathy, which is ever ready to come forward as soon as the obstacle in its path is removed.

It follows from this analysis that the feeling of

the beautiful is no specific feeling, but that every

Stages in the aesthetic emotion. feeling experienced by us will assume an aesthetic character, provided that it has been _suggested,_ and not _caused._ It will now be understood why the aesthetic emotion seems to us to admit of degrees of intensity, and also of degrees of elevation. Sometimes the feeling which is suggested scarcely makes a break in the compact texture of psychic phenomena of which our history consists ; sometimes it draws our attention from them, but not so that they become lost to sight ; sometimes, finally, it puts itself in their place, engrosses us and completely monopolizes our soul. There are thus distinct phases in the progress of an aesthetic feeling, as in the state of hypnosis ; and these phases correspond less to variations of degree than to differences of state or of nature. But the merit of a work of art is not measured so much by the power with which the suggested feeling takes hold of us as by the richness of this feeling itself : in other words, besides degrees of intensity we instinctively distinguish degrees of depth or elevation. If this last concept be analysed, it will be seen that the feelings and thoughts which the artist suggests to us express and sum up a more or less considerable part of his history. If the art which gives only sensations is an inferior art, the reason is that analysis often fails to discover in a sensation anything beyond the sensation itself. But the greater number of emotions are instinct with a thousand sensations, feelings or ideas which pervade them : each one is then a state unique of its kind and indefinable, and it seems that we should have to re-live the life of the subject who experiences it if we wished to grasp it in its original complexity. Yet the artist aims at giving us a share in this emotion, so rich, so personal, so novel, and at enabling us to experience what he cannot make us understand. This he will bring about by choosing, among the outward signs of his emotions, those which our body is likely to imitate mechanically, though slightly, as soon as it perceives them, so as to transport us all at once into the indefinable psychological state which called them forth. Thus will be broken down the barrier interposed by time and space between his consciousness and ours : and the richer in ideas and the more pregnant with sensations and emotions is the feeling within whose limits the artist has brought us, the deeper and the higher shall we find the beauty thus expressed. The successive intensities of the æsthetic feeling thus correspond to changes of state occurring in us, and the degrees of depth to the larger or smaller number of elementary psychic phenomena which we dimly discern in the fundamental emotion.

The moral feelings might be studied in the same way. Let us take pity as an example. It consists in the first place in putting oneself mentally in the place of others, in suffering their pain. But if it were

The moral feelings. Pity. Its increasing intensity is a qualitative progress.

nothing more, as some have maintained, it would inspire us with the idea of avoiding the wretched rather than helping them, for pain is naturally abhorrent to us. This feeling of horror may indeed be at the root of pity ; but a new element soon comes in, the need of helping our fellow-men and of alleviating their suffering. Shall we say with La Rochefoucauld that this so-called sympathy is a calculation, " a shrewd insurance against evils to come " ? Perhaps a dread of some future evil to ourselves does hold a place in our compassion for other people's evil. These however are but lower forms of pity. True pity consists not so much in fearing suffering as in desiring it. The desire is a faint one and we should hardly wish to see it realized ; yet we form it in spite of ourselves, as if Nature were committing some great injustice and it were necessary to get rid of all suspicion of complicity with her. The essence of pity is thus a need for self-abasement, an aspiration downwards. This painful aspiration nevertheless has a charm about it, because it raises us in our own estimation and makes us feel superior to those sensuous goods from which our thought is temporarily detached. The increasing intensity of pity thus consists in a qualitative progress, in a transition from repugnance to fear, from fear to sympathy, and from sympathy itself to humility.

We do not propose to carry this analysis any further.   The psychic states whose intensity we have just defined are deep-seated states which

Conscious states connected with external causes or involving physical symptoms.

do not seem to have any close relation to their external cause or to involve the perception of muscular contraction. But such states are rare.   There is hardly any passion or desire, any joy or sorrow, which is not accompanied by physical symptoms ; and, where these symptoms occur, they probably count for something in the estimate of intensities.   As for the sensations properly so called, they are manifestly connected with their external cause, and though the intensity of the sensation cannot be defined by the magnitude of its cause, there undoubtedly exists some relation between these two terms. In some of its manifestations consciousness even appears to spread outwards, as if intensity were being developed into extensity, e.g. in the case of muscular effort.   Let us face this last phenomenon at once : we shall thus be transported at a bound to the opposite extremity of the series of psychic phenomena.

If there is a phenomenon which seems to be presented immediately to consciousness under the

Muscular effort seems at first sight to be quantitative.

form of quantity or at least of magnitude, it is undoubtedly muscular effort. We picture to our minds a psychic force imprisoned in the soul like the winds in the cave of Aeolus, and only waiting for an opportunity to burst forth : our will is supposed to watch over

this force and from time to time to open a passage
for it, regulating the outflow by the effect which
it is desired to produce.   If we consider the matter
carefully, we shall see that this somewhat crude
conception of effort plays a large part in our belief
in intensive magnitudes.   Muscular force, whose
sphere of action is space and which manifests itself
in phenomena admitting of measure, seems to us
to have existed previous to its manifestations, but
in smaller volume, and, so to speak, in a compressed
state :   hence we do not hesitate to reduce this
volume more and more, and finally we believe that
we can understand how a purely psychic state,
which does not occupy space, can nevertheless
possess magnitude.   Science, too, tends to strength-
en the illusion of common sense with regard to
this point.   Bain, for example, declares that " the
sensibility accompanying muscular movement
coincides with the *outgoing* stream of nervous
energy : "[1] it is thus just the emission of nervous force which consciousness perceives.   Wundt
also speaks of a sensation, central in its origin,
accompanying the voluntary innervation of the
muscles, and quotes the example of the paralytic
" who has a very distinct sensation of the force
which he employs in the effort to raise his leg,
although it remains motionless." [2]   Most of the

[1] *The Senses and the Intellect*, 4th ed., (1894), p. 79.
[2] *Grundzüge der Physiologischen Psychologie*, 2nd ed.
(1880), Vol. i, p. 375

authorities adhere to this opinion, which would
be the unanimous view of positive science were it
not that several years ago Professor William James
drew the attention of physiologists to certain
phenomena which had been but little remarked,
although they were very remarkable.

When a paralytic strives to raise his useless
limb, he certainly does not execute this movement, but, with or without his will,
he executes another. Some movement
is carried out somewhere : otherwise
there is no sensation of effort.[1] Vulpian
had already called attention to the
fact that if a man affected with hemiplegia is told to clench his paralysed fist, he
unconsciously carries out this action with the
fist which is not affected. Ferrier described a
still more curious phenomenon.[2] Stretch out
your arm while slightly bending your forefinger,
as if you were going to press the trigger of a
pistol ; without moving the finger, without
contracting any muscle of the hand, without
producing any apparent movement, you will yet
be able to feel that you are expending energy.
On a closer examination, however, you will
perceive that this sensation of effort coincides

The feeling of effort. We are conscious not of an expenditure of force but of the resulting muscular movement.

---

[1] W. James, *Le sentiment de l'effort* (*Critique philosophique*,
1880, Vol. ii,) [cf. *Principles of Psychology*, (1891), Vol. ii,
chap. xxvi.]

[2] *Functions of the Brain*, 2nd ed. (1886), p. 386.

with the fixation of the muscles of your chest, that you keep your glottis closed and actively contract your respiratory muscles. As soon as respiration resumes its normal course the consciousness of effort vanishes, unless you really move your finger. These facts already seemed to show that we are conscious, not of an expenditure of force, but of the movement of the muscles which results from it. The new feature in Professor James's investigation is that he has verified the hypothesis in the case of examples which seemed to contradict it absolutely. Thus when the external rectus muscle of the right eye is paralysed, the patient tries in vain to turn his eye towards the right ; yet objects seem to him to recede towards the right, and since the act of volition has produced no effect, it follows, said Helmholtz,[1] that he is conscious of the effort of volition. But, replies Professor James, no account has been taken of what goes on in the other eye. This remains covered during the experiments ; nevertheless it moves and there is not much trouble in proving that it does. It is the movement of the left eye, perceived by consciousness, which produces the sensation of effort together with the impression that the objects perceived by the right eye are moving. These and similar observations lead Professor James to assert that the feeling

[1] *Handbuch der Physiologischen Optik*, 1st ed. (1867), pp. 600-601.

of effort is centripetal and not centrifugal. We are not conscious of a force which we are supposed to launch upon our organism : our feeling of muscular energy at work " is a complex afferent sensation, which comes from contracted muscles, stretched ligaments, compressed joints, an immobilized chest, a closed glottis, a knit brow, clenched jaws," in a word, from all the points of the periphery where the effort causes an alteration.

It is not for us to take a side in the dispute. After all, the question with which we have to deal is not whether the feeling of effort comes from the centre or the periphery, but in what does our perception of its intensity exactly consist ? Now, it is sufficient to observe oneself attentively to reach a conclusion on this point which Professor James has not formulated, but which seems to us quite in accord with the spirit of his teaching. We maintain that the more a given effort seems to us to increase, the greater is the number of muscles which contract in sympathy with it, and that the apparent consciousness of a greater intensity of effort at a given point of the organism is reducible, in reality, to the perception of a larger surface of the body being affected.

Try, for example, to clench the fist with increasing force. You will have the impression of a sensation of effort entirely localized in your hand and running up a scale of magnitudes. In reality, what you experience in your hand

Intensity of feeling of effort proportional to extent of our body affected.

remains the same, but the sensation which was at first localized there has affected your arm and ascended to the shoulder; finally, the other arm stiffens, both legs do the same, the respiration is checked; it is the whole body which is at work. But you fail to notice distinctly all these concomitant movements unless you are warned of them : till then you thought you were dealing with a single state of consciousness which changed in magnitude. When you press your lips more and more tightly against one another, you believe that you are experiencing in your lips one and the same sensation which is continually increasing in strength : here again further reflection will show you that this sensation remains identical, but that certain muscles of the face and the head and then of all the rest of the body have taken part in the operation. You felt this gradual encroachment, this increase of the surface affected, which is in truth a change of quantity ; but, as your attention was concentrated on your closed lips, you localized the increase there and you made the psychic force there expended into a magnitude, although it possessed no extensity. Examine carefully somebody who is lifting heavier and heavier weights : the muscular contraction gradually spreads over his whole body. As for the special sensation which he experiences in the arm which is at work, it remains constant for a very long time and hardly changes except in quality, the weight becoming at a certain moment fatigue, and the fatigue pain. Yet the subject will imagine that he is conscious of a continual increase in the psychic force flowing into his arm. He will not recognize his mistake unless he is warned of it, so inclined is he to measure a given psychic state by the conscious movements which accompany it! From these facts and from many others of the same kind we believe we can deduce the following conclusion : our consciousness of an increase of muscular effort is reducible to the twofold perception of a greater number of peripheral sensations, and of a qualitative change occurring in some of them.

We are thus led to define the intensity of a superficial effort in the same way as that of a deep-seated psychic feeling. In both cases there is a qualitative progress and an increasing complexity, indistinctly perceived. But consciousness, accustomed to think in terms of space and to translate its thoughts into words, will denote the feeling by a single word and will localize the effort at the exact point where it yields a useful result : it will then become aware of an effort which is always of the same nature and increases at the spot assigned to it, and a feeling which, retaining the same name, grows without changing its nature. Now, the same illusion of consciousness is likely to be met with again in the case of the states which are inter-

The same definition of intensity applies to superficial efforts, deep-seated feelings and states intermediate between the two.

mediate between superficial efforts and deep-
seated feelings. A large number of psychic states
are accompanied, in fact, by muscular contractions
and peripheral sensations. Sometimes these superficial elements are co-ordinated by a purely specu-
lative idea, sometimes by an idea of a practical
order. In the first case there is intellectual effort
or attention ; in the second we have the emotions
which may be called violent or acute : anger, terror,
and certain varieties of joy, sorrow, passion and
desire. Let us show briefly that the same definition of intensity applies to these intermediate
states.

Attention is not a purely physiological phenomenon, but we cannot deny that it is accompanied
by movements. These movements are
neither the cause nor the result of the
phenomenon ; they are part of it, they
express it in terms of space, as Ribot
has so remarkably proved.[1] Fechner had already
reduced the effort of attention in a sense-organ to
the muscular feeling " produced by putting in
motion, by a sort of reflex action, the muscles
which are correlated with the different sense
organs." He had noticed the very distinct sensation of tension and contraction of the scalp, the
pressure from without inwards over the whole
skull, which we experience when we make a great
effort to recall something. Ribot has studied

The interme-
diate states.
Attention and
its relation to
muscular con-
traction.

---

[1] *Le mécanisme de l'attention.* Alcan, 1888.

more closely the movements which are characteristic of voluntary attention. " Attention con-
tracts the frontal muscle : this muscle . . .
draws the eyebrow towards itself, raises it and
causes transverse wrinkles on the forehead. . . .
In extreme cases the mouth is opened wide. With
children and with many adults eager attention gives
rise to a protrusion of the lips, a kind of pout."
Certainly, a purely psychic factor will always
enter into voluntary attention, even if it be
nothing more than the exclusion by the will of all
ideas foreign to the one with which the subject
wishes to occupy himself. But, once this exclusion
is made, we believe that we are still conscious of a
growing tension of soul, of an immaterial effort
which increases. Analyse this impression and
you will find nothing but the feeling of a muscular
contraction which spreads over a wider surface or
changes its nature, so that the tension becomes
pressure, fatigue and pain.

Now, we do not see any essential difference
between the effort of attention and what may be
The intensity called the effort of psychic tension :
of violent emo-
tions as mus- acute desire, uncontrolled anger, passion-
cular tension. ate love, violent hatred. Each of these
states may be reduced, we believe, to a system of
muscular contractions co-ordinated by an idea ; but
in the case of attention, it is the more or less reflective idea of knowing ; in the case of emotion, the
unreflective idea of acting. The intensity of these
violent emotions is thus likely to be nothing but

the muscular tension which accompanies them.
Darwin has given a remarkable description of the
physiological symptoms of rage. " The action of
the heart is much accelerated. . . . The face red-
dens or may turn deadly pale. The respiration is
laboured, the chest heaves, and the dilated nostrils
quiver. The whole body often trembles. The
voice is affected. The teeth are clenched or ground
together and the muscular system is commonly
stimulated to violent, almost frantic action. The
gestures . . . represent more or less plainly the
act of striking or fighting with an enemy." [1] We
shall not go so far as to maintain, with Professor
James, [2] that the emotion of rage is reducible to the
sum of these organic sensations : there will always
be an irreducible psychic element in anger, if this
be only the idea of striking or fighting, of which
Darwin speaks, and which gives a common direction
to so many diverse movements. But, though this
idea determines the direction of the emotional state
and the accompanying movements, the growing intensity of the state itself is, we believe, nothing but
the deeper and deeper disturbance of the organism,
a disturbance which consciousness has no difficulty
in measuring by the number and extent of the
bodily surfaces concerned. It will be useless to
assert that there is a restrained rage which is all
the more intense. The reason is that, where
emotion has free play, consciousness does not

---

[1] *The Expression of the Emotions.* 1st ed., (1872), p. 74.
[2] " What is an Emotion ? " *Mind*, 1884, p. 189.

dwell on the details of the accompanying movements, but it does dwell upon them and is concentrated upon them when its object is to conceal them.
Eliminate, in short, all trace of organic disturbance,
all tendency towards muscular contraction, and
all that will be left of anger will be the idea, or, if
you still insist on making it an emotion, you will
be unable to assign it any intensity.

"Fear, when strong," says Herbert Spencer,
"expresses itself in cries, in efforts to escape, in
palpitations, in tremblings." [1] We go
further, and maintain that these movements form part of the terror itself : by
their means the terror becomes an
emotion capable of passing through
different degrees of intensity. Suppress
them entirely, and the more or less
intense state of terror will be succeeded by an
idea of terror, the wholly intellectual representation
of a danger which it concerns us to avoid. There
are also high degrees of joy and sorrow, of desire,
aversion and even shame, the height of which will
be found to be nothing but the reflex movements
begun by the organism and perceived by consciousness. "When lovers meet," says Darwin, " we
know that their hearts beat quickly, their breathing
is hurried and their faces flushed." [2] Aversion
is marked by movements of repugnance which we
repeat without noticing when we think of the

Intensity and reflex move-ments. No essential dif-ference be-tween inten-sity of deep-seated feelings and that of violent emo-tions.

[1] *Principles of Psychology*, 3rd. ed., (1890), Vol. i, p. 482.
[2] *The Expression of the Emotions.* 1st ed., p. 78.

object of our dislike. We blush and involuntarily clench the fingers when we feel shame, even if it be retrospective. The acuteness of these emotions is estimated by the number and nature of the peripheral sensations which accompany them. Little by little, and in proportion as the emotional state loses its violence and gains in depth, the peripheral sensations will give place to inner states; it will be no longer our outward movements but our ideas, our memories, our states of consciousness of every description, which will turn in larger or smaller numbers in a definite direction. There is, then, no essential difference from the point of view of intensity between the deep-seated feelings, of which we spoke at the beginning, and the acute or violent emotions which we have just passed in review. To say that love, hatred, desire, increase in violence is to assert that they are projected outwards, that they radiate to the surface, that peripheral sensations are substituted for inner states: but superficial or deep-seated, violent or reflective, the intensity of these feelings always consists in the multiplicity of simple states which consciousness dimly discerns in them.

We have hitherto confined ourselves to feelings and efforts, complex states the intensity of which **Magnitude of sensations.** does not absolutely depend on an ex**Affective and representative sensations.** ternal cause. But sensations seem to us simple states: in what will their magnitude

consist ?   The intensity of sensations varies with
the external cause of which they are said to be
the conscious equivalent : how shall we explain the
presence of quantity in an effect which is inextensive, and in this case indivisible?   To answer this
question, we must first distinguish between the
so-called affective and the representative sensations.   There is no doubt that we pass gradually
from the one to the other and that some affective
element enters into the majority of our simple
representations.   But nothing prevents us from
isolating this element and inquiring separately,
in what does the intensity of an affective sensation,
a pleasure or a pain, consist ?

Perhaps the difficulty of the latter problem is principally due to the fact that we are unwilling to see
Affective sen- in the affective state anything but the
sations and
organic dis- conscious expression of an organic disturb-
turbance. ance, the inward echo of an outward cause.
We notice that a more intense sensation generally
corresponds to a greater nervous disturbance ;
but inasmuch as these disturbances are unconscious as movements, since they come before consciousness in the guise of a sensation which has
no resemblance at all to motion, we do not see
how they could transmit to the sensation anything
of their own magnitude.   For there is nothing
in common, we repeat, between superposable
magnitudes such as, for example, vibration-
amplitudes, and sensations which do not occupy

space. If the more intense sensation seems to us to contain the less intense, if it assumes for us, like the physical impression itself, the form of a magnitude, the reason probably is that it retains something of the physical impression to which it corresponds. And it will retain nothing of it if it is merely the conscious translation of a movement of molecules ; for, just because this movement is translated into the sensation of pleasure or pain, it remains unconscious as molecular movement.

But it might be asked whether pleasure and pain, instead of expressing only what has just occurred, or what is actually occurring, in the organism, as is usually believed, could not also point out what is going to, or what is tending to take place. It seems indeed somewhat improbable that nature, so profoundly utilitarian, should have here assigned to consciousness the merely scientific task of informing us about the past or the present, which no longer depend upon us. It must be noticed in addition that we rise by imperceptible stages from automatic to free movements, and that the latter differ from the former principally in introducing an affective sensation between the external action which occasions them and the volitional reaction which ensues. Indeed, all our actions might have been automatic, and we can surmise that there are many organized beings in whose case an external stimulus causes a definite reaction without calling up consciousness as an

Pleasure and pain as signs of the future reaction rather than psychic translations of the past stimulus.

intermediate agent. If pleasure and pain make
their appearance in certain privileged beings, it is
probably to call forth a resistance to the automatic
reaction which would have taken place: either
sensation has nothing to do, or it is nascent freedom. But how would it enable us to resist the
reaction which is in preparation if it did not
acquaint us with the nature of the latter by some
definite sign? And what can this sign be except
the sketching, and, as it were, the prefiguring of
the future automatic movements in the very
midst of the sensation which is being experienced?
The affective state must then correspond not merely
to the physical disturbances, movements or phenomena which have taken place, but also, and
especially, to those which are in preparation, those
which are getting ready to be.

It is certainly not obvious at first sight how this
hypothesis simplifies the problem. For we are
Intensity of
affective sen-
sations would
then be our
consciousness
of the involun-
tary move-
ments tending
to follow the
stimulus. trying to find what there can be in
common, from the point of view of magnitude, between a physical phenomenon
and a state of consciousness, and we
seem to have merely turned the difficulty
round by making the present state of
consciousness a sign of the future reaction, rather
than a psychic translation of the past stimulus.
But the difference between the two hypotheses is
considerable. For the molecular disturbances
which were mentioned just now are necessarily
unconscious, since no trace of the movements

themselves can be actually perceived in the sensation which translates them. But the automatic movements which tend to follow the stimulus as its natural outcome are likely to be conscious as movements : or else the sensation itself, whose function is to invite us to choose between this automatic reaction and other possible movements, would be of no avail. The intensity of affective sensations might thus be nothing more than our consciousness of the involuntary movements which are being begun and outlined, so to speak, within these states, and which would have gone on in their own way if nature had made us automata instead of conscious beings.

If such be the case, we shall not compare a pain of increasing intensity to a note which grows louder and louder, but rather to a

Intensity of a
pain estim-
ated by extent
of organism
affected.

symphony, in which an increasing number of instruments make themselves heard. Within the characteristic sensation, which gives the tone to all the others, consciousness distinguishes a larger or smaller number of sensations arising at different points of the periphery, muscular contractions, organic movements of every kind : the choir of these elementary psychic states voices the new demands of the organism, when confronted by a new situation. In other words, we estimate the intensity of a pain by the larger or smaller part of the organism which takes interest in it. Richet [1]

[1] *L'homme et l'intelligence*, p. 36.

has observed that the slighter the pain, the more precisely is it referred to a particular spot ; if it becomes more intense, it is referred to the whole of the member affected. And he concludes by saying that " the pain spreads in proportion as it is more intense." [1] We should rather reverse the sentence, and define the intensity of the pain by the very number and extent of the parts of the body which sympathize with it and react, and whose reactions are perceived by consciousness. To convince ourselves of this, it will be enough to read the remarkable description of disgust given by the same author : " If the stimulus is slight there may be neither nausea nor vomiting. . . . If the stimulus is stronger, instead of being confined to the pneumo-gastric nerve, it spreads and affects almost the whole organic system. The face turns pale, the smooth muscles of the skin contract, the skin is covered with a cold perspiration, the heart stops beating : in a word there is a general organic disturbance following the stimulation of the medulla oblongata, and this disturbance is the supreme expression of disgust." [2] But is it nothing more than its expression ? In what will the general sensation of disgust consist, if not in the sum of these elementary sensations ? And what can we understand here by increasing intensity, if it is not the constantly increasing number of sensations

[1] Ibid. p. 37.   [2] Ibid. p. 43.

which join in with the sensations already experienced ? Darwin has drawn a striking picture of the reactions following a pain which becomes more and more acute. " Great pain urges all animals . . . to make the most violent and diversified efforts to escape from the cause of suffering. . . . With men the mouth may be closely compressed, or more commonly the lips are retracted with the teeth clenched or ground together. . . . The eyes stare wildly . . . or the brows are heavily contracted. Perspiration bathes the body. . . . The circulation and respiration are much affected." [1] Now, is it not by this very contraction of the muscles affected that we measure the intensity of a pain ? Analyse your idea of any suffering which you call extreme : do you not mean that it is unbearable, that is to say, that it urges the organism to a thousand different actions in order to escape from it ? I can picture to myself a nerve transmitting a pain which is independent of all automatic reaction ; and I can equally understand that stronger or weaker stimulations influence this nerve differently. But I do not see how these differences of sensation would be interpreted by our consciousness as differences of quantity unless we connected them with the reactions which usually accompany them, and which are more or less extended and more or

---

[1] *The Expression of the Emotions.* 1st ed., pp. 72, 69, 70.

less important. Without these subsequent reactions, the intensity of the pain would be a
quality, and not a magnitude.

We have hardly any other means of comparing
several pleasures with one another. What do
we mean by a greater pleasure except a
pleasure that is preferred? And what
can our preference be, except a certain
disposition of our organs, the effect of which
is that, when two pleasures are offered simultaneously to our mind, our body inclines towards one
of them? Analyse this inclination itself and
you will find a great many little movements which
begin and become perceptible in the organs concerned, and even in the rest of the body, as if the
organism were coming forth to meet the pleasure
as soon as it is pictured. When we define inclination as a movement, we are not using a metaphor.
When confronted by several pleasures pictured
by our mind, our body turns towards one of them
spontaneously, as though by a reflex action.
It rests with us to check it, but the attraction
of the pleasure is nothing but this movement
that is begun, and the very keenness of the pleasure, while we enjoy it, is merely the inertia
of the organism, which is immersed in it and
rejects every other sensation. Without this *vis
inertiae* of which we become conscious by the
very resistance which we offer to anything that
might distract us, pleasure would be a state,
but no longer a magnitude. In the moral as in

*Pleasures com-
pared by bod-
ily inclination.*

the physical world, attraction serves to define movement rather than to produce it.

We have studied the affective sensations separately, but we must now notice that many representative sensations possess an affective character, and thus call forth a reaction on our part which we take into account in estimating their intensity. A considerable increase of light is represented for us by a characteristic sensation which is not yet pain, but which is analogous to dazzling. In proportion as the amplitude of sound-vibrations increases, our head and then our body seem to us to vibrate or to receive a shock. Certain representative sensations, those of taste, smell and temperature, have a fixed character of pleasantness or unpleasantness. Between flavours which are more or less bitter you will hardly distinguish anything but differences of quality; they are like different shades of one and the same colour. But these differences of quality are at once interpreted as differences of quantity, because of their affective character and the more or less pronounced movements of reaction, pleasure or repugnance, which they suggest to us. Besides, even when the sensation remains purely representative, its external cause cannot exceed a certain degree of strength or weakness without inciting us to movements which enable us to measure it. Sometimes indeed

The intensity of representative sensations. Many also affective and intensity is measured by reaction called forth. In others a new element enters.

we have to make an effort to perceive this sensation, as if it were trying to escape notice ; sometimes on the other hand it obsesses us, forces
itself upon us and engrosses us to such an extent
that we make every effort to escape from it and
to remain ourselves. In the former case the
sensation is said to be of slight intensity, and in
the latter case very intense. Thus, in order to
perceive a distant sound, to distinguish what
we call a faint smell or a dim light, we strain all
our faculties, we " pay attention." And it is
just because the smell and the light thus require
to be reinforced by our efforts that they seem
to us feeble. And, inversely, we recognize a
sensation of extreme intensity by the irresistible
reflex movements to which it incites us, or by
the powerlessness with which it affects us. When
a cannon is fired off close to our ears or a dazzling
light suddenly flares up, we lose for an instant
the consciousness of our personality ; this state
may even last some time in the case of a very
nervous subject. It must be added that, even
within the range of the so-called medium intensities, when we are dealing on even terms with a
representative sensation, we often estimate its
importance by comparing it with another which
it drives away, or by taking account of the per-
sistence with which it returns. Thus the ticking
of a watch seems louder at night because it easily
monopolizes a consciousness almost empty of
sensations and ideas. Foreigners talking to one

another in a language which we do not understand seem to us to speak very loudly, because
their words no longer call up any ideas in our
mind, and thus break in upon a kind of intellectual
silence and monopolize our attention like the
ticking of a watch at night. With these so-called
medium sensations, however, we approach a
series of psychic states, the intensity of which
is likely to possess a new meaning. For, in
most cases, the organism hardly reacts at all, at
least in a way that can be perceived ; and yet
we still make a magnitude out of the pitch of
a sound, the intensity of a light, the saturation
of a colour. Doubtless, a closer observation of
what takes place in the whole of the organism
when we hear such and such a note or perceive
such and such a colour has more than one surprise in store for us. Has not C. Féré shown
that every sensation is accompanied by an increase in muscular force which can be measured
by the dynamometer ?[1] But of an increase of this
kind there is hardly any consciousness at all,
and if we reflect on the precision with which we
distinguish sounds and colours, nay, even weights
and temperatures, we shall easily guess that
some new element must come into play in our
estimate of them.

Now, the nature of this element is easy to deter-

---

[1] C. Féré, *Sensation et Mouvement.* Paris, 1887.

mine. For, in proportion as a sensation loses its affective character and becomes representative, the reactions which it called forth on our part tend to dis-appear, but at the same time we per-ceive the external object which is its cause, or if we do not now perceive it, we have perceived it, and we think of it. Now, this cause is ex-tensive and therefore measurable : a constant experience, which began with the first glimmer-ings of consciousness and which continues throughout the whole of our life, shows us a definite shade of sensation corresponding to a definite amount of stimulation. We thus associ-ate the idea of a certain quantity of cause with a certain quality of effect ; and finally, as happens in the case of every acquired perception, we trans-fer the idea into the sensation, the quantity of the cause into the quality of the effect. At this very moment the intensity, which was nothing but a certain shade or quality of the sensation, becomes a magnitude. We shall easily understand this process if, for example, we hold a pin in our right hand and prick our left hand more and more deeply. At first we shall feel as it were a tickling, then a touch which is succeeded by a prick, then a pain localized at a point, and finally the spreading of this pain over the surrounding zone. And the more we reflect on it, the more clearly shall we see that we are here dealing with so many qualitatively distinct sensations,

The purely re-presentative sensations are measured by their external causes.

so many varieties of a single species. But yet
we spoke at first of one and the same sensation
which spread further and further, of one prick
which increased in intensity. The reason is that,
without noticing it, we localized in the sensation
of the left hand, which is pricked, the progressive
effort of the right hand, which pricks. We thus
introduced the cause into the effect, and unconsciously interpreted quality as quantity, intensity as magnitude. Now, it is easy to see that
the intensity of every representative sensation
ought to be understood in the same way.

The sensations of sound display well marked
degrees of intensity. We have already spoken
of the necessity of taking into account
the affective character of these sensations, the shock received by the whole
of the organism. We have shown that
a very intense sound is one which engrosses our attention, which supplants all the
others. But take away the shock, the well-
marked vibration, which you sometimes feel
in your head or even throughout your body :
take away the clash which takes place between
sounds heard simultaneously : what will be left
except an indefinable quality of the sound which
is heard ? But this quality is immediately interpreted as quantity because you have obtained
it yourself a thousand times, e.g. by striking
some object and thus expending a definite quantity of effort. You know, too, how far you would

The sensa-
tions of sound.
Intensity mea-
sured by effort
necessary to
produce a sim-
ilar sound.

have to raise your voice to produce a similar sound, and the idea of this effort immediately comes into your mind when you transform the intensity of the sound into a magnitude. Wundt [1] has drawn attention to the quite special connexions of vocal and auditory nervous filaments which are met with in the human brain. And has it not been said that to hear is to speak to oneself? Some neuropaths cannot be present at a conversation without moving their lips; this is only an exaggeration of what takes place in the case of every one of us. How will the expressive or rather suggestive power of music be explained, if not by admitting that we repeat to ourselves the sounds heard, so as to carry ourselves back into the psychic state out of which they emerged, an original state, which nothing will express, but which something may suggest, viz., the very motion and attitude which the sound imparts to our body?

Thus, when we speak of the intensity of a sound of medium force as a magnitude, we allude principally to the greater or less effort which we should have ourselves to expend in order to summon, by our own effort, the same auditory sensation. Now, besides the intensity, we distinguish another characteristic property of the sound, its pitch.

Intensity and pitch. The part played by muscular effort.

[1] *Grundzüge der Physiologischen Psychologie*, 2nd ed., (1880), Vol. ii, p. 437.

Are the differences in pitch, such as our ear
perceives, quantitative differences ? I grant that
a sharper sound calls up the picture of a higher
position in space. But does it follow from
this that the notes of the scale, as auditory
sensations, differ otherwise than in quality ?
Forget what you have learnt from physics, examine carefully your idea of a higher or lower note,
and see whether you do not think simply of the
greater or less effort which the tensor muscle
of your vocal chords has to make in order to
produce the note ? As the effort by which your
voice passes from one note to another is discontinuous, you picture to yourself these successive
notes as points in space, to be reached by a series
of sudden jumps, in each of which you cross an
empty separating interval : this is why you
establish intervals between the notes of the scale.
Now, why is the line along which we dispose
them vertical rather than horizontal, and why
do we say that the sound ascends in some cases
and descends in others ? It must be remembered
that the high notes seem to us to produce some
sort of resonance in the head and the deep notes
in the thorax : this perception, whether real or
illusory, has undoubtedly had some effect in
making us reckon the intervals vertically. But
we must also notice that the greater the tension
of the vocal chords in the chest voice, the greater
is the surface of the body affected, if the singer
is inexperienced ; this is just the reason why the

effort is felt by him as more intense. And as
he breathes out the air upwards, he will attribute
the same direction to the sound produced by the
current of air ; hence the sympathy of a larger
part of the body with the vocal muscles will be
represented by a movement upwards. We shall
thus say that the note is higher because the body
makes an effort as though to reach an object which
is more elevated in space. In this way it became
customary to assign a certain height to each note
of the scale, and as soon as the physicist was able
to define it by the number of vibrations in a given
time to which it corresponds, we no longer hesitated to declare that our ear perceived differences of quantity directly. But the sound would
remain a pure quality if we did not bring in the
muscular effort which produces it or the vibrations which explain it.

The experiments of Blix, Goldscheider and
Donaldson [1] have shown that the points on the
The sensations surface of the body which feel cold are
of heat and
cold.   These not the same as those which feel heat.
soon become
affective and Physiology is thus disposed to set up a
are measured
by   reactions distinction of nature, and not merely of
called forth. degree, between the sensations of heat
and cold. But psychological observation goes
further, for close attention can easily discover
specific differences between the different sensations of heat, as also between the sensations of

[1] "On the Temperature Sense" *Mind*, 1885.

cold. A more intense heat is really another kind of heat. We call it more intense because we have experienced this same change a thousand times when we approached nearer and nearer a source of heat, or when a growing surface of our body was affected by it. Besides, the sensations of heat and cold very quickly become affective and incite us to more or less marked reactions by which we measure their external cause : hence, we are inclined to set up similar quantitative differences among the sensations which correspond to lower intensities of the cause. But I shall not insist any further ; every one must question himself carefully on this point, after making a clean sweep of everything which his past experience has taught him about the cause of his sensations and coming face to face with the sensations themselves. The result of this examination is likely to be as follows : it will be perceived that the magnitude of a representative sensation depends on the cause having been put into the effect, while the intensity of the affective element depends on the more or less important reactions which prolong the external stimulations and find their way into the sensation itself.

The same thing will be experienced in the case of pressure and even weight. When you say

The sensations of pressure and weight measured by extent of organism affected. that a pressure on your hand becomes stronger and stronger, see whether you do not mean that there first was a contact, then a pressure, afterwards a

pain, and that this pain itself, after having gone
through a series of qualitative changes, has spread
further and further over the surrounding region.
Look again and see whether you do not bring in
the more and more intense, i.e. more and more
extended, effort of resistance which you oppose to
the external pressure. When the psychophysicist lifts a heavier weight, he experiences, he
says, an increase of sensation. Examine whether
this increase of sensation ought not rather to be
called a sensation of increase. The whole question
is centred in this, for in the first case the sensation
would be a quantity like its external cause, whilst
in the second it would be a quality which had
become representative of the magnitude of its
cause. The distinction between the heavy and
the light may seem to be as old-fashioned and as
childish as that between the hot and the cold.
But the very childishness of this distinction makes
it a psychological reality. And not only do the
heavy and the light impress our consciousness as
generically different, but the various degrees of
lightness and heaviness are so many species of
these two genera. It must be added that the
difference of quality is here translated spontaneously into a difference of quantity, because of the
more or less extended effort which our body makes
in order to lift a given weight. Of this you will
soon become aware if you are asked to lift a basket
which, you are told, is full of scrap-iron, whilst
in fact there is nothing in it. You will think you

are losing your balance when you catch hold of
it, as though distant muscles had interested themselves beforehand in the operation and experienced a sudden disappointment. It is chiefly
by the number and nature of these sympathetic
efforts, which take place at different points of the
organism, that you measure the sensation of
weight at a given point ; and this sensation would
be nothing more than a quality if you did not thus
introduce into it the idea of a magnitude. What
strengthens the illusion on this point is that we
have become accustomed to believe in the immediate perception of a homogeneous movement in a
homogeneous space. When I lift a light weight
with my arm, all the rest of my body remaining
motionless, I experience a series of muscular sensations each of which has its " local sign," its peculiar shade : it is this series which my consciousness interprets as a continuous movement in space.
If I afterwards lift a heavier weight to the same
height with the same speed, I pass through a new
series of muscular sensations, each of which differs
from the corresponding term of the preceding
series. Of this I could easily convince myself
by examining them closely. But as I interpret
this new series also as a continuous movement,
and as this movement has the same direction, the
same duration and the same velocity as the preceding, my consciousness feels itself bound to
localize the difference between the second series
of sensations and the first elsewhere than in the

movement itself. It thus materializes this difference at the extremity of the arm which moves ;
it persuades itself that the sensation of movement
has been identical in both cases, while the sensation of weight differed in magnitude. But movement and weight are but distinctions of the reflective consciousness : what is present to consciousness immediately is the sensation of, so to speak,
a heavy movement, and this sensation itself can
be resolved by analysis into a series of muscular
sensations, each of which represents by its shade
its place of origin and by its colour the magnitude
of the weight lifted.

Shall we call the intensity of light a quantity, or
shall we treat it as a quality ? It has not perhaps
been sufficiently noticed what a large
number of different factors co-operate in
daily life in giving us information about
the nature of the luminous source. We
know from long experience that, when we
have a difficulty in distinguishing the
outlines and details of objects, the light
is at a distance or on the point of going out.
Experience has taught us that the affective sensation or nascent dazzling that we experience in certain cases must be attributed to a higher intensity
of the cause. Any increase or diminution in the
number of luminous sources alters the way in
which the sharp lines of bodies stand out and also
the shadows which they project. Still more
important are the changes of hue which coloured

The sensation
of light. Qua-
litative
changes of
colour inter-
preted as
quantitative
changes in
intensity of
luminous
source.

surfaces, and even the pure colours of the spectrum, undergo under the influence of a brighter
or dimmer light. As the luminous source is
brought nearer, violet takes a bluish tinge, green
tends to become a whitish yellow, and red a bril-
liant yellow. Inversely, when the light is moved
away, ultramarine passes into violet and yellow
into green ; finally, red, green and violet tend to become a whitish yellow. Physicists have remarked
these changes of hue for some time ;[1] but what
is still more remarkable is that the majority of men
do not perceive them, unless they pay attention to
them or are warned of them. Having made up
our mind, once for all, to interpret changes of
quality as changes of quantity, we begin by asserting that every object has its own peculiar colour,
definite and invariable. And when the hue of
objects tends to become yellow or blue, instead of
saying that we see their colour change under the
influence of an increase or diminution of light, we
assert that the colour remains the same but that
our sensation of luminous intensity increases or
diminishes. We thus substitute once more, for
the qualitative impression received by our consciousness, the quantitative interpretation given
by our understanding. Helmholtz has described
a case of interpretation of the same kind, but still
more complicated : " If we form white with two
colours of the spectrum, and if we increase or

---

[1] Rood, *Modern Chromatics*, (1879), pp. 181–187.

diminish the intensities of the two coloured lights in the same ratio, so that the proportions of the combination remain the same, the resultant colour remains the same although the relative intensity of the sensations undergoes a marked change. . . . This depends on the fact that the light of the sun, which we consider as the normal white light during the day, itself undergoes similar modifications of shade when the luminous intensity varies." [1]

But yet, if we often judge of variations in the luminous source by the relative changes of hue of the objects which surround us, this is no longer the case in simple instances where a single object, e.g. a white surface, passes successively through different degrees of luminosity. We are bound to insist particularly on this last point. For the physicist speaks of degrees of luminous intensity as of real quantities : and, in fact, he measures them by the photometer. The psychophysicist goes still further : he maintains that our eye itself estimates the intensities of light. Experiments have been attempted, at first by Delbœuf,[2] and afterwards by Lehmann and Neiglick,[3] with

Does experiment prove that we can measure directly our sensations of light?

---

[1] *Handbuch der Physiologischen Optik,* 1st ed. (1867), pp. 318-319.

[2] *Éléments de psychophysique.* Paris, 1883.

[3] See the account given of these experiments in the *Revue philosophique,* 1887, Vol. i, p. 71, and Vol. ii, p. 180.

the view of constructing a psychophysical formula from the direct measurement of our luminous sensations. Of these experiments we shall not dispute the result, nor shall we deny the value of photometric processes ; but we must see how we have to interpret them.

Look closely at a sheet of paper lighted e.g. by four candles, and put out in succession one, two, three of them. You say that the surface remains white and that its brightness diminishes. But you are aware that one candle has just been put out ; or, if you do not know it, you have often observed a similar change in the appearance of a white surface when the illumination was diminished. Put aside what you remember of your past experiences and what you are accustomed to say of the present ones ; you will find that what you really perceive is not a diminished illumination of the white surface, it is a *layer of shadow* passing over this surface at the moment the candle is extinguished. This shadow is a reality to your consciousness, like the light itself. If you call the first surface in all its brilliancy white, you will have to give another name to what you now see, for it is a different thing : it is, if we may say so, a new shade of white. We have grown accustomed, through the combined influence of our past experience and of physical theories, to regard black as the absence, or at least as the minimum, of luminous sensation, and the succes-

Photometric experiments. We perceive different shades and afterwards interpret them as decreasing intensities of white light.

sive shades of grey as decreasing intensities of white light. But, in point of fact, black has just as much reality for our consciousness as white, and the decreasing intensities of white light illuminating a given surface would appear to an unprejudiced consciousness as so many different shades, not unlike the various colours of the spectrum. This is the reason why the change in the sensation is not continuous, as it is in the external cause, and why the light can increase or decrease for a certain period without producing any apparent change in the illumination of our white surface : the illumination will not appear to change until the increase or decrease of the external light is sufficient to produce a new quality. The variations in brightness of a given colour—the affective sensations of which we have spoken above being left aside—would thus be nothing but qualitative changes, were it not our custom to transfer the cause to the effect and to replace our immediate impressions by what we learn from experience and science. The same thing might be said of degrees of saturation. Indeed, if the different intensities of a colour correspond to so many different shades existing between this colour and black, the degrees of saturation are like shades intermediate between this same colour and pure white. Every colour, we might say, can be regarded under two aspects, from the point of view of black and from the point of view of white. And black is then to intensity what white is to saturation.

The meaning of the photometric experiments will now be understood. A candle placed at a

certain distance from a sheet of paper illuminates it in a certain way : you double the distance and find that four candles are required to produce the same sensation. From this you conclude that if you had doubled the distance without increasing the intensity of the luminous source, the resultant illumination would have been only one-fourth as bright. But it is quite obvious that you are here dealing with the physical and not the psychological effect. For it cannot be said that you have compared two sensations with one another : you have made use of a single sensation in order to compare two different luminous sources with each other, the second four times as strong as the first but twice as far off. In a word, the physicist never brings in sensations which are twice or three times as great as others, but only identical sensations, destined to serve as intermediaries between two physical quantities which can then be equated with one another. The sensation of light here plays the part of the auxiliary unknown quantity which the mathematician introduces into his calculations, and which is not intended to appear in the final result.

But the object of the psychophysicist is entirely different : it is the sensation of light itself which he studies, and claims to measure. Sometimes he will proceed to integrate infinitely small

differences, after the method of Fechner ; some-
The psycho-
physicist
claims to com-
pare and
measure sensa-
tions. Del-
bœuf's ex-
periments.
times he will compare one sensation
directly with another. The latter
method, due to Plateau and Delbœuf,
differs far less than has hitherto been
believed from Fechner's : but, as it bears
more especially on the luminous sensations, we shall
deal with it first. Delbœuf places an observer
in front of three concentric rings which vary in
brightness. By an ingenious arrangement he can
cause each of these rings to pass through all the
shades intermediate between white and black.
Let us suppose that two hues of grey are simultaneously produced on two of the rings and kept
unchanged ; let us call them A and B. Delbœuf
alters the brightness, C, of the third ring, and asks
the observer to tell him whether, at a certain
moment, the grey, B, appears to him equally distant from the other two. A moment comes, in
fact, when the observer states that the contrast
A B is equal to the contrast B C, so that, according
to Delbœuf, a scale of luminous intensities could
be constructed on which we might pass from each
sensation to the following one by equal sensible
contrasts : our sensations would thus be measured
by one another. I shall not follow Delbœuf
into the conclusions which he has drawn from
these remarkable experiments : the essential question, the only question, as it seems to me, is whether
a contrast A B, formed of the elements A and B, is
really equal to a contrast B C, which is differently

composed. As soon as it is proved that two sensations can be equal without being identical, psychophysics will be established. But it is this
equality which seems to me open to question : it
is easy to explain, in fact, how a sensation of
luminous intensity can be said to be at an equal
distance from two others.

Let us assume for a moment that from our birth
onwards the growing intensity of a luminous source
In what case had always called up in our conscious-
differences of
colour might ness, one after the other, the different
be interpreted
as differences colours of the spectrum. There is no
of magnitude. doubt that these colours would then
appear to us as so many notes of a gamut, as
higher or lower degrees in a scale, in a word, as
magnitudes. Moreover it would be easy for us to
assign each of them its place in the series. For
although the extensive cause varies continuously,
the changes in the sensation of colour are discontinuous, passing from one shade to another shade.
However numerous, then, may be the shades intermediate between the two colours, A and B, it
will always be possible to count them in thought,
at least roughly, and ascertain whether this number is almost equal to that of the shades which
separate B from another colour C. In the latter
case it will be said that B is equally distant from
A and C, that the contrast is the same on one
side as on the other. But this will always be
merely a convenient interpretation : for although
the number of intermediate shades may be equal

on both sides, although we may pass from one to the other by sudden leaps, we do not know whether these leaps are magnitudes, still less whether they are *equal* magnitudes : above all it would be necessary to show that the intermediaries which have helped us throughout our measurement could be found again inside the object which we have measured. If not, it is only by a metaphor that a sensation can be said to be an equal distance from two others.

Now, if the views which we have before enumerated with regard to luminous intensities are accepted, it will be recognized that the different hues of grey which Delbœuf displays to us are strictly analogous, for our consciousness, to colours, and that if we declare that a grey tint is equi-distant from two other grey tints, it is in the same sense in which it might be said that orange, for example, is at an equal distance from green and red. But there is this difference, that in all our past experience the succession of grey tints has been produced in connexion with a progressive increase or decrease in illumination. Hence we do for the differences of brightness what we do not think of doing for the differences of colour : we promote the changes of quality into variations of magnitude. Indeed, there is no difficulty here about the measuring, because the successive shades of grey produced by a continuous decrease of illumination are discontinuous, as being

This is just the case with differences of intensity in sensations of light. Delbœuf's underlying postulate.

qualities, and because we can count approximately
the principal intermediate shades which separate
any two kinds of grey.   The contrast A B will
thus be declared equal to the contrast B C when
our imagination, aided by our memory, inserts
between A and B the same number of intermediate
shades as between B and C.   It is needless to say
that this will necessarily be a very rough estimate.
We may anticipate that it will vary considerably
with different persons.   Above all it is to be ex-
pected that the person will show more hesitation
and that the estimates of different persons will
differ more widely in proportion as the difference
in brightness between the rings A and B is increased,
for a more and more laborious effort will be required
to estimate the number of intermediate hues.
This is exactly what happens, as we shall easily
perceive by glancing at the two tables drawn up
by Delbœuf.[1]   In proportion as he increases the
difference in brightness between the exterior
ring and the middle ring, the difference between
the numbers on which one and the same observer
or different observers successively fix increases
almost continuously from 3 degrees to 94, from
5 to 73, from 10 to 25, from 7 to 40.   But let
us leave these divergences on one side : let
us assume that the observers are always consistent and always agree with one another ; will it
then be established that the contrasts A B and
B C are equal ?   It would first be necessary to

---

[1] *Éléments de psychophysique*, pp. 61, 69.

prove that two successive elementary contrasts
are equal quantities, whilst, in fact, we only know
that they are successive.   It would then be necessary to prove that inside a given tint of grey we
perceive the less intense shades which our imagination has run through in order to estimate the
objective intensity of the source of light.   In a
word, Delbœuf's psychophysics assumes a theoretical postulate of the greatest importance,
which is disguised under the cloak of an experimental result, and which we should formulate as
follows : " When the objective quantity of light
is continuously increased, the differences between
the hues of grey successively obtained, each of
which represents the smallest perceptible increase
of physical stimulation, are quantities equal to one
another.   And besides, any one of the sensations
obtained can be equated with the sum of the
differences which separate from one another all
previous sensations, going from zero upwards."
Now, this is just the postulate of Fechner's psychophysics, which we are going to examine.

Fechner   took   as   his   starting-point   a   law
discovered by Weber, according to which, given
Fechner's psy-   a   certain   stimulus   which   calls   forth
chophysics.   a   certain   sensation,   the   amount   by
Weber's Law.   which   the   stimulus   must   be   increased
for consciousness to become aware of any change
bears a fixed relation to the original stimulus.
Thus, if we denote by E the stimulus which
corresponds   to   the   sensation   S,   and   by ΔE

the amount by which the original stimulus must be increased in order that a sensation of difference may be produced, we shall have $\dfrac{\Delta E}{E} = const.$

This formula has been much modified by the disciples of Fechner, and we prefer to take no part in the discussion ; it is for experiment to decide between the relation established by Weber and its substitutes. Nor shall we raise any difficulty about granting the probable existence of a law of this nature. It is here really a question not of measuring a sensation but only of determining the exact moment at which an increase of stimulus produces a change in it. Now, if a definite amount of stimulus produces a definite shade of sensation, it is obvious that the minimum amount of stimulus required to produce a change in this shade is also definite ; and since it is not constant, it must be a function of the original stimulus. But how are we to pass from a relation between the stimulus and its minimum increase to an equation which connects the "amount of sensation" with the corresponding stimulus ? The whole of psychophysics is involved in this transition, which is therefore worthy of our closest consideration.

We shall distinguish several different artifices in the process of transition from Weber's experiments, or from any other series of similar observations, to a psychophysical law like Fechner's. It is

The underlying assumptions and the process by which Fechner's Law is reached.

first of all agreed to consider our consciousness of an increase of stimulus as an increase of the sensation S : this is therefore called S. It is the n asserted that all the sensations ΔS, which correspond to the smallest perceptible increase of stimulus, are equal to one another. They are therefore treated as quantities, and while, on the one hand, these quantities are supposed to be always equal, and, on the other, experiment has given a certain relation $\Delta E = f(E)$ between the stimulus E and its minimum increase, the constancy of ΔS is expressed by writing $\Delta S = C \dfrac{\Delta E}{f(E)}$, C being a constant quantity. Finally it is agreed to replace the very small differences ΔS and ΔE by the infinitely small differences dS and dE, whence an equation which is, this time, a differential one : $dS = C \dfrac{dE}{f(E)}$. We shall now simply have to integrate on both sides to obtain the desired relation[1]: $S = C \displaystyle\int_0^E \dfrac{dE}{f(E)}$. And the transition will thus be made from a proved law, which only concerned the *occurrence* of a sensation, to an unprovable law which gives its *measure*.

Without entering upon any thorough discussion

---

[1] In the particular case where we admit without restriction Weber's Law $\dfrac{\Delta E}{E} = const.$, integration gives $S = C$ log. $\dfrac{E}{Q}$, Q being a constant. This is Fechner's " logarithmic law."

of this ingenious operation, let us show in a few words how Fechner has grasped the real difficulty of the problem, how he has tried to overcome it, and where, as it seems to us, the flaw in his reasoning lies.

Fechner realized that measurement could not be introduced into psychology without first defining what is meant by the equality and addition of two simple states, e.g. two sensations. But, unless they are identical, we do not at first see how two sensations can be equal. Undoubtedly in the physical world equality is not synonymous with identity. But the reason is that every phenomenon, every object, is there presented under two aspects, the one qualitative and the other extensive : nothing prevents us from putting the first one aside, and then there remains nothing but terms which can be directly or indirectly superposed on one another and consequently seen to be identical. Now, this qualitative element, which we begin by eliminating from external objects in order to measure them, is the very thing which psychophysics retains and claims to measure. And it is no use trying to measure this quality Q by some physical quantity Q' which lies beneath it : for it would be necessary to have previously shown that Q is a function of Q', and this would not be possible unless the quality Q had first been measured with some fraction of itself. Thus nothing prevents us from measuring the sensation of heat by

Can two sensations be equal without being identical?

the degree of temperature ; but this is only a convention, and the whole point of psychophysics lies in rejecting this convention and seeking how the sensation of heat varies when you change the temperature. In a word, it seems, on the one hand, that two different sensations cannot be said to be equal unless some identical residuum remains after the elimination of their qualitative difference ; but, on the other hand, this qualitative difference being all that we perceive, it does not appear what could remain once it was eliminated.

The novel feature in Fechner's treatment is that he did not consider this difficulty insurmountable. Taking advantage of the fact that sensation varies by sudden jumps while the stimulus increases continuously, he did not hesitate to call these differ-
ences of sensation by the same name : they are all, he says, *minimum* differences, since each cor-
responds to the smallest perceptible increase in the external stimulus. Therefore you can set aside the specific shade or quality of these suc-
cessive differences ; a common residuum will remain in virtue of which they will be seen to be in a manner identical : they all have the common character of being *minima*. Such will be the defini-
tion of equality which we were seeking. Now, the definition of addition will follow naturally. For if we treat as a quantity the difference perceived by consciousness between two sensations which succeed one another in the course of a continuous increase

Fechner's method of minimum differences.

of stimulus, if we call the first sensation S, and the second S+ΔS, we shall have to consider every sensation S as a sum, obtained by the addition of the minimum differences through which we pass before reaching it. The only remaining step will then be to utilize this twofold definition in order to establish, first of all, a relation between the differences ΔS and ΔE, and then, through the substitution of the differentials, between the two variables. True, the mathematicians may here lodge a protest against the substitution of differential for difference ; the psychologists may ask, too, whether the quantity ΔS, instead of being constant, does not vary as the sensation S itself ;¹ finally, taking the psychophysical law for granted, we may all debate about its real meaning. But, by the mere fact that ΔS is regarded as a quantity and S as a sum, the fundamental postulate of the whole process is accepted.

Now it is just this postulate which seems to us open to question, even if it can be understood. **Break-down of the assumption that the sensation is a sum, and the minimum differences quantities.** Assume that I experience a sensation S, and that, increasing the stimulus continuously, I perceive this increase after a certain time. I am now notified of the increase of the cause : but why should I call this notification an arithmetical difference ? No doubt the notification consists in the fact that the original state S has changed :

¹ Latterly it has been assumed that ΔS is proportional to S.

it has become S'; but the transition from S to S'
could only be called an arithmetical difference
if I were conscious, so to speak, of an interval
between S and S', and if my sensation were felt
to rise from S to S' by the addition of something.
By giving this transition a name, by calling it ΔS,
you make it first a reality and then a quantity.
Now, not only are you unable to explain in what
sense this transition is a quantity, but reflection
will show you that it is not even a reality ; the
only realities are the states S and S' through which
I pass. No doubt, if S and S' were numbers,
I could assert the reality of the difference S'—S
even though S and S' alone were given ; the
reason is that the number S'—S, which is a certain
sum of units, will then represent just the successive
moments of the addition by which we pass from
S to S'. But if S and S' are simple states, in
what will the *interval* which separates them consist ? And what, then, can the transition from
the first state to the second be, if not a mere act
of your thought, which, arbitrarily and for the
sake of the argument, assimilates a succession of
two states to a differentiation of two magnitudes ?

Either you keep to what consciousness presents
to you or you have recourse to a conventional
mode of representation. In the first
case you will find a difference between
S and S' like that between the shades
of the rainbow, and not at all an interval
of magnitude. In the second case you may intro-

We can speak
of " arithme-
tical differ-
ence " only in
a conventional
sense.

duce the symbol ΔS if you like, but it is only
in a conventional sense that you will speak here
of an arithmetical difference, and in a conventional
sense, also, that you will assimilate a sensation
to a sum. The most acute of Fechner's critics,
Jules Tannery, has made the latter point perfectly clear. "It will be said, for example, that
a sensation of 50 degrees is expressed by the number of differential sensations which would succeed
one another from the point where sensation is
absent up to the sensation of 50 degrees. . . . I
do not see that this is anything but a definition,
which is as legitimate as it is arbitrary." [1]

We do not believe, in spite of all that has been
said, that the method of mean gradations has
Delbœuf's re- set psychophysics on a new path. The
sults seem
more plausible, novel feature in Delbœuf's investi-
but, in the end, gation was that he chose a particular
all psychophy-
sics revolves case, in which consciousness seemed to
in a vicious
circle. decide in Fechner's favour, and in which
common sense itself played the part of the psychophysicist. He inquired whether certain sensations did not appear to us immediately as equal
although different, and whether it would not be
possible to draw up, by their help, a table of
sensations which were double, triple or quadruple
those which preceded them. The mistake which
Fechner made, as we have just seen, was that
he believed in an interval between two successive

[1] *Revue scientifique*, March 13 and April 24, 1875.

sensations S and S', when there is simply a *passing* from one to the other and not a *difference* in the arithmetical sense of the word. But if the two terms between which the passing takes place could be given simultaneously, there would then be a contrast besides the transition ; and although the contrast is not yet an arithmetical difference, it resembles it in a certain respect ; for the two terms which are compared stand here side by side as in a case of subtraction of two numbers. Suppose now that these sensations belong to the same *genus* and that in our past experience we have constantly been present at their march past, so to speak, while the physical stimulus increased continuously : it is extremely probable that we shall thrust the cause into the effect, and that the idea of contrast will thus melt into that of arithmetical difference. As we shall have noticed, moreover, that the sensation changed abruptly while the stimulus rose continuously, we shall no doubt estimate the distance between two given sensations by a rough guess at the number of these sudden jumps, or at least of the intermediate sensations which usually serve us as landmarks. To sum up, the contrast will appear to us as a difference, the stimulus as a quantity, the sudden jump as an element of equality : combining these three factors, we shall reach the idea of equal quantitative differences. Now, these conditions are nowhere so well realized as when surfaces of the same

colour, more or less illuminated, are simultaneously
presented to us. Not only is there here a contrast between similar sensations, but these sensations correspond to a cause whose influence
has always been felt by us to be closely connected
with its distance ; and, as this distance can vary
continuously, we cannot have escaped noticing
in our past experience a vast number of shades
of sensation which succeeded one another along
with the continuous increase in the cause. We
are therefore able to say that the contrast between
one shade of grey and another, for example, seems
to us almost equal to the contrast between the
latter and a third one ; and if we define two equal
sensations by saying that they are sensations
which a more or less confused process of reasoning
interprets as such, we shall in fact reach a law
like that proposed by Delbœuf. But it must
not be forgotten that consciousness has here
passed through the same intermediate steps as
the psychophysicist, and that its judgment is
worth here just what psychophysics is worth ;
it is a symbolical interpretation of quality as
quantity, a more or less rough estimate of the
number of sensations which can come in between
two given sensations. The difference is thus
not as great as is believed between the method of
least noticeable differences and that of mean
gradations, between the psychophysics of Fechner
and that of Delbœuf. The first led to a conventional measurement of sensation ; the second

appeals to common sense in the particular cases where common sense adopts a similar convention. In a word, all psychophysics is condemned by its origin to revolve in a vicious circle, for the theoretical postulate on which it rests condemns it to experimental verification, and it cannot be experimentally verified unless its postulate is first granted. The fact is that there is no point of contact between the unextended and the extended, between quality and quantity. We can interpret the one by the other, set up the one as the equivalent of the other ; but sooner or later, at the beginning or at the end, we shall have to recognize the conventional character of this assimilation.

In truth, psychophysics merely formulates with precision and pushes to its extreme consequences a conception familiar to common sense. As speech dominates over thought, as external objects, which are common to us all, are more important to us than the subjective states through which each of us passes, we have everything to gain by objectifying these states, by introducing into them, to the largest possible extent, the representation of their external cause. And the more our knowledge increases, the more we perceive the extensive behind the intensive, quantity behind quality, the more also we tend to thrust the former into the latter, and to treat our sensations as magnitudes. Physics,

Psychophysics merely pushes to its extreme consequences the fundamental but natural mistake of regarding sensations as magnitudes.

whose particular function it is to calculate the external cause of our internal states, takes the least possible interest in these states themselves : constantly and deliberately it confuses them with their cause. It thus encourages and even exaggerates the mistake which common sense makes on the point. The moment was inevitably bound to come at which science, familiarized with this confusion between quality and quantity, between sensation and stimulus, should seek to measure the one as it measures the other : such was the object of psychophysics. In this bold attempt Fechner was encouraged by his adversaries themselves, by the philosophers who speak of intensive magnitudes while declaring that psychic states cannot be submitted to measurement. For if we grant that one sensation can be stronger than another, and that this inequality is inherent in the sensations themselves, independently of all association of ideas, of all more or less conscious consideration of number and space, it is natural to ask by how much the first sensation exceeds the second, and to set up a quantitative relation between their intensities. Nor is it any use to reply, as the opponents of psychophysics sometimes do, that all measurement implies superposition, and that there is no occasion to seek for a numerical relation between intensities, which are not superposable objects. For it will then be necessary to explain why one sensation is said to be more intense than another, and how the conceptions of greater and smaller can be applied to things which, it has just been acknowledged, do not admit among themselves of the relations of container to contained. If, in order to cut short any question of this kind, we distinguish two kinds of quantity, the one intensive, which admits only of a " more or less," the other extensive, which lends itself to measurement, we are not far from siding with Fechner and the psychophysicists. For, as soon as a thing is acknowledged to be capable of increase and decrease, it seems natural to ask by how much it decreases or by how much it increases. And, because a measurement of this kind does not appear to be possible directly, it does not follow that science cannot successfully accomplish it by some indirect process, either by an integration of infinitely small elements, as Fechner proposes, or by any other roundabout way. Either, then, sensation is pure quality, or, if it is a magnitude, we ought to try to measure it.

To sum up what precedes, we have found the notion of intensity to present itself under a double aspect, according as we study the states of consciousness which represent an external cause, or those which are self-sufficient. In the former case the perception of intensity consists in a certain estimate of the magnitude of the cause by means of a certain quality in the effect : it is, as the Scottish philoso-

Thus intensity judged (1) in representative states by an estimate of the magnitude of the cause (2) in affective states by multiplicity of psychic phenomena involved.

phers would have said, an acquired perception. In the second case, we give the name of intensity to the larger or smaller number of simple psychic phenomena which we conjecture to be involved in the fundamental state : it is no longer an *acquired* perception, but a *confused* perception. In fact, these two meanings of the word usually intermingle, because the simpler phenomena involved in an emotion or an effort are generally representative, and because the majority of representative states, being at the same time affective, themselves include a multiplicity of elementary psychic phenomena. The idea of intensity is thus situated at the junction of two streams, one of which brings us the idea of extensive magnitude from without, while the other brings us from within, in fact from the very depths of consciousness, the image of an inner multiplicity. Now, the point is to determine in what the latter image consists, whether it is the same as that of number, or whether it is quite different from it. In the following chapter we shall no longer consider states of consciousness in isolation from one another, but in their concrete multiplicity, in so far as they unfold themselves in pure duration. And, in the same way as we have asked what would be the intensity of a representative sensation if we did not introduce into it the idea of its cause, we shall now have to inquire what the multiplicity of our inner states becomes, what form duration assumes, when the space in which it unfolds is eliminated. This second question is even more important than the first. For, if the confusion of quality with quantity were confined to each of the phenomena of consciousness taken separately, it would give rise to obscurities, as we have just seen, rather than to problems. But by invading the series of our psychic states, by introducing space into our perception of duration, it corrupts at its very source our feeling of outer and inner change, of movement, and of freedom. Hence the paradoxes of the Eleatics, hence the problem of free will. We shall insist rather on the second point ; but instead of seeking to solve the question, we shall show the mistake of those who ask it.

CHAPTER II

THE MULTIPLICITY OF CONSCIOUS STATES [1]
THE IDEA OF DURATION

NUMBER may be defined in general as a collection of units, or, speaking more exactly, as the synthesis *What is number?* of the one and the many. Every number ber is one, since it is brought before the

---

[1] I had already completed the present work when I read in the *Critique philosophique* (for 1883 and 1884) F. Pillon's very remarkable refutation of an interesting article by G. Noël on the interconnexion of the notions of number and space. But I have not found it necessary to make any alterations in the following pages, seeing that Pillon does not distinguish between time as quality and time as quantity, between the multiplicity of juxtaposition and that of interpenetration. Without this vital distinction, which it is the chief aim of the present chapter to establish, it would be possible to maintain, with Pillon, that number may be built up from the relation of co-existence. But what is here meant by co-existence? If the co-existing terms form an organic whole, they will never lead us to the notion of number; if they remain distinct, they are in juxtaposition and we are dealing with space. It is no use to quote the example of simultaneous impressions received by several senses. We either leave these sensations their specific differences, which amounts to saying that we do not count them; or else we eliminate their differences, and then how are we to distinguish them if not by their position or that of their symbols? We shall see that the verb " to distinguish " has two meanings, the one qualitative, the other

mind by a simple intuition and is given a name ; but the unity which attaches to it is that of a sum, it covers a multiplicity of parts which can be considered separately. Without attempting for the present any thorough examination of these conceptions of unity and multiplicity, let us inquire whether the idea of number does not imply the representation of something else as well.

It is not enough to say that number is a collection of units ; we must add that these units are identical with one another, or at least that they are assumed to be identical when they are counted. No doubt we can count the sheep in a flock and say that there are fifty, although they are all different from one another and are easily recognized by the shepherd : but the reason is that we agree in that case to neglect their individual differences and to take into account only what they have in common. On the other hand, as soon as we fix our attention on the particular features of objects or individuals, we can of course make an enumeration of them, but not a total. We place ourselves at these two very different points of view when we count the soldiers in a battalion and when we call the roll. Hence we may conclude that the idea of number implies the simple intuition of a multiplicity of parts or units, which are absolutely alike.

The units which make up a number must be identical.

quantitative : these two meanings have been confused, in my opinion, by the philosophers who have dealt with the relations between number and space.

And yet they must be somehow distinct from one another, since otherwise they would merge into a single unit. Let us assume that all the sheep in the flock are identical ; they differ at least by the position which they occupy in space, otherwise they would not form a flock. But now let us even set aside the fifty sheep themselves and retain only the idea of them. Either we include them all in the same image, and it follows as a necessary consequence that we place them side by side in an ideal space, or else we repeat fifty times in succession the image of a single one, and in that case it does seem, indeed, that the series lies in duration rather than in space. But we shall soon find out that it cannot be so. For if we picture to ourselves each of the sheep in the flock in succession and separately, we shall never have to do with more than a single sheep. In order that the number should go on increasing in proportion as we advance, we must retain the successive images and set them alongside each of the new units which we picture to ourselves : now, it is in space that such a juxtaposition takes place and not in pure duration. In fact, it will be easily granted that counting material objects means thinking all these objects together, thereby leaving them in space. But does this intuition of space accompany every idea of number, even of an abstract number ?

Any one can answer this question by reviewing

But they must also be distinct.

the various forms which the idea of number has
assumed for him since his childhood.
It will be seen that we began by imagin-
ing e.g. a row of balls, that these balls
afterwards became points, and, finally,
this image itself disappeared, leaving

We cannot form an image or idea of number without the accompanying intuition of space.

behind it, as we say, nothing but *abstract* number.
But at this very moment we ceased to have an
image or even an idea of it ; we kept only the
symbol which is necessary for reckoning and
which is the conventional way of *expressing* number. For we can confidently assert that 12 is
half of 24 without thinking either the number 12
or the number 24 : indeed, as far as quick calculation is concerned, we have everything to gain
by not doing so. But as soon as we wish to picture
number to ourselves, and not merely figures or
words, we are compelled to have recourse to an
extended image. What leads to misunderstanding
on this point seems to be the habit we have fallen
into of counting in time rather than in space. In
order to imagine the number 50, for example,
we repeat all the numbers starting from unity,
and when we have arrived at the fiftieth, we
believe we have built up the number in duration
and in duration only. And there is no doubt that
in this way we have counted moments of duration
rather than points in space ; but the question is
whether we have not counted the moments of
duration by means of points in space. It is certainly possible to perceive in time, and in time

only, a succession which is nothing but a succession, but not an addition, i.e. a succession which culminates in a sum. For though we reach a sum by taking into account a succession of different terms, yet it is necessary that each of these terms should remain when we pass to the following, and should wait, so to speak, to be added to the others : how could it wait, if it were nothing but an instant of duration ? And where could it wait if we did not localize it in space ? We involuntarily fix at a point in space each of the moments which we count, and it is only on this condition that the abstract units come to form a sum. No doubt it is possible, as we shall show later, to conceive the successive moments of time independently of space ; but when we add to the present moment those which have preceded it, as is the case when we are adding up units, we are not dealing with these moments themselves, since they have vanished for ever, but with the lasting traces which they seem to have left in space on their passage through it. It is true that we generally dispense with this mental image, and that, after having used it for the first two or three numbers, it is enough to know that it would serve just as well for the mental picturing of the others, if we needed it. But every clear idea of number implies a visual image in space ; and the direct study of the units which go to form a discrete multiplicity will lead us to the same conclusion on this point as the examination of number itself.

Every number is a collection of units, as we have said, and on the other hand every number is itself a unit, in so far as it is a synthesis of the units which compose it. But is the word *unit* taken in the same sense in both cases ? When we assert that number is a unit, we understand by this that we master the whole of it by a simple and indivisible intuition of the mind ; this unity thus includes a multiplicity, since it is the unity of a whole. But when we speak of the units which go to form number, we no longer think of these units as sums, but as pure, simple, irreducible units, intended to yield the natural series of numbers by an indefinitely continued process of accumulation. It seems, then, that there are two kinds of units, the one ultimate, out of which a number is formed by a process of addition, and the other provisional, the number so formed, which is multiple in itself, and owes its unity to the simplicity of the act by which the mind perceives it. And there is no doubt that, when we picture the units which make up number, we believe that we are thinking of indivisible components : this belief has a great deal to do with the idea that it is possible to conceive number independently of space. Nevertheless, by looking more closely into the matter, we shall see that all unity is the unity of a simple act of the mind, and that, as this is an act of unification, there must be some multiplicity for it to unify. No doubt, at the moment at which I think each of these units separately, I look upon it as indivisible, since I am determined to think of its unity alone. But as soon as I put it aside in order to pass to the next, I objectify it, and by that very deed I make it a thing, that is to say, a multiplicity. To convince oneself of this, it is enough to notice that the units by means of which arithmetic forms numbers are *provisional* units, which can be subdivided without limit, and that each of them is the sum of fractional quantities as small and as numerous as we like to imagine. How could we divide the unit, if it were here that ultimate unity which characterizes a simple act of the mind? How could we split it up into fractions whilst affirming its unity, if we did not regard it implicitly as an extended object, one in intuition but multiple in space? You will never get out of an idea which you have formed anything which you have not put into it ; and if the unity by means of which you make up your number is the unity of an act and not of an object, no effort of analysis will bring out of it anything but unity pure and simple. No doubt, when you equate the number 3 to the sum of 1 + 1 + 1, nothing prevents you from regarding the units which compose it as indivisible : but the reason is that you do not choose to make use of the multiplicity which is enclosed within each of these units. Indeed, it is probable that the number 3 first assumes to our mind this simpler shape, because we think rather of the way in which we have obtained it than of the use which we might make of it. But we soon perceive that, while all multiplication implies the possibility of treating any number whatever as a provisional unit which can be added to itself, inversely the units in their turn are true numbers which are as big as we like, but are regarded as provisionally indivisible for the purpose of compounding them with one another. Now, the very admission that it is possible to divide the unit into as many parts as we like, shows that we regard it as extended.

For we must understand what is meant by the *discontinuity* of number. It cannot be denied that the formation or construction of a number implies discontinuity. In other words, as we remarked above, each of the units with which we form the number 3 seems to be indivisible while we are dealing with it, and we pass abruptly from one to the other. Again, if we form the same number with halves, with quarters, with any units whatever, these units, in so far as they serve to form the said number, will still constitute elements which are provisionally indivisible, and it is always by jerks, by sudden jumps, so to speak, that we advance from one to the other. And the reason is that, in order to get a number, we are compelled to fix our attention successively on each of the units of which it is compounded. The indivisibility of the act by which

Number in process of formation is discontinuous, but, when formed, is invested with the continuity of space.

we conceive any one of them is then represented under the form of a mathematical point which is separated from the following point by an interval of space. But, while a series of mathematical points arranged in empty space expresses fairly well the process by which we form the idea of number, these mathematical points have a tendency to develop into lines in proportion as our attention is diverted from them, as if they were trying to reunite with one another. And when we look at number in its finished state, this union is an accomplished fact : the points have become lines, the divisions have been blotted out, the whole displays all the characteristics of continuity. This is why number, although we have formed it according to a definite law, can be split up on any system we please. In a word, we must distinguish between the unity which we think of and the unity which we set up as an object after having thought of it, as also between number in process of formation and number once formed. The unit is irreducible while we are thinking it and number is discontinuous while we are building it up : but, as soon as we consider number in its finished state, we objectify it, and it then appears to be divisible to an unlimited extent. In fact, we apply the term *subjective* to what seems to be completely and adequately known, and the term *objective* to what is known in such a way that a constantly increasing number of new impressions could be substituted for the idea which we actually have of it. Thus, a complex feeling will contain a fairly large number of simple elements ; but, as long as these elements do not stand out with perfect clearness, we cannot say that they were completely realized, and, as soon as consciousness has a distinct perception of them, the psychic state which results from their synthesis will have changed for this very reason. But there is no change in the general appearance of a body, however it is analysed by thought, because these different analyses, and an infinity of others, are already visible in the mental image which we form of the body, though they are not realized : this actual and not merely virtual perception of subdivisions in what is undivided is just what we call objectivity. It then becomes easy to determine the exact part played by the subjective and the objective in the idea of number. What properly belongs to the mind is the indivisible process by which it concentrates attention successively on the different parts of a given space ; but the parts which have thus been isolated remain in order to join with the others, and, once the addition is made, they may be broken up in any way whatever. They are therefore parts of space, and space is, accordingly, the material with which the mind builds up number, the medium in which the mind places it.

Properly speaking, it is arithmetic which teaches us to split up without limit the units of which number consists. Common sense is very much inclined to build up number with indivisibles.

And this is easily understood, since the provisional simplicity of the component units
is just what they owe to the mind, and
the latter pays more attention to its
own acts than to the material on which it
works. Science confines itself, here, to drawing
our attention to this material : if we did not
already localize number in space, science would
certainly not succeed in making us transfer it
thither. From the beginning, therefore, we must
have thought of number as of a juxtaposition in
space. This is the conclusion which we reached
at first, basing ourselves on the fact that all addition implies a multiplicity of parts simultaneously
perceived.

It follows that number is actually thought of as a juxtaposition in space.

Now, if this conception of number is granted,
it will be seen that everything is not counted in
the same way, and that there are two
very different kinds of multiplicity.
When we speak of material objects, we
refer to the possibility of seeing and
touching them ; we localize them in
space. In that case, no effort of the
inventive faculty or of symbolical representation is necessary in order to count
them ; we have only to think them, at first separately, and then simultaneously, within the very
medium in which they come under our observation.
The case is no longer the same when we consider
purely affective psychic states, or even mental

Two kinds of multiplicity: (1) material objects, counted in space ; (2) conscious states, not countable un-less symbolic-ally repre-sented in space.

images other than those built up by means of
sight and touch.   Here, the terms being no longer
given in space, it seems, *a priori*, that we can
hardly count them except by some process of
symbolical representation.   In fact, we are well
aware of a representation of this kind when
we are dealing with sensations the cause of
which is obviously situated in space.   Thus, when
we hear a noise of steps in the street, we have
a confused vision of somebody walking along :
each of the successive sounds is then localized at
a point in space where the passer-by might tread :
we count our sensations in the very space in which
their tangible causes are ranged.   Perhaps some
people count the successive strokes of a distant
bell in a similar way, their imagination pictures
the bell coming and going ; this spatial sort of
image is sufficient for the first two units, and the
others follow naturally.   But most people's minds
do not proceed in this way.   They range the successive sounds in an ideal space and then fancy
that they are counting them in pure duration.
Yet we must be clear on this point.   The sounds
of the bell certainly reach me one after the other ;
but one of two alternatives must be true.   Either
I retain each of these successive sensations in order
to combine it with the others and form a group
which reminds me of an air or rhythm which I
know : in that case I do not *count* the sounds, I
limit myself to gathering, so to speak, the qualitative impression produced by the whole series.   Or

else I intend explicitly to count them, and then I shall have to separate them, and this separation must take place within some homogeneous medium in which the sounds, stripped of their qualities, and in a manner emptied, leave traces of their presence which are absolutely alike. The question now is, whether this medium is time or space. But a moment of time, we repeat, cannot persist in order to be added to others. If the sounds are separated, they must leave empty intervals between them. If we count them, the intervals must remain though the sounds disappear : how could these intervals remain, if they were pure duration and not space ? It is in space, therefore, that the operation takes place. It becomes, indeed, more and more difficult as we penetrate further into the depths of consciousness. Here we find ourselves confronted by a confused multiplicity of sensations and feelings which analysis alone can distinguish. Their number is identical with the number of the moments which we take up when we count them ; but these moments, as they can be added to one another, are again points in space. Our final conclusion, therefore, is that there are two kinds of multiplicity : that of material objects, to which the conception of number is immediately applicable ; and the multiplicity of states of consciousness, which cannot be regarded as numerical without the help of some symbolical representation, in which a necessary element is *space*.

As a matter of fact, each of us makes a distinction between these two kinds of multiplicity whenever he speaks of the impenetrability of matter. We sometimes set up impenetrability as a fundamental property of bodies, known in the same way and put on the same level as e.g. weight or resistance. But a purely negative property of this kind cannot be revealed by our senses ; indeed, certain experiments in mixing and combining things might lead us to call it in question if our minds were not already made up on the point. Try to picture one body penetrating another : you will at once assume that there are empty spaces in the one which will be occupied by the particles of the other ; these particles in their turn cannot penetrate one another unless one of them divides in order to fill up the interstices of the other ; and our thought will prolong this operation indefinitely in preference to picturing two bodies in the same place. Now, if impenetrability were really a quality of matter which was known by the senses, it is not at all clear why we should experience more difficulty in conceiving two bodies merging into one another than a surface devoid of resistance or a weightless fluid. In reality, it is not a physical but a logical necessity which attaches to the proposition : "Two bodies cannot occupy the same place at the same time." The contrary assertion involves an absurdity which no conceivable experience could succeed in dispelling.

The impenetrability of matter is not a physical but a logical necessity.

In a word, it implies a contradiction. But does not this amount to recognizing that the very idea of the number 2, or, more generally, of any number whatever, involves the idea of juxtaposition in space ? If impenetrability is generally regarded as a quality of matter, the reason is that the idea of number is thought to be independent of the idea of space. We thus believe that we are adding something to the idea of two or more objects by saying that they cannot occupy the same place : as if the idea of the number 2, even the abstract number, were not already, as we have shown, that of two different positions in space ! Hence to assert the impenetrability of matter is simply to recognize the inter-connexion between the notions of number and space, it is to state a property of number rather than of matter.—Yet, it will be said, do we not count feelings, sensations, ideas, all of which permeate one another, and each of which, for its part, takes up the whole of the soul ?—Yes, undoubtedly ; but, just because they permeate one another, we cannot count them unless we represent them by homogeneous units which occupy separate positions in space and consequently no longer permeate one another. Impenetrability thus makes its appearance at the same time as number ; and when we attribute this quality to matter in order to distinguish it from everything which is not matter, we simply state under another form the distinction established above between extended objects, to which the conception of number is immediately applicable, and states of consciousness, which have first of all to be represented symbolically in space.

It is advisable to dwell on the last point. If, in order to count states of consciousness, we have to represent them symbolically in space, is it not likely that this symbolical representation will alter the normal conditions of inner perception? Let us recall what we said a short time ago about the intensity of certain psychic states. Representative sensation, looked at in itself, is pure quality; but, seen through the medium of extensity, this quality becomes in a certain sense quantity, and is called intensity. In the same way, our projection of our psychic states into space in order to form a discrete multiplicity is likely to influence these states themselves and to give them in reflective consciousness a new form, which immediate perception did not attribute to them. Now, let us notice that when we speak of *time*, we generally think of a homogeneous medium in which our conscious states are ranged alongside one another as in space, so as to form a discrete multiplicity. Would not time, thus understood, be to the multiplicity of our psychic states what intensity is to certain of them, —a sign, a symbol, absolutely distinct from true duration? Let us ask consciousness to isolate itself from the external world, and, by a vigorous effort of abstraction, to become itself again. We

[Marginal note:] Homogeneous time as the medium in which conscious states form discrete series. This time is nothing but space, and pure duration is something different.

shall then put this question to it : does the multiplicity of our conscious states bear the slightest
resemblance to the multiplicity of the units of a
number ?   Has true duration anything to do
with space ?   Certainly, our analysis of the idea
of number could not but make us doubt this
analogy, to say no more.   For if time, as the
reflective consciousness represents it, is a medium
in which our conscious states form a discrete series
so as to admit of being counted, and if on the other
hand our conception of number ends in spreading
out in space everything which can be directly
counted, it is to be presumed that time, understood in the sense of a medium in which we make
distinctions and count, is nothing but space.   That
which goes to confirm this opinion is that we are
compelled to borrow from space the images by
which we describe what the reflective consciousness
feels about time and even about succession ; it
follows that pure duration must be something
different.   Such are the questions which we have
been led to ask by the very analysis of the notion
of discrete multiplicity.   But we cannot throw any
light upon them except by a direct study of the
ideas of space and time in their mutual relations.

We shall not lay too much stress on the question
of the absolute reality of space : perhaps we might
as well ask whether space is or is not in
space.   In short, our senses perceive
the qualities of bodies and space along

Does space
exist inde-
pendently of
its contents, as
Kant held ?

with them : the great difficulty seems to
have been to discover whether extensity is an
aspect of these physical qualities—a quality of
quality—or whether these qualities are essentially
unextended, space coming in as a later addition,
but being self-sufficient and existing without
them. On the first hypothesis, space would be
reduced to an abstraction, or, speaking more
correctly, an extract ; it would express the common element possessed by certain sensations called
representative. In the second case, space would
be a reality as solid as the sensations themselves,
although of a different order. We owe the exact
formulation of this latter conception to Kant :
the theory which he works out in the Transcendental Aesthetic consists in endowing space
with an existence independent of its content, in
laying down as *de jure* separable what each of
us separates *de facto*, and in refusing to regard
extensity as an abstraction like the others. In
this respect the Kantian conception of space differs
less than is usually imagined from the popular belief. Far from shaking our faith in the reality of
space, Kant has shown what it actually means
and has even justified it.

Moreover, the solution given by Kant does not
seem to have been seriously disputed since his
time : indeed, it has forced itself, sometimes
without their knowledge, on the majority of
those who have approached the problem anew,
whether nativists or empiricists. Psychologists

agree in assigning a Kantian origin to the nativistic explanation of Johann Müller ;
but Lotze's hypothesis of local signs,
Bain's theory, and the more comprehensive explanation suggested by Wundt,
may seem at first sight quite independent
of the Transcendental Aesthetic. The
authors of these theories seem indeed to
have put aside the problem of the nature of space, in
order to investigate simply by what process our
sensations come to be situated in space and to be
set, so to speak, alongside one another : but this
very question shows that they regard sensations
as inextensive and make a radical distinction, just
as Kant did, between the matter of representation
and its form. The conclusion to be drawn from
the theories of Lotze and Bain, and from Wundt's
attempt to reconcile them, is that the sensations
by means of which we come to form the notion of
space are themselves unextended and simply
qualitative : extensity is supposed to result from
their synthesis, as water from the combination of
two gases. The empirical or genetic explanations
have thus taken up the problem of space at the
very point where Kant left it : Kant separated
space from its contents : the empiricists ask how
these contents, which are taken out of space by
our thought, manage to get back again. It is true
that they have apparently disregarded the activity
of the mind, and that they are obviously inclined
to regard the extensive form under which we repre-

sent things as produced by a kind of alliance of the
sensations with one another : space, without being
extracted from the sensations, is supposed to
result from their co-existence. But how can we
explain such an origination without the active
intervention of the mind ? The extensive differs
by hypothesis from the inextensive : and even if
we assume that extension is nothing but a relation
between inextensive terms, this relation must still
be established by a mind capable of thus associating several terms. It is no use quoting the
example of chemical combinations, in which the
whole seems to assume, of its own accord, a form
and qualities which did not belong to any of the
elementary atoms. This form and these qualities
owe their origin just to the fact that we gather up
the multiplicity of atoms in a single perception :
get rid of the mind which carries out this synthesis
and you will at once do away with the qualities,
that is to say, the aspect under which the synthesis
of elementary parts is presented to our consciousness. Thus inextensive sensations will remain
what they are, viz., inextensive sensations, if
nothing be added to them. For their co-existence
to give rise to space, there must be an act of the
mind which takes them in all at the same time and
sets them in juxtaposition : this unique act is
very like what Kant calls an *a priori* form of
sensibility.

If we now seek to characterize this act, we see
that it consists essentially in the intuition, or

rather the conception, of an empty homogeneous medium. For it is scarcely
possible to give any other definition of
space : space is what enables us to distinguish a number of identical and
simultaneous sensations from one another; it is thus a principle of differentiation other than that of qualitative differentiation,
and consequently it is a reality with no quality.
Some one may say, with the believers in the theory of
local signs, that simultaneous sensations are never
identical, and that, in consequence of the diversity
of the organic elements which they affect, there
are no two points of a homogeneous surface which
make the same impression on the sight or the
touch. We are quite ready to grant it, for if these
two points affected us in the same way, there would
be no reason for placing one of them on the right
rather than on the left. But, just because we afterwards interpret this difference of quality in the sense
of a difference of situation, it follows that we must
have a clear idea of a homogeneous medium, i.e.
of a simultaneity of terms which, although identical
in quality, are yet distinct from one another. The
more you insist on the difference between the
impressions made on our retina by two points
of a homogeneous surface, the more do you
thereby make room for the activity of the mind,
which perceives under the form of extensive
homogeneity what is given it as qualitative
heterogeneity. No doubt, though the repre-

*This act con-
sists in the
intuition of
an empty
homogeneous
medium :
perhaps pecu-
liar to man and
not shared by
animals.*

sentation of a homogeneous space grows out of an effort of the mind, there must be within the qualities themselves which differentiate two sensations some reason why they occupy this or that definite position in space. We must thus distinguish between the perception of extensity and the conception of space : they are no doubt implied in one another, but, the higher we rise in the scale of intelligent beings, the more clearly do we meet with the independent idea of a homogeneous space. It is therefore doubtful whether animals perceive the external world quite as we do, and especially whether they represent externality in the same way as ourselves. Naturalists have pointed out, as a remarkable fact, the surprising ease with which many verte-brates, and even some insects, manage to find their way through space. Animals have been seen to return almost in a straight line to their old home, pursuing a path which was hitherto unknown to them over a distance which may amount to several hundreds of miles. Attempts have been made to explain this feeling of direction by sight or smell, and, more recently, by the perception of magnetic currents which would enable the animal to take its bearings like a living compass. This amounts to saying that space is not so homogeneous for the animal as for us, and that determinations of space, or directions, do not assume for it a purely geome-trical form. Each of these directions might appear to it with its own shade, its peculiar quality. We shall understand how a perception of this kind is possible if we remember that we ourselves distinguish our right from our left by a natural feeling, and that these two parts of our own extensity do then appear to us as if they bore a different *quality* ; in fact, this is the very reason why we cannot give a proper definition of right and left.   In truth, qualitative differences exist everywhere in nature, and I do not see why two concrete directions should not be as marked in immediate perception as two colours.   But the conception of an empty homogeneous medium is something far more extraordinary, being a kind of reaction against that heterogeneity which is the very ground of our experience. Therefore, instead of saying that animals have a special sense of direction, we may as well say that men have a special faculty of perceiving or conceiving a space without quality.   This faculty is not the faculty of abstraction : indeed, if we notice that abstraction assumes clean-cut distinctions and a kind of externality of the concepts or their symbols with regard to one another, we shall find that the faculty of abstraction already implies the intuition of a homogeneous medium.   What we must say is that we have to do with two different kinds of reality, the one heterogeneous, that of sensible qualities, the other homogeneous, namely space.   This latter, clearly conceived by the human intellect, enables us to use clean-cut distinctions, to count, to abstract, and perhaps also to speak.

Now, if space is to be defined as the homogeneous, it seems that inversely every homogeneous
and unbounded medium will be space.
For, homogeneity here consisting in the
absence of every quality, it is hard to
see how two forms of the homogeneous
could be distinguished from one another.
Nevertheless it is generally agreed to regard time
as an unbounded medium, different from space
but homogeneous like the latter : the homogeneous is thus supposed to take two forms, according
as its contents co-exist or follow one another. It
is true that, when we make time a homogeneous
medium in which conscious states unfold themselves, we take it to be given all at once, which
amounts to saying that we abstract it from duration.   This simple consideration ought to warn us
that we are thus unwittingly falling back upon
space, and really giving up time.   Moreover, we
can understand that material objects, being exterior to one another and to ourselves, derive both
exteriorities from the homogeneity of a medium
which inserts intervals between them and sets off
their outlines : but states of consciousness, even
when successive, permeate one another, and in the
simplest of them the whole soul can be reflected.
We may therefore surmise that time, conceived
under the form of a homogeneous medium, is
some spurious concept, due to the trespassing of
the idea of space upon the field of pure consciousness.   At any rate we cannot finally admit two

Time, in so far as it is a homogeneous medium, and not concrete duration, is reducible to space.

forms of the homogeneous, time and space, without first seeking whether one of them cannot be reduced to the other. Now, externality is the distinguishing mark of things which occupy space, while states of consciousness are not essentially external to one another, and become so only by being spread out in time, regarded as a homogeneous medium. If, then, one of these two supposed forms of the homogeneous, namely time and space, is derived from the other, we can surmise *a priori* that the idea of space is the fundamental datum. But, misled by the apparent simplicity of the idea of time, the philosophers who have tried to reduce one of these ideas to the other have thought that they could make extensity out of duration. While showing how they have been misled, we shall see that time, conceived under the form of an unbounded and homogeneous medium, is nothing but the ghost of space haunting the reflective consciousness.

The English school tries, in fact, to reduce relations of extensity to more or less complex relations of succession in time. When, with our eyes shut, we run our hands along a surface, the rubbing of our fingers against the surface, and especially the varied play of our joints, provide a series of sensations, which differ only by their *qualities* and which exhibit a certain order in time. Moreover, experience teaches us that this series can be reversed, that we can, by an

Mistake of the attempt to derive relations of extensity from those of succession. The conception of " pure duration."

effort of a different kind (or, as we shall call it later, *in an opposite direction*), obtain the same sensations over again in an inverse order : relations of position in space might then be defined as reversible relations of succession in time. But such a definition involves a vicious circle, or at least a very superficial idea of time. There are, indeed, as we shall show a little later, two possible conceptions of time, the one free from all alloy, the other surreptitiously bringing in the idea of space. Pure duration is the form which the succession of our conscious states assumes when our ego lets itself *live*, when it refrains from separating its present state from its former states. For this purpose it need not be entirely absorbed in the passing sensation or idea; for then, on the contrary, it would no longer *endure*. Nor need it forget its former states : it is enough that, in recalling these states, it does not set them alongside its actual state as one point alongside another, but forms both the past and the present states into an organic whole, as happens when we recall the notes of a tune, melting, so to speak, into one another. Might it not be said that, even if these notes succeed one another, yet we perceive them in one another, and that their totality may be compared to a living being whose parts, although distinct, permeate one another just because they are so closely connected ? The proof is that, if we interrupt the rhythm by dwelling longer than is right on one

note of the tune, it is not its exaggerated length,
as length, which will warn us of our mistake, but
the qualitative change thereby caused in the
whole of the musical phrase. We can thus conceive of succession without distinction, and think
of it as a mutual penetration, an interconnexion
and organization of elements, each one of which
represents the whole, and cannot be distinguished
or isolated from it except by abstract thought.
Such is the account of duration which would be
given by a being who was ever the same and ever
changing, and who had no idea of space. But,
familiar with the latter idea and indeed beset by
it, we introduce it unwittingly into our feeling of
pure succession ; we set our states of consciousness
side by side in such a way as to perceive them
simultaneously, no longer in one another, but
alongside one another ; in a word, we project
time into space, we express duration in terms of
extensity, and succession thus takes the form of a
continuous line or a chain, the parts of which touch
without penetrating one another. Note that the
mental image thus shaped implies the perception,
no longer successive, but simultaneous, of a *before*
and *after*, and that it would be a contradiction to
suppose a succession which was only a succession,
and which nevertheless was contained in one and
the same instant. Now, when we speak of an
order of succession in duration, and of the reversi-
bility of this order, is the succession we are dealing
with pure succession, such as we have just defined

it, without any admixture of extensity, or is it succession developing in space, in such a way that we can take in at once a number of elements which are both distinct and set side by side ?   There is no doubt about the answer : we could not introduce *order* among terms without first distinguishing them and then comparing the places which they occupy ; hence we must perceive them as multiple, simultaneous and distinct ; in a word, we set them side by side, and if we introduce an order in what is successive, the reason is that succession is converted into simultaneity and is projected into space.   In short, when the movement of my finger along a surface or a line provides me with a series of sensations of different qualities, one of two things happens : either I picture these sensations to myself as in duration only, and in that case they succeed one another in such a way that I cannot at a given moment perceive a number of them as simultaneous and yet distinct ; or else I make out an order of succession, but in that case I display the faculty not only of perceiving a succession of elements, but also of setting them out in line after having distinguished them : in a word, I already possess the idea of space.   Hence the idea of a reversible series in duration, or even simply of a certain *order* of succession in time, itself implies the representation of space, and cannot be used to define it.

To give this argument a stricter form, let us imagine a straight line of unlimited length, and on this line a material point A, which moves.

Succession cannot be symbolized as a line without introducing the idea of space of three dimensions. If this point were conscious of itself, it would feel itself change, since it moves : it would perceive a succession; but would this succession assume for it the form of a line ? No doubt it would, if it could rise, so to speak, above the line which it traverses, and perceive simultaneously several points of it in juxtaposition : but by doing so it would form the idea of space, and it is in space and not in pure duration that it would see displayed the changes which it undergoes. We here put our finger on the mistake of those who regard pure duration as something similar to space, but of a simpler nature. They are fond of setting psychic states side by side, of forming a chain or a line of them, and do not imagine that they are introducing into this operation the idea of space properly so called, the idea of space in its totality, because space is a medium of three dimensions. But how can they fail to notice that, in order to perceive a line as a line, it is necessary to take up a position outside it, to take account of the void which surrounds it, and consequently to think a space of three dimensions ? If our conscious point A does not yet possess the idea of space— and this is the hypothesis which we have agreed to adopt—the succession of states through which it passes cannot assume for it the form of a line ; but its sensations will add themselves dynamically to one another and will organize themselves, like

the successive notes of a tune by which we allow
ourselves to be lulled and soothed. In a word,
pure duration might well be nothing but a succession of qualitative changes, which melt into
and permeate one another, without precise outlines, without any tendency to externalize themselves in relation to one another, without any
affiliation with number : it would be pure heterogeneity. But for the present we shall not insist
upon this point; it is enough for us to have shown
that, from the moment when you attribute the
least homogeneity to duration, you surreptitiously
introduce space.

It is true that we count successive moments
of duration, and that, because of its relations with
number, time at first seems to us to be
a measurable magnitude, just like space.
But there is here an important distinction to be made. I say, e.g., that
a minute has just elapsed, and I mean
by this that a pendulum, beating the
seconds, has completed sixty oscillations. If I
picture these sixty oscillations to myself all at
once by a single mental perception, I exclude by
hypothesis the idea of a succession. I do not think
of sixty strokes which succeed one another, but
of sixty points on a fixed line, each one of which
symbolizes, so to speak, an oscillation of the
pendulum. If, on the other hand, I wish to picture
these sixty oscillations in succession, but without
altering the way they are produced in space, I shall

*Pure dura-
tion is
wholly quali-
tative. It
cannot be
measured un-
less symbol-
ically repre-
sented in
space.*

be compelled to think of each oscillation to the
exclusion of the recollection of the preceding one,
for space has preserved no trace of it ; but by
doing so I shall condemn myself to remain for
ever in the present ; I shall give up the attempt
to think a succession or a duration.　Now if,
finally, I retain the recollection of the preceding
oscillation together with the image of the present
oscillation, one of two things will happen.　Either
I shall set the two images side by side, and we then
fall back on our first hypothesis, or I shall perceive one in the other, each permeating the other and
organizing themselves like the notes of a tune, so
as to form what we shall call a continuous or
qualitative multiplicity with no resemblance to
number.　I shall thus get the image of pure duration ; but I shall have entirely got rid of the idea
of a homogeneous medium or a measurable quantity.　By carefully examining our consciousness
we shall recognize that it proceeds in this way
whenever it refrains from representing duration
symbolically.　When the regular oscillations of the
pendulum make us sleepy, is it the last sound
heard, the last movement perceived, which produces this effect ?　No, undoubtedly not, for why
then should not the first have done the same ?
Is it the recollection of the preceding sounds or
movements, set in juxtaposition to the last one ?
But this same recollection, if it is later on set in
juxtaposition to a single sound or movement, will
remain without effect.　Hence we must admit

that the sounds combined with one another and acted, not by their quantity as quantity, but by the quality which their quantity exhibited, i.e. by the rhythmic organization of the whole. Could the effect of a slight but continuous stimulation be understood in any other way? If the sensation remained always the same, it would continue to be indefinitely slight and indefinitely bearable. But the fact is that each increase of stimulation is taken up into the preceding stimulations, and that the whole produces on us the effect of a musical phrase which is constantly on the point of ending and constantly altered in its totality by the addition of some new note. If we assert that it is always the *same* sensation, the reason is that we are thinking, not of the sensation itself, but of its objective cause situated in space. We then set it out in space in its turn, and in place of an organism which develops, in place of changes which permeate one another, we perceive one and the same sensation stretching itself out lengthwise, so to speak, and setting itself in juxtaposition to itself without limit. Pure duration, that which consciousness perceives, must thus be reckoned among the so-called intensive magnitudes, if intensities can be called magnitudes : strictly speaking, however, it is not a quantity, and as soon as we try to measure it, we unwittingly replace it by space.

But we find it extraordinarily difficult to think of duration in its original purity ; this is due, no doubt, to the fact that we do not *endure*

Time, as dealt
with by the
astronomer
and the phy-
sicist, does in-
deed *seem* to
be measura-
ble and there-
fore homo-
geneous. alone, external objects, it seems, *endure*
as we do, and time, regarded from
this point of view, has every appearance of a homogeneous medium.   Not
only do the moments of this duration
seem to be external to one another, like
bodies in space, but the movement perceived by
our senses is the, so to speak, palpable sign of a
homogeneous and measurable duration.   Nay
more, time enters into the formulae of mechanics,
into the calculations of the astronomer, and even
of the physicist, under the form of a quantity.
We measure the velocity of a movement, implying
that time itself is a magnitude.   Indeed, the
analysis which we have just attempted requires
to be completed, for if duration properly so-called
cannot be measured, what is it that is measured
by the oscillations of the pendulum ?   Granted
that inner duration, perceived by consciousness,
is nothing else but the melting of states of
consciousness into one another, and the gradual
growth of the ego, it will be said, notwithstanding,
that the time which the astronomer introduces
into his formulae, the time which our clocks
divide into equal portions, this time, at least, is
something different : it must be a measurable
and therefore homogeneous magnitude.—It is
nothing of the sort, however, and a close examination will dispel this last illusion.

When I follow with my eyes on the dial of a

clock the movement of the hand which corresponds to the oscillations of the pendulum, I do not measure duration, as
seems to be thought ; I merely count
simultaneities, which is very different.
Outside of me, in space, there is never
more than a single position of the hand and
the pendulum, for nothing is left of the
past positions. Within myself a process of
organization or interpenetration of conscious
states is going on, which constitutes true duration.
It is because I *endure* in this way that I picture
to myself what I call the past oscillations of the
pendulum at the same time as I perceive the
present oscillation. Now, let us withdraw for a
moment the ego which thinks these so-called successive oscillations : there will never be more
than a single oscillation, and indeed only a single
position, of the pendulum, and hence no duration.
Withdraw, on the other hand, the pendulum and
its oscillations ; there will no longer be anything
but the heterogeneous duration of the ego,
without moments external to one another, without relation to number. Thus, within our ego,
there is succession without mutual externality ;
outside the ego, in pure space, mutual externality
without succession : mutual externality, since
the present oscillation is radically distinct from
the previous oscillation, which no longer exists ;
but no succession, since succession exists solely
for a conscious spectator who keeps the past in

But what we call measuring time is nothing but count- ing simultanei- ties. The clock taken as an illustration.

mind and sets the two oscillations or their symbols side by side in an auxiliary space. Now,
between this succession without externality and
this externality without succession, a kind of
exchange takes place, very similar to what physicists call the phenomenon of endosmosis. As the
successive phases of our conscious life, although
interpenetrating, correspond individually to an
oscillation of the pendulum which occurs at the
same time, and as, moreover, these oscillations
are sharply distinguished from one another, we
get into the habit of setting up the same distinction between the successive moments of our conscious life : the oscillations of the pendulum
break it up, so to speak, into parts external to
one another : hence the mistaken idea of a homogeneous inner duration, similar to space, the
moments of which are identical and follow, without penetrating, one another. But, on the other
hand, the oscillations of the pendulum, which
are distinct only because one has disappeared
when the other appears on the scene, profit, as
it were, from the influence which they have thus
exercised over our conscious life. Owing to the
fact that our consciousness has organized them
as a whole in memory, they are first preserved
and afterwards disposed in a series : in a word,
we create for them a fourth dimension of space,
which we call homogeneous time, and which
enables the movement of the pendulum, although
taking place at one spot, to be continually set in

juxtaposition to itself. Now, if we try to determine the exact part played by the real and the imaginary in this very complex process, this is what we find. There is a real space, without duration, in which phenomena appear and disappear simultaneously with our states of consciousness. There is a real duration, the heterogeneous moments of which permeate one another ; each moment, however, can be brought into relation with a state of the external world which is contemporaneous with it, and can be separated from the other moments in consequence of this very process. The comparison of these two realities gives rise to a symbolical representation of duration, derived from space. Duration thus assumes the illusory form of a homogeneous medium, and the connecting link between these two terms, space and duration, is simultaneity, which might be defined as the intersection of time and space.

If we analyse in the same way the concept of motion, the living symbol of this seemingly homogeneous duration, we shall be led to make a distinction of the same kind. We generally say that a movement takes place *in* space, and when we assert that motion is homogeneous and divisible, it is of the space traversed that we are thinking, as if it were interchangeable with the motion itself. Now, if we reflect further, we shall see that the successive positions of the moving body really do occupy

Two elements in motion : (1) the space traversed, which is homogeneous and divisible ; (2) the act of traversing, indivisible and real only for consciousness.

space, but that the process by which it passes
from one position to the other, a process which
occupies duration and which has no reality except for a conscious spectator, eludes space. We
have to do here not with an *object* but with a
progress : motion, in so far as it is a passage from
one point to another, is a mental synthesis, a
psychic and therefore unextended process. Space
contains only parts of space, and at whatever point
of space we consider the moving body, we shall
get only a position. If consciousness is aware
of anything more than positions, the reason is
that it keeps the successive positions in mind and
synthesizes them. But how does it carry out a
synthesis of this kind ? It cannot be by a fresh
setting out of these same positions in a homogeneous medium, for a fresh synthesis would be
necessary to connect the positions with one
another, and so on indefinitely. We are thus compelled to admit that we have here to do with a
synthesis which is, so to speak, qualitative, a
gradual organization of our successive sensations,
a unity resembling that of a phrase in a melody.
This is just the idea of motion which we form
when we think of it by itself, when, so to speak,
from motion we extract mobility. Think of
what you experience on suddenly perceiving a
shooting star : in this extremely rapid motion
there is a natural and instinctive separation between the space traversed, which appears to you
under the form of a line of fire, and the absolutely

indivisible sensation of motion or mobility. A rapid gesture, made with one's eyes shut, will assume for consciousness the form of a purely qualitative sensation as long as there is no thought of the space traversed. In a word, there are two elements to be distinguished in motion, the space traversed and the act by which we traverse it, the successive positions and the synthesis of these positions. The first of these elements is a homogeneous quantity : the second has no reality except in a consciousness : it is a quality or an intensity, whichever you prefer. But here again we meet with a case of endosmosis, an inter-mingling of the purely intensive sensation of mobility with the extensive representation of the space traversed. On the one hand we attribute to the motion the divisibility of the space which it traverses, forgetting that it is quite possible to divide an *object*, but not an *act* : and on the other hand we accustom ourselves to projecting this act itself into space, to applying it to the whole of the line which the moving body traverses, in a word, to solidifying it : as if this localizing of a *progress* in space did not amount to asserting that, even outside consciousness, the past co-exists along with the present !

It is to this confusion between motion and the space traversed that the paradoxes of the Eleatics are due ; for the interval which separates two points is infinitely divisible, and if motion con-sisted of parts like those of the interval itself,

the interval would never be crossed. But the
truth is that each of Achilles' steps is
a simple indivisible act, and that, after
a given number of these acts, Achilles
will have passed the tortoise.   The mistake of the Eleatics arises from their
identification of this series of acts, each of which is
of a definite kind and *indivisible*, with the homogeneous space which underlies them. As this
space can be divided and put together again according to any law whatever, they think they are
justified in reconstructing Achilles' whole movement, not with Achilles' kind of step, but with the
tortoise's kind : in place of Achilles pursuing the
tortoise they really put two tortoises, regulated
by each other, two tortoises which agree to make
the same kind of steps or simultaneous acts, so as
never to catch one another.   Why does Achilles
outstrip the tortoise ?   Because each of Achilles'
steps and each of the tortoise's steps are indivisible
acts in so far as they are movements, and are
different magnitudes in so far as they are space :
so that addition will soon give a greater length
for the space traversed by Achilles than is obtained
by adding together the space traversed by the
tortoise and the handicap with which it started.
This is what Zeno leaves out of account when he
reconstructs the movement of Achilles according
to the same law as the movement of the tortoise,
forgetting that space alone can be divided and ·
put together again in any way we like, and thus

The common confusion between motion and the space traversed gives rise to the paradoxes of the Eleatics.

confusing space with motion. Hence we do not think it necessary to admit, even after the acute and profound analysis of a contemporary thinker,[1] that the meeting of the two moving bodies implies a discrepancy between real and imaginary motion, between *space in itself* and indefinitely divisible space, between concrete time and abstract time. Why resort to a metaphysical hypothesis, however ingenious, about the nature of space, time, and motion, when immediate intuition shows us motion within duration, and duration outside space ? There is no need to assume a limit to the divisibility of concrete space ; we can admit that it is infinitely divisible, provided that we make a distinction between the simultaneous positions of the two moving bodies, which are in fact in space, and their movements, which cannot occupy space, being duration rather than extent, quality and not quantity. To measure the velocity of a movement, as we shall see, is simply to ascertain a simultaneity ; to introduce this velocity into calculations is simply to use a convenient means of anticipating a simultaneity. Thus mathematics confines itself to its own province as long as it is occupied with determining the simultaneous positions of Achilles and the tortoise at a given moment, or when it admits *a priori* that the two moving bodies meet at a point X—a meeting which is itself a simultaneity. But it goes

---

[1] Évellin, *Infini et quantité*. Paris, 1881.

beyond its province when it claims to reconstruct what takes place in the interval between two simultaneities ; or rather it is inevitably led, even then, to consider simultaneities once more, fresh simultaneities, the indefinitely increasing number of which ought to be a warning that we cannot make movement out of immobilities, nor time out of space. In short, just as nothing will be found homogeneous in duration except a symbolical medium with no duration at all, namely space, in which simultaneities are set out in line, in the same way no homogeneous element will be found in motion except that which least belongs to it, the traversed space, which is motionless.

Now, just for this reason, science cannot deal with time and motion except on condition of first **Science has to** eliminating the essential and qualita- **eliminate dur-** tive element—of time, duration, and of **ation from** **time and mo-** motion, mobility. We may easily con- **bility from** **motion before** vince ourselves of this by examining the **it can deal** **with them.** part played in astronomy and mechanics by considerations of time, motion, and velocity.

Treatises on mechanics are careful to announce that they do not intend to define duration itself but only the equality of two durations. " Two intervals of time are equal when two identical bodies, in identical conditions at the beginning of each of these intervals and subject to the same actions and influences of every kind, have traversed the same space at the end of these intervals." In other words, we are to note the exact moment at

which the motion begins, i.e. the coincidence of an
external change with one of our psychic states ;
we are to note the moment at which the motion
ends, that is to say, another simultaneity ; finally
we are to measure the space traversed, the only
thing, in fact, which is really measurable.   Hence
there is no question here of duration, but only of
space and simultaneities.   To announce that something will take place at the end of a time t is to
declare that consciousness will note between now
and then a number t of simultaneities of a certain
kind.   And we must not be led astray by the
words " between now and then," for the interval
of duration exists only for us and on account of
the interpenetration of our conscious states.
Outside ourselves we should find only space, and
consequently nothing but simultaneities, of which
we could not even say that they are objectively
successive, since succession can only be thought
through *comparing* the present with the past.—That
the interval of duration itself cannot be taken into
account by science is proved by the fact that, if
all the motions of the universe took place twice or
thrice as quickly, there would be nothing to alter
either in our formulae or in the figures which are
to be found in them.   Consciousness would have
an indefinable and as it were qualitative impression
of the change, but the change would not make
itself felt outside consciousness, since the same
number of simultaneities would go on taking place
in space.   We shall see, later on, that when the

astronomer predicts, e.g., an eclipse, he does something of this kind : he shortens infinitely the intervals of duration, as these do not count for science, and thus perceives in a very short time—a few seconds at the most—a succession of simultaneities which may take up several centuries for the concrete consciousness, compelled to live through the intervals instead of merely counting their extremities.

A direct analysis of the notion of velocity will bring us to the same conclusion.   Mechanics gets

This is seen in the definition of *velocity*.

this notion through a series of ideas, the connexion of which it is easy enough to trace.   It first builds up the idea of uniform motion by picturing, on the one hand, the path AB of a certain moving body, and, on the other, a physical phenomenon which is repeated indefinitely under the same conditions, e.g., a stone always falling from the same height on to the same spot.   If we mark on the path AB the points   M, N, P . . .   reached   by   the   moving body at each of the moments when the stone touches the ground, and if the intervals AM, MN and NP are found to be equal to one another, the motion will be said to be uniform : and any one of these intervals will be called the velocity of the moving body, provided that it is agreed to adopt as unit of duration the physical phenomenon which has been chosen as the term of comparison.   Thus, the velocity of a uniform motion is defined by mechanics without appealing to any other notions

than those of space and simultaneity.   Now let us
turn to the case of a variable motion, that is, to the
case when the elements AM, MN, NP . . . are
found to be unequal.   In order to define the
velocity of the moving body A at the point M, we
shall only have to imagine an unlimited number of
moving bodies A_1, A_2, A_3 . . . all moving uni-
formly with velocities v_1, v_2, v_3 . . . which are
arranged, e.g., in an ascending scale and which
correspond to all possible magnitudes.   Let us
then consider on the path of the moving body A
two points M' and M'', situated on either side of
the point M but very near it.   At the same time
as this moving body reaches the points M', M, M'',
the other moving bodies reach points M'_1 M_1 M''_1,
M'_2 M_2 M''_2 . . . on their respective paths ; and
there must be two moving bodies A_h and A_p such
that we have on the one hand M' M = M'_h M_h and
on the other hand MM'' = M_p M''_p.   We shall then
agree to say that the velocity of the moving body
A at the point M lies between v_h and v_p.   But
nothing prevents our assuming that the points
M' and M'' are still nearer the point M, and it will
then be necessary to replace v_h and v_p by two
fresh velocities v_l and v_m, the one greater than
v_h and the other less than v_p.   And in proportion
as we reduce the two intervals M'M and MM'', we
shall lessen the difference between the velocities
of the uniform corresponding movements.   Now,
the two intervals being capable of decreasing right
down to zero, there evidently exists between v_l

and v_n a certain velocity v_m, such that the difference between this velocity and v_h, v_i . . . on the one hand, and v_p, v_n . . . on the other, can become smaller than any given quantity.   It is this common limit v_m which we shall call the velocity of the moving body A at the point M.—Now, in this analysis of variable motion, as in that of uniform motion, it is a question only of spaces once traversed and of simultaneous positions once reached.   We were thus justified in saying that, while all that mechanics retains of time is simultaneity, all that it retains of motion itself — restricted, as it is, to a *measurement* of motion — is immobility.

This result might have been foreseen by noticing that mechanics necessarily deals with equations, and that an algebraic equation always expresses something already done.   Now, it is of the very essence of duration and motion, as they appear to our consciousness, to be something that is unceasingly being done ; thus algebra can represent the results gained at a certain moment of duration and the positions occupied by a certain moving body in space, but not duration and motion themselves.   Mathematics may, indeed, increase the number of simultaneities and positions which it takes into consideration by making the intervals very small : it may even, by using the differential instead of the difference, show that it is possible to increase without limit the number of these

Mechanics deals with equations, which express something finished, and not processes, such as duration and motion.

intervals of duration. Nevertheless, however small the interval is supposed to be, it is the extremity of the interval at which mathematics always places itself. As for the interval itself, as for the duration and the motion, they are necessarily left out of the equation. The reason is that duration and motion are mental syntheses, and not objects; that, although the moving body occupies, one after the other, points on a line, motion itself has nothing to do with a line; and finally that, although the positions occupied by the moving body vary with the different moments of duration, though it even creates distinct moments by the mere fact of occupying different positions, duration properly so called has no moments which are identical or external to one another, being essentially heterogeneous, continuous, and with no analogy to number.

It follows from this analysis that space alone is homogeneous, that objects in space form a discrete multiplicity, and that every discrete multiplicity is got by a process of unfolding in space. It also follows that there is neither duration nor even succession in space, if we give to these words the meaning in which consciousness takes them: each of the so-called successive states of the external world exists alone; their multiplicity is real only for a consciousness that can first retain them and then set them side by side by externalizing them in relation

Conclusion: space alone is homogeneous: duration and succession belong not to the external world, but to the conscious mind.

to one another. If it retains them, it is because these distinct states of the external world give rise to states of consciousness which permeate one another, imperceptibly organize themselves into a whole, and bind the past to the present by this very process of connexion. If it externalizes them in relation to one another, the reason is that, thinking of their radical distinctness (the one having ceased to be when the other appears on the scene), it perceives them under the form of a discrete multiplicity, which amounts to settingthem out in line, in the space in which each of them existed separately. The space employed for this purpose is just that which is called homogeneous time.

But another conclusion results from this analysis, namely, that the multiplicity of conscious states, regarded in its original purity, is not at all like the discrete multiplicity which goes to form a number. In such a case there is, as we said, a qualitative multiplicity. In short, we must admit two kinds of multiplicity, two possible senses of the word " distinguish," two conceptions, the one qualitative and the other quantitative, of the difference between *same* and *other*. Sometimes this multiplicity, this distinctness, this heterogeneity contains number only potentially, as Aristotle would have said. Consciousness, then, makes a qualitative discrimination without any further thought of counting the qualities or even of distinguishing them as *several*. In such

Two kinds of multiplicity : two senses of the word "distinguish," the one qualitative and the other quantitative.

a case we have multiplicity without quantity. Sometimes, on the other hand, it is a question of a multiplicity of terms which are counted or which are conceived as capable of being counted ; but we think then of the possibility of externalizing them in relation to one another, we set them out in space. Unfortunately, we are so accustomed to illustrate one of these two meanings of the same word by the other, and even to perceive the one in the other, that we find it extraordinarily difficult to distinguish between them or at least to express this distinction in words. Thus I said that several conscious states are organized into a whole, permeate one another, gradually gain a richer content, and might thus give any one ignorant of space the feeling of pure duration ; but the very use of the word " several " shows that I had already isolated these states, externalized them in relation to one another, and, in a word, set them side by side ; thus, by the very language which I was compelled to use, I betrayed the deeply ingrained habit of setting out time in space. From this spatial setting out, already accomplished, we are compelled to borrow the terms which we use to describe the state of a mind which has not yet accomplished it : these terms are thus misleading from the very beginning, and the idea of a multiplicity without relation to number or space, although clear for pure reflective thought, cannot be translated into the language of common sense. And yet we cannot even form the idea of discrete multiplicity without considering at the same time a qualitative multiplicity. When we explicitly count units by stringing them along a spatial line, is it not the case that, alongside this addition of identical terms standing out from a homogeneous background, an organization of these units is going on in the depths of the soul, a wholly dynamic process, not unlike the purely qualitative way in which an anvil, if it could feel, would realize a series of blows from a hammer ? In this sense we might almost say that the numbers in daily use have each their emotional equivalent. Tradesmen are well aware of it, and instead of indicating the price of an object by a round number of shillings, they will mark the next smaller number, leaving themselves to insert afterwards a sufficient number of pence and farthings. In a word, the process by which we count units and make them into a discrete multiplicity has two sides ; on the one hand we assume that they are identical, which is conceivable only on condition that these units are ranged alongside each other in a homogeneous medium ; but on the other hand the third unit, for example, when added to the other two, alters the nature, the appearance and, as it were, the rhythm of the whole ; without this interpenetration and this, so to speak, qualitative progress, no addition would be possible. Hence it is through the quality of quantity that we form the idea of quantity without quality.

It is therefore obvious that, if it did not betake itself to a symbolical substitute, our consciousness would never regard time as a homogeneous medium, in which the terms of a succession remain outside one another. But we naturally reach this symbolical representation by the mere fact that, in a series of identical terms, each term assumes a double aspect for our consciousness : one aspect which is the same for all of them, since we are thinking then of the sameness of the external object, and another aspect which is characteristic of each of them, because the supervening of each term brings about a new organization of the whole. Hence the possibility of setting out in space, under the form of numerical multiplicity, what we have called a qualitative multiplicity, and of regarding the one as the equivalent of the other. Now, this twofold process is nowhere accomplished so easily as in the perception of the external phenomenon which takes for us the form of motion. Here we certainly have a series of identical terms, since it is always the same moving body ; but, on the other hand, the synthesis carried out by our consciousness between the actual position and what our memory calls the former positions, causes these images to permeate, complete, and, so to speak, continue one another. Hence, it is principally by the help of motion that duration assumes the form of a homogeneous medium, and that time is projected

Our successive sensations are regarded as mutually external, like their objective causes, and this reacts on our deeper psychic life.

into space. But, even if we leave out motion, any repetition of a well-marked external pheno- menon would suggest to consciousness the same mode of representation. Thus, when we hear a series of blows of a hammer, the sounds form an indivisible melody in so far as they are pure sensations, and, here again, give rise to a dynamic progress ; but, knowing that the same objective cause is at work, we cut up this progress into phases which we then regard as identical ; and this multiplicity of elements no longer being con- ceivable except by being set out in space, since they have now become identical, we are necessarily led to the idea of a homogeneous time, the sym- bolical image of real duration. In a word, our ego comes in contact with the external world at its surface ; our successive sensations, although dissolving into one another, retain something of the mutual externality which belongs to their objective causes ; and thus our superficial psychic life comes to be pictured without any great effort as set out in a homogeneous medium. But the symbolical character of such a picture becomes more striking as we advance further into the depths of consciousness : the deep-seated self which ponders and decides, which heats and blazes up, is a self whose states and changes permeate one another and undergo a deep alteration as soon as we separate them from one another in order to set them out in space. But as this deeper self forms one and the same person with the superficial ego, the two seem to *endure* in the same way. And as the repeated picture of one identical objective phenomenon, ever recurring, cuts up our superficial psychic life into parts external to one another, the moments which are thus determined determine in their turn distinct segments in the dynamic and undivided progress of our more personal conscious states. Thus the mutual externality which material objects gain from their juxtaposition in homogeneous space reverberates and spreads into the depths of consciousness : little by little our sensations are distinguished from one another like the external causes which gave rise to them, and our feelings or ideas come to be separated like the sensations with which they are contemporaneous.

That our ordinary conception of duration depends on a gradual incursion of space into the domain of pure consciousness is proved by the fact that, in order to deprive the ego of the faculty of perceiving a homogeneous time, it is enough to take away from it this outer circle of psychic states which it uses as a balance-wheel. These conditions are realized when we dream ; for sleep, by relaxing the play of the organic functions, alters the communicating surface between the ego and external objects. Here we no longer measure duration, but we feel it ; from quantity it returns to the state of quality ; we no longer estimate past time mathematically : the mathematical estimate gives place to a confused instinct,

Eliminate the superficial psychic states, and we no longer perceive a homogeneous time or measure duration, but feel it as a quality.

capable, like all instincts, of committing gross errors, but also of acting at times with extraordinary skill. Even in the waking state, daily experience ought to teach us to distinguish between duration as quality, that which consciousness reaches immediately and which is probably what animals perceive, and time so to speak materialized, time that has become quantity by being set out in space. Whilst I am writing these lines, the hour strikes on a neighbouring clock, but my inattentive ear does not perceive it until several strokes have made themselves heard. Hence I have not counted them ; and yet I only have to turn my attention backwards to count up the four strokes which have already sounded and add them to those which I hear. If, then, I question myself carefully on what has just taken place, I perceive that the first four sounds had struck my ear and even affected my consciousness, but that the sensations produced by each one of them, instead of being set side by side, had melted into one another in such a way as to give the whole a peculiar quality, to make a kind of musical phrase out of it. In order, then, to estimate retrospectively the number of strokes sounded, I tried to reconstruct this phrase in thought : my imagination made one stroke, then two, then three, and as long as it did not reach the exact number four, my feeling, when consulted, answered that the total effect was qualitatively different. It had thus ascertained in its own way the succession of four strokes, but quite otherwise than by a process of addition, and without bringing in the image of a juxtaposition of distinct terms. In a word, the number of strokes was perceived as a quality and not as a quantity : it is thus that duration is presented to immediate consciousness, and it retains this form so long as it does not give place to a symbolical representation derived from extensity.

We should therefore distinguish two forms of multiplicity, two very different ways of regarding duration, two aspects of conscious life.

There are therefore two forms of multiplicity, of duration and conscious life. Below homogeneous duration, which is the extensive symbol of true duration, a close psychological analysis distinguishes a duration whose heterogeneous moments permeate one another ; below the numerical multiplicity of conscious states, a qualitative multiplicity ; below the self with well-defined states, a self in which *succeeding each other* means *melting into one another* and forming an organic whole. But we are generally content with the first, i.e. with the shadow of the self projected into homogeneous space. Consciousness, goaded by an insatiable desire to separate, substitutes the symbol for the reality, or perceives the reality only through the symbol. As the self thus refracted, and thereby broken to pieces, is much better adapted to the requirements of social life in general and language in particular, consciousness prefers it, and gradually loses sight of the fundamental self.

In order to recover this fundamental self, as
the unsophisticated consciousness would perceive
it, a vigorous effort of analysis is necessary, which will isolate the fluid inner
states from their image, first refracted,
then solidified in homogeneous space.   In other
words, our perceptions, sensations, emotions and
ideas occur under two aspects : the one clear and
precise, but impersonal; the other confused, ever
changing, and inexpressible, because language
cannot get hold of it without arresting its mobility
or fit it into its common-place forms without
making it into public property.   If we have been
led to distinguish two forms of multiplicity, two
forms of duration, we must expect each conscious
state, taken by itself, to assume a different aspect
according as we consider it within a discrete
multiplicity or a confused multiplicity, in the
time as quality, in which it is produced, or in the
time as quantity, into which it is projected.

When e.g. I take my first walk in a town in
which I am going to live, my environment produces on me two impressions at the
same time, one of which is destined to
last while the other will constantly
change.   Every day I perceive the
same houses, and as I know that they
are the same objects, I always call them by
the same name and I also fancy that they always
look the same to me.   But if I recur, at the
end of a sufficiently long period, to the impression

The two aspects of our conscious states.

One of which is due to the solidifying influence of external objects and language on our constantly changing feelings.

which I experienced during the first few years, I am surprised at the remarkable, inexplicable, and indeed inexpressible change which has taken place. It seems that these objects, continually perceived by me and constantly impressing themselves on my mind, have ended by borrowing from me something of my own conscious existence ; like myself they have lived, and like myself they have grown old. This is not a mere illusion ; for if to-day's impression were absolutely identical with that of yesterday, what difference would there be between perceiving and recognizing, between learning and remembering ? Yet this difference escapes the attention of most of us ; we shall hardly perceive it, unless we are warned of it and then carefully look into ourselves. The reason is that our outer and, so to speak, social life is more practically important to us than our inner and individual existence. We instinctively tend to solidify our impressions in order to express them in language. Hence we confuse the feeling itself, which is in a perpetual state of becoming, with its permanent external object, and especially with the word which expresses this object. In the same way as the fleeting duration of our ego is fixed by its projection in homogeneous space, our constantly changing impressions, wrapping themselves round the external object which is their cause, take on its definite outlines and its immobility.

Our simple sensations, taken in their natural

state, are still more fleeting. Such and such a
flavour, such and such a scent, pleased
me when I was a child though I dislike
them to-day. Yet I still give the same
name to the sensation experienced, and
I speak as if only my taste had changed, whilst the
scent and the flavour have remained the same.
Thus I again solidify the sensation ; and when
its changeableness becomes so obvious that I cannot
help recognizing it, I abstract this changeableness
to give it a name of its own and solidify it in the
shape of a *taste*.   But in reality there are neither
identical sensations nor multiple tastes : for
sensations and tastes seem to me to be *objects* as
soon as I isolate and name them, and in the
human soul there are only *processes*. What I
ought to say is that every sensation is altered by
repetition, and that if it does not seem to me to
change from day to day, it is because I perceive
it through the object which is its cause, through
the word which translates it. This influence of
language on sensation is deeper than is usually
thought.   Not only does language make us believe
in the unchangeableness of our sensations, but it
will sometimes deceive us as to the nature of the
sensation felt. Thus, when I partake of a dish
that is supposed to be exquisite, the name which
it bears, suggestive of the approval given to it,
comes between my sensation and my consciousness;
I may believe that the flavour pleases me when a
slight effort of attention would prove the contrary.

In short, the word with well-defined outlines, the rough and ready word, which stores up the stable, common, and consequently impersonal element in the impressions of mankind, over-whelms or at least covers over the delicate and fugitive impressions of our individual conscious-ness. To maintain the struggle on equal terms, the latter ought to express themselves in precise words ; but these words, as soon as they were formed, would turn against the sensation which gave birth to them, and, invented to show that the sensation is unstable, they would impose on it their own stability.

This overwhelming of the immediate conscious-ness is nowhere so striking as in the case of our *How analysis* feelings. A violent love or a deep *and descrip-* melancholy takes possession of our *tion distort* *the feelings.* soul : here we feel a thousand different elements which dissolve into and permeate one another without any precise outlines, without the least tendency to externalize themselves in relation to one another ; hence their originality. We distort them as soon as we distinguish a numerical multiplicity in their confused mass : what will it be, then, when we set them out, isolated from one another, in this homogeneous medium which may be called either time or space, whichever you prefer ?   A moment ago each of them was borrowing an indefinable colour from its surroundings : now we have it colourless, and ready to accept a name.   The feeling itself is a

being which lives and develops and is therefore constantly changing ; otherwise how could it gradually
lead us to form a resolution ?   Our resolution
would be immediately taken.   But it lives because
the duration in which it develops is a duration
whose moments permeate one another.   By
separating these moments from each other, by
spreading out time in space, we have caused this
feeling to lose its life and its colour.   Hence, we
are now standing before our own shadow : we
believe that we have analysed our feeling, while
we have really replaced it by a juxtaposition
of lifeless states which can be translated into words,
and each of which constitutes the common element,
the impersonal residue, of the impressions felt in a
given case by the whole of society.   And this is
why we reason about these states and apply our
simple logic to them : having set them up as
genera by the mere fact of having isolated them
from one another, we have prepared them for
use in some future deduction.   Now, if some bold
novelist, tearing aside the cleverly woven curtain
of our conventional ego, shows us under this
appearance of logic a fundamental absurdity,
under this juxtaposition of simple states an
infinite permeation of a thousand different impressions which have already ceased to exist the
instant they are named, we commend him for
having known us better than we knew ourselves.
This is not the case, however, and the very fact
that he spreads out our feeling in a homogeneous

time, and expresses its elements by words, shows
that he in his turn is only offering us its shadow :
but he has arranged this shadow in such a way as
to make us suspect the extraordinary and illogical
nature of the object which projects it ; he has
made us reflect by giving outward expression to
something of that contradiction, that interpenetration, which is the very essence of the elements
expressed. Encouraged by him, we have put
aside for an instant the veil which we interposed
between our consciousness and ourselves. He
has brought us back into our own presence.

We should experience the same sort of surprise
if we strove to seize our ideas themselves in their
natural state, as our consciousness would
perceive them if it were no longer beset
by space. This breaking up of the
constituent elements of an idea, which
issues in abstraction, is too convenient
for us to do without it in ordinary life
and even in philosophical discussion. But when
we fancy that the parts thus artificially separated are the genuine threads with which the
concrete idea was woven, when, substituting for
the interpenetration of the real terms the juxtaposition of their symbols, we claim to make
duration out of space, we unavoidably fall into the
mistakes of associationism. We shall not insist
on the latter point, which will be the subject of a
thorough examination in the next chapter. Let
it be enough to say that the impulsive zeal with

On the sur-
face our con-
scious states
obey the laws
of association.
Deeper down
they interpene-
trate and
form a part of
ourselves.

which we take sides on certain questions shows how
our intellect has its instincts—and what can an
instinct of this kind be if not an impetus common
to all our ideas, i.e. their very interpenetration ?
The beliefs to which we most strongly adhere are
those of which we should find it most difficult to
give an account, and the reasons by which we
justify them are seldom those which have led us to
adopt them.   In a certain sense we have adopted
them without any reason, for what makes them
valuable in our eyes is that they match the colour
of all our other ideas, and that from the very
first we have seen in them something of ourselves.
Hence they do not take in our minds that common
looking form which they will assume as soon as we
try to give expression to them in words; and,
although they bear the same name in other minds,
they are by no means the same thing.   The fact
is that each of them has the same kind of life as a
cell in an organism : everything which affects the
general state of the self affects it also.   But while
the cell occupies a definite point in the organism,
an idea which is truly ours fills the whole of our
self.   Not all our ideas, however, are thus incorporated in the fluid mass of our conscious states.
Many float on the surface, like dead leaves on the
water of a pond: the mind, when it thinks
them over and over again, finds them ever the
same, as if they were external to it. Among
these are the ideas which we receive ready made,
and which remain in us without ever being

properly assimilated, or again the ideas which we have omitted to cherish and which have withered in neglect. If, in proportion as we get away from the deeper strata of the self, our conscious states tend more and more to assume the form of a numerical multiplicity, and to spread out in a homogeneous space, it is just because these conscious states tend to become more and more lifeless, more and more impersonal. Hence we need not be surprised if only those ideas which least belong to us can be adequately expressed in words : only to these, as we shall see, does the associationist theory apply. External to one another, they keep up relations among themselves in which the inmost nature of each of them counts for nothing, relations which can therefore be classified. It may thus be said that they are associated by contiguity or for some logical reason. But if, digging below the surface of contact between the self and external objects, we penetrate into the depths of the organized and living intelligence, we shall witness the joining together or rather the blending of many ideas which, when once dissociated, seem to exclude one another as logically contradictory terms. The strangest dreams, in which two images overlie one another and show us at the same time two different persons, who yet make only one, will hardly give us an idea of the interweaving of concepts which goes on when we are awake. The imagination of the dreamer, cut off from the external world, imitates with

mere images, and parodies in its own way, the
process which constantly goes on with regard
to ideas in the deeper regions of the intellectual life.

Thus may be verified, thus, too, will be illus-
trated by a further study of deep-seated psychic
phenomena the principle from which
we started : conscious life displays two
aspects according as we perceive it
directly or by refraction through space.
Considered in themselves, the deep-
seated conscious states have no relation
to quantity, they are pure quality ; they
intermingle in such a way that we cannot tell
whether they are one or several, nor even examine
them from this point of view without at once
altering their nature. The duration which they
thus create is a duration whose moments do not
constitute a numerical multiplicity : to characterize these moments by saying that they encroach
on one another would still be to distinguish them.
If each of us lived a purely individual life, if there
were neither society nor language, would our
consciousness grasp the series of inner states in
this unbroken form ? Undoubtedly it would not
quite succeed, because we should still retain the
idea of a homogeneous space in which objects are
sharply distinguished from one another, and
because it is too convenient to set out in such a
medium the somewhat cloudy states which first
attract the attention of consciousness, in order to

By separating
our conscious
states we pro-
mote social
life, but raise
problems sol-
uble only by
recourse to
the concrete
and living
self.

resolve them into simpler terms. But mark that
the intuition of a homogeneous space is already
a step towards social life. Probably animals do
not picture to themselves, beside their sensations,
as we do, an external world quite distinct from
themselves, which is the common property of all
conscious beings. Our tendency to form a clear
picture of this externality of things and the homogeneity of their medium is the same as the impulse which leads us to live in common and to
speak. But, in proportion as the conditions of
social life are more completely realized, the current which carries our conscious states from
within outwards is strengthened; little by little
these states are made into objects or things; they
break off not only from one another, but from
ourselves. Henceforth we no longer perceive
them except in the homogeneous medium in which
we have set their image, and through the word
which lends them its commonplace colour. Thus
a second self is formed which obscures the first,
a self whose existence is made up of distinct
moments, whose states are separated from one
another and easily expressed in words. I do not
mean, here, to split up the personality, nor to
bring back in another form the numerical multiplicity which I shut out at the beginning. It is
the same self which perceives distinct states at
first, and which, by afterwards concentrating its
attention, will see these states melt into one another like the crystals of a snow-flake when touched

for some time with the finger.   And, in truth, for
the sake of language, the self has everything to
gain by not bringing back confusion where order
reigns, and in not upsetting this ingenious arrangement of almost impersonal states by which it has
ceased to form " a kingdom within a kingdom."
An inner life with well distinguished moments
and with clearly characterized states will answer
better the requirements of social life.   Indeed, a
superficial psychology may be content with describing it without thereby falling into error, on
condition, however, that it restricts itself to the
study of what has taken place and leaves out what
is going on.   But if, passing from statics to dynamics, this psychology claims to reason about
things in the making as it reasoned about things
made, if it offers us the concrete and living self as
an association of terms which are distinct from
one another and are set side by side in a homogeneous medium, it will see difficulty after difficulty rising in its path.   And these difficulties
will multiply the greater the efforts it makes to
overcome them, for all its efforts will only bring
into clearer light the absurdity of the fundamental
hypothesis by which it spreads out time in space and
puts succession at the very centre of simultaneity.
We shall see that the contradictions implied in the
problems of causality, freedom, personality, spring
from no other source, and that, if we wish to get
rid of them, we have only to go back to the real and
concrete self and give up its symbolical substitute.

CHAPTER III

THE ORGANIZATION OF CONSCIOUS STATES
FREE WILL

IT is easy to see why the question of free will brings into conflict these two rival systems of nature, mechanism and dynamism. Dyna-

Mechanism, dynamism, and free will.

mism starts from the idea of voluntary activity, given by consciousness, and comes to represent inertia by gradually emptying this idea : it has thus no difficulty in conceiving free force on the one hand and matter governed by laws on the other. Mechanism follows the opposite course. It assumes that the materials which it synthesizes are governed by necessary laws, and although it reaches richer and richer combinations, which are more and more difficult to foresee, and to all appearance more and more contingent, yet it never gets out of the narrow circle of necessity within which it at first shut itself up.

A thorough examination of these two conceptions of nature will show that they involve two

For dynamism facts more real than laws : mechanism reverses this attitude. The idea of spontaneity simpler than that of inertia.

very different hypotheses as to the relations between laws and the facts which they govern. As he looks higher and higher, the believer in dynamism thinks that he perceives facts which more and more elude the grasp of laws : he thus

sets up the fact as the absolute reality, and the
law as the more or less symbolical expression of
this reality. Mechanism, on the contrary, dis-
covers within the particular fact a certain number of laws of which the fact is thus made to be the
meeting point, and nothing else : on this hypothesis it is the law which becomes the genuine reality.
Now, if it is asked why the one party assigns a
higher reality to the fact and the other to the
law, it will be found that mechanism and dynamism take the word *simplicity* in two very different
senses. For the first, any principle is simple of
which the effects can be foreseen and even calcu-
lated : thus, by the very definition, the notion of
inertia becomes simpler than that of freedom, the
homogeneous simpler than the heterogeneous, the
abstract simpler than the concrete. But dynamism
is not anxious so much to arrange the notions
in the most convenient order as to find out their
real relationship : often, in fact, the so-called
simple notion—that which the believer in mechanism regards as primitive—has been obtained by the
blending together of several richer notions which
seem to be derived from it, and which have
more or less neutralized one another in this very
process of blending, just as darkness may be produced by the interference of two lights. Regarded from this new point of view, the idea of
spontaneity is indisputably simpler than that of
inertia, since the second can be understood and
defined only by means of the first, while the first

is self-sufficient. For each of us has the immediate knowledge (be it thought true or fallacious) of his free spontaneity, without the notion of inertia having anything to do with this knowledge. But, if we wish to define the inertia of matter, we must say that it cannot move or stop of its own accord, that every body perseveres in the state of rest or motion so long as it is not acted upon by any force : and in both cases we are unavoidably carried back to the idea of activity. It is therefore natural that, *a priori*, we should reach two opposite conceptions of human activity, according to the way in which we understand the relation between the concrete and the abstract, the simple and the complex, facts and laws.

A posteriori, however, definite facts are appealed to against freedom, some physical, others psychological. Sometimes it is asserted that our actions are necessitated by our feelings, our ideas, and the whole preceding series of our conscious states ; sometimes freedom is denounced as being incompatible with the fundamental properties of matter, and in particular with the principle of the conservation of energy. Hence two kinds of determinism, two apparently different empirical proofs of universal necessity. We shall show that the second of these two forms is reducible to the first, and that all determinism, even physical determinism, involves a psychological hypothesis : we shall then prove

Determinism : (1) physical (2) psychological. Former reducible to latter, which itself rests on inaccurate conception of multiplicity of conscious states or duration.

that psychological determinism itself, and the refutations which are given of it, rest on an inaccurate conception of the multiplicity of conscious states, or rather of duration. Thus, in the light of the principles worked out in the foregoing chapter, we shall see a self emerge whose activity cannot be compared to that of any other force.

Physical determinism, in its latest form, is closely bound up with mechanical or rather kinetic Physical de- theories of matter. The universe is terminism stated in the pictured as a heap of matter which the language of the molecular imagination resolves into molecules and theory of mat- ter. atoms. These particles are supposed to carry out unceasingly movements of every kind, sometimes of vibration, sometimes of translation ; and physical phenomena, chemical action, the qualities of matter which our senses perceive, heat, sound, electricity, perhaps even attraction, are thought to be reducible objectively to these elementary movements. The matter which goes to make up organized bodies being subject to the same laws, we find in the nervous system, for example, only molecules and atoms which are in motion and attract and repel one another. Now if all bodies, organized or unorganized, thus act and react on one another in their ultimate parts, it is obvious that the molecular state of the brain at a given moment will be modified by the shocks which the nervous system receives from the sur-

rounding matter, so that the sensations, feelings
and ideas which succeed one another in us can be
defined as mechanical resultants, obtained by the
compounding of shocks received from without
with the previous movements of the atoms of the
nervous substance. But the opposite phenomenon
may occur ; and the molecular movements which
go on in the nervous system, if compounded with
one another or with others, will often give as resultant a reaction of our organism on its environment :
hence the reflex movements, hence also the so-
called free and voluntary actions. As, moreover,
the principle of the conservation of energy has
been assumed to admit of no exception, there is
not an atom, either in the nervous system or in
the whole of the universe, whose position is not
determined by the sum of the mechanical actions
which the other atoms exert upon it. And the
mathematician who knew the position of the
molecules or atoms of a human organism at a
given moment, as well as the position and motion
of all the atoms in the universe capable of
influencing it, could calculate with unfailing
certainty the past, present and future actions
of the person to whom this organism belongs,
just as one predicts an astronomical phenomenon.[1]

We shall not raise any difficulty about recog-

[1] On this point see Lange, *History of Materialism*, Vol. ii,
Part ii.

nizing that this conception of physiological phenomena in general, and nervous phenomena in particular, is a very natural
deduction from the law of the conservation of energy. Certainly, the atomic
theory of matter is still at the hypothetical stage, and the purely kinetic explanations of physical facts lose more than they
gain by being too closely bound up with it. We
must observe, however, that, even if we leave aside
the atomic theory as well as any other hypothesis
as to the nature of the ultimate elements of matter,
the necessitating of physiological facts by their
antecedents follows from the theorem of the conservation of energy, as soon as we extend this
theorem to all processes going on in all living bodies.
For to admit the universality of this theorem is to
assume, at bottom, that the material points of
which the universe is composed are subject solely
to forces of attraction and repulsion, arising from
these points themselves and possessing intensities
which depend only on their distances : hence the
relative position of these material points at a given
moment—whatever be their nature—would be
strictly determined by relation to what it was at
the preceding moment. Let us then assume for
a moment that this last hypothesis is true : we
propose to show, in the first place, that it does not
involve the absolute determination of our conscious
states by one another, and then that the very
universality of the principle of the conservation

If principle of conservation of energy is universal, physiological and nervous phenomena are necessitated, but perhaps not conscious states.

of energy cannot be admitted except in virtue of some psychological hypothesis.

Even if we assumed that the position, the direction and the velocity of each atom of cerebral matter are determined at every moment of time, it would not at all follow that our psychic life is subject to the same necessity. For we should first have to prove that a strictly determined psychic state corresponds to a definite cerebral state, and the proof of this is still to be given. As a rule we do not think of demanding it, because we know that a definite vibration of the tympanum, a definite stimulation of the auditory nerve, gives a definite note on the scale, and because the parallelism of the physical and psychical series has been proved in a fairly large number of cases. But then, nobody has ever contended that we were free, under given conditions, to hear any note or perceive any colour we liked. Sensations of this kind, like many other psychic states, are obviously bound up with certain determining conditions, and it is just for this reason that it has been possible to imagine or discover beneath them a system of movements which obey our abstract mechanics. In short, wherever we succeed in giving a mechanical explanation, we observe a fairly strict parallelism between the physiological and the psychological series, and we need not be surprised at it, since explanations of this kind will assuredly not be met with except where the two

To prove conscious states determined, we should have to show a necessary connexion between them and cerebral states. No such proof.

series exhibit parallel terms.   But to extend this parallelism to the series themselves in their totality is to settle *a priori* the problem of freedom. Certainly this may be done, and some of the greatest thinkers have set the example; but then, as we said at first, it was not for reasons of a physical order that they asserted the strict correspondence between states of consciousness and modes of extension.   Leibniz ascribed it to a preestablished harmony, and would never have admitted that a motion could give rise to a perception as a cause produces an effect.   Spinoza said that the modes of thought and the modes of extension correspond with but never influence one another : they only express in two different languages the same eternal truth.   But the theories of physical determinism which are rife at the present day are far from displaying the same clearness, the same geometrical rigour.   They point to molecular movements taking place in the brain : consciousness is supposed to arise out of these at times in some mysterious way, or rather to follow their track like the phosphorescent line which results from the rubbing of a match.   Or yet again we are to think of an invisible musician playing behind the scenes while the actor strikes a keyboard the notes of which yield no sound : consciousness must be supposed to come from an unknown region and to be superimposed on the molecular vibrations, just as the melody is on the rhythmical movements of the actor.   But, what-

ever image we fall back upon, we do not prove
and we never shall prove by any reasoning that
the psychic fact is fatally determined by the molecular movement. For in a movement we may
find the reason of another movement, but not the
reason of a conscious state : only observation
can prove that the latter accompanies the former.
Now the unvarying conjunction of the two
terms has not been verified by experience except
in a very limited number of cases and with regard
to facts which all confess to be almost independent
of the will. But it is easy to understand why
physical determinism extends this conjunction to
all possible cases.

Consciousness indeed informs us that the majority of our actions can be explained by motives.
Physical But it does not appear that determina-
determinism,
when assumed tion here means necessity, since common
to be universal,
postulates sense believes in free will. The deter-
psychological
determinism. minist, however, led astray by a conception of duration and causality which we shall
criticise a little later, holds that the determination of conscious states by one another is absolute.
This is the origin of associationist determinism,
an hypothesis in support of which the testimony
of consciousness is appealed to, but which cannot,
in the beginning, lay claim to scientific rigour. It
seems natural that this, so to speak, approximate
determinism, this determinism of quality, should
seek support from the same mechanism that
underlies the phenomena of nature : the latter

would thus convey to the former its own
geometrical character, and the transaction would
be to the advantage both of psychological
determinism, which would emerge from it in a
stricter form, and of physical mechanism, which
would then spread over everything.   A fortunate
circumstance favours this alliance.   The simplest
psychic states do in fact occur as accessories
to well-defined physical phenomena, and the
greater number of sensations seem to be bound
up with definite molecular movements.   This
mere beginning of an experimental proof is
quite enough for the man who, for psychological
reasons, is already convinced that our conscious
states are the necessary outcome of the circumstances under which they happen.   Henceforth
he no longer hesitates to hold that the drama
enacted in the theatre of consciousness is a literal
and even slavish translation of some scenes performed by the molecules and atoms of organized
matter.   The physical determinism which is
reached in this way is nothing but psychological
determinism, seeking to verify itself and fix its
own outlines by an appeal to the sciences of nature.

But we must own that the amount of freedom
which is left to us after strictly complying with the
Is the princi- principle of the conservation of energy
ple of conser-
vation of   is rather limited.   For, even if this law
energy uni-
versally valid? does not exert a necessitating influence
over the course of our ideas, it will at least
determine our movements.   Our inner life will

still depend upon ourselves up to a certain point ; but, to an outside observer, there will be nothing to distinguish our activity from absolute automatism. We are thus led to inquire whether the very extension of the principle of the conservation of energy to all the bodies in nature does not itself involve some psychological theory, and whether the scientist who did not possess *a priori* any prejudice against human freedom would think of setting up this principle as a universal law.

We must not overrate the part played by the principle of the conservation of energy in the history of the natural sciences. In its

It implies that a system can return to its original state. Neglects duration, hence inapplicable to living beings and conscious states.

present form it marks a certain phase in the evolution of certain sciences ; but it has not been the governing factor in this evolution and we should be wrong in making it the indispensable postulate of all scientific research. Certainly, every mathematical operation which we carry out on a given quantity implies the permanence of this quantity throughout the course of the operation, in whatever way we may split it up. In other words, what is given is given, what is not given is not given, and in whatever order we add up the same terms we shall get the same result. Science will for ever remain subject to this law, which is nothing but the law of non-contradiction ; but this law does not involve any special hypothesis as to the nature of what we ought to take as given, or what will remain constant. No doubt it informs us that something cannot come from nothing ; but experience alone will tell us which aspects or functions of reality must count for something, and which for nothing, from the point of view of positive science. In short, in order to foresee the state of a determinate system at a determinate moment, it is absolutely necessary that something should persist as a constant quantity throughout a series of combinations ; but it belongs to experience to decide as to the nature of this something, and especially to let us know whether it is found in all possible systems, whether, in other words, all possible systems lend themselves to our calculations. It is not certain that all the physicists before Leibniz believed, like Descartes, in the conservation of a fixed quantity of motion in the universe : were their discoveries less valuable on this account or their researches less successful ? Even when Leibniz had substituted for this principle that of the conservation of *vis viva*, it was not possible to regard the law as quite general, since it admitted of an obvious exception in the case of the direct impact of two inelastic bodies. Thus science has done for a very long time without a universal conservative principle. In its present form, and since the development of the mechanical theory of heat, the principle of the conservation of energy certainly seems to apply to the whole range of physico-chemical phenomena. But no one can tell whether the study of physiological phenomena in general, and of nervous phenomena in particular, will not reveal to us, besides the *vis viva* or kinetic energy of which Leibniz spoke, and the potential energy which was a later and neces- • sary adjunct, some new kind of energy which may differ from the other two by rebelling against calculation. Physical science would not thereby lose any of its exactitude or geometrical rigour, as has lately been asserted : only it would be realized that conservative systems are not the only systems possible, and even, perhaps, that in the whole of concrete reality each of these systems plays the same part as the chemist's atom in bodies and their combinations. Let us note that the most radical of mechanical theories is that which makes consciousness an *epiphenomenon* which, in given circumstances, may supervene on certain molecular movements. But, if molecular movement can create sensation out of a zero of consciousness, why should not consciousness in its turn create movement either out of a zero of kinetic and potential energy, or by making use of this energy in its own way ? Let us also note that the law of the conservation of energy can only be intelligibly applied to a system of which the points, after moving, can return to their former positions. This return is at least conceived of as possible, and it is supposed that under these conditions nothing would be changed in the original state of the system as a whole or of its elements. In short, time cannot bite into it ; and the instinctive, though vague, belief of mankind in the conservation of a fixed quantity of matter, a fixed quantity of energy, perhaps has its root in the very fact that inert matter does not seem to endure or to preserve any trace of past time. But this is not the case in the realm of life. Here duration certainly seems to act like a cause, and the idea of putting things back in their place at the end of a certain time involves a kind of absurdity, since such a turning backwards has never been accomplished in the case of a living being. But let us admit that the absurdity is a mere appearance, and that the impossibility for living beings to come back to the past is simply owing to the fact that the physico-chemical phenomena which take place in living bodies, being infinitely complex, have no chance of ever occurring again all at the same time : at least it will be granted to us that the hypothesis of a turning backwards is almost meaningless in the sphere of conscious states. A sensation, by the mere fact of being prolonged, is altered to the point of becoming unbearable. The same does not here remain the same, but is reinforced and swollen by the whole of its past. In short, while the material point, as mechanics understands it, remains in an eternal present, the past is a reality perhaps for living bodies, and certainly for conscious beings. While past time is neither a gain nor a loss for a system assumed to be conservative, it may be a gain for the living being, and it is indisputably one for the conscious being. Such

being the case, is there not much to be said for the
hypothesis of a conscious force or free will, which,
subject to the action of time and storing up duration, may thereby escape the law of the conservation of energy ?

In truth, it is not a wish to meet the requirements
of positive science, but rather a psychological
The idea of mistake which has caused this abstract
the universal-
ity of conser- principle of mechanics to be set up as a
vation depends
on confusion universal law. As we are not accustomed
between con-
crete duration to observe ourselves directly, but per-
and abstract
time. ceive ourselves through forms borrowed
from the external world, we are led to believe that
real duration, the duration lived by consciousness,
is the same as the duration which glides over the
inert atoms without penetrating and altering
them. Hence it is that we do not see any absurdity in putting things back in their place after a
lapse of time, in supposing the same motives
acting afresh on the same persons, and in concluding that these causes would again produce the
same effect. That such an hypothesis has no real
meaning is what we shall prove later on. For the
present let us simply show that, if once we enter
upon this path, we are of course led to set up
the principle of the conservation of energy as a
universal law. For we have thereby got rid of
just that difference between the outer and the inner
world which a close examination shows to be the
main one : we have identified true duration with
apparent duration. After this it would be absurd

to consider time, even *our* time, as a cause of gain or loss, as a concrete reality, or a force in its own way.   Thus, while we ought only to say (if we kept aloof from all presuppositions concerning free will) that the law of the conservation of energy governs physical phenomena and *may*, one day, be extended to all phenomena if psychological facts also prove favourable to it, we go far beyond this, and, under the influence of a metaphysical prepossession, we lay down the principle of the conservation of energy as a law which *should* govern all phenomena whatever, or must be supposed to do so until psychological facts have actually spoken against it.   Science, properly so called, has therefore nothing to do with all this. We are simply confronted with a confusion between concrete duration and abstract time, two very different things.   In a word, the so-called physical determinism is reducible at bottom to a psychological determinism, and it is this latter doctrine, as we hinted at first, that we have to examine.

Psychological determinism, in its latest and most precise shape, implies an associationist conception of mind.   The existing state of consciousness is first thought of as necessitated by the preceding states, but it is soon realized that this cannot be a geometrical necessity, such as that which connects a resultant, for example, with its components. For between successive conscious states there

Psychological determinism depends on associationist conception of mind.

exists a difference of quality which will always
frustrate any attempt to deduce any one of them
a priori from its predecessors. So experience is
appealed to, with the object of showing that the
transition from one psychic state to another can
always be explained by some simple reason, the
second obeying as it were the call of the first.
Experience really does show this : and, as for ourselves, we shall willingly admit that there always
is some relation between the existing state of
consciousness and any new state to which
consciousness passes. But is this relation,
which explains the transition, the cause of
it ?

May we here give an account of what we have
personally observed ?   In resuming a conversation
The series of which had been interrupted for a few
associations
may be merely moments we have happened to notice
an *ex post facto*
attempt to that both we ourselves and our friend
account for a
new idea. were thinking of some new object at the
same time.—The reason is, it will be said, that
each has followed up for his own part the natural
development of the idea at which the conversation
had stopped : the same series of associations has
been formed on both sides.—No doubt this interpretation holds good in a fairly large number of
cases ; careful inquiry, however, has led us to an
unexpected result.   It is a fact that the two
speakers do connect the new subject of conversation with the former one : they will even point
out the intervening ideas ; but, curiously enough,

they will not always connect the new idea, which they have both reached, with the same point of the preceding conversation, and the two series of intervening associations may be quite different. What are we to conclude from this, if not that this common idea is due to an unknown cause—perhaps to some physical influence—and that, in order to justify its emergence, it has called forth a series of antecedents which explain it and which seem to be its cause, but are really its effect ?

When a patient carries out at the appointed time the suggestion received in the hypnotic state,

Illustration from hypnotic suggestion.

the act which he performs is brought about, according to him, by the preceding series of his conscious states. Yet these states are really effects, and not causes : it was necessary that the act should take place ; it was also necessary that the patient should explain it to himself ; and it is the future act which determined, by a kind of attraction, the whole series of psychic states of which it is to be the natural consequence. The determinists will seize on this argument : it proves as a matter of fact that we are sometimes irresistibly subject to another's will. But does it not also show us how our own will is capable of willing for willing's sake, and of then leaving the act which has been performed to be explained by antecedents of which it has really been the cause ?

If we question ourselves carefully, we shall see

that we sometimes weigh motives and deliberate

Illustration from delibera- tion.
over them, when our mind is already made up. An inner voice, hardly perceivable, whispers : " Why this deliberation ? You know the result and you are quite certain of what you are going to do." But no matter ! it seems that we make a point of safe-guarding the principle of mechanism and of conforming to the laws of the association of ideas. The abrupt intervention of the will is a kind of *coup d'état* which our mind foresees and which it tries to legitimate beforehand by a formal deliberation. True, it could be asked whether the will, even when it wills for willing's sake, does not obey some decisive reason, and whether willing for willing's sake is free willing. We shall not insist on this point for the moment. It will be enough for us to have shown that, even when adopting the point of view of associationism, it is difficult to maintain that an act is absolutely determined by its motive and our conscious states by one another. Beneath these deceptive appearances a more attentive psychology sometimes reveals to us effects which precede their causes, and phenomena of psychic attraction which elude the known laws of the association of ideas. But the time has come to ask whether the very point of view which associationism adopts does not involve a defective conception of the self and of the multiplicity of conscious states.

Associationist determinism represents the self as

a collection of psychic states, the strongest of
Association- which exerts a prevailing influence and
ism involves a
defective con- carries the others with it.   This doctrine
ception of the thus sharply distinguishes co-existing
self.
psychic phenomena from one another.   " I could
have abstained from murder," says Stuart Mill,
" if my aversion to the crime and my dread of its
consequences had been weaker than the temptation
which impelled me to commit it."[1]   And a little
further on :   " His desire to do right and his
aversion to doing wrong are strong enough to
overcome . . . any other desire or aversion which
may conflict with them."[2]   Thus desire, aversion,
fear, temptation are here presented as distinct
things which there is no inconvenience in naming
separately.   Even when he connects these states
with the self which experiences them, the English
philosopher still insists on setting up clear-cut
distinctions :   " The conflict is between me and
myself ;   between (for instance) me desiring a
pleasure and me dreading self-reproach."[3]   Bain,
for his part, devotes a whole chapter to the " Conflict of Motives."[4]   In it he balances pleasures
and pains as so many terms to which one might
attribute, at least by abstraction, an existence of
their own.   Note that the opponents of determinism agree to follow it into this field.   They too
speak of associations of ideas and conflicts of

[1] Cf. *Examination of Sir W. Hamilton's Philosophy.* 5th ed.,
(1878), p. 583.   [2] *Ibid.* p. 585.   [3] *Ibid.* p. 585.
[4] *The Emotions and the Will*, Chap. vi.

motives, and one of the ablest of these philosophers, Alfred Fouillée, goes so far as to make the idea of freedom itself a motive capable of counterbalancing others.[1] Here, however, lies the danger. Both parties commit themselves to a confusion which arises from language, and which is due to the fact that language is not meant to convey all the delicate shades of inner states.

I rise, for example, to open the window, and I have hardly stood up before I forget what I had to do.—All right, it will be said ; you have associated two ideas, that of an end to be attained and that of a movement to be accomplished : one of the ideas has vanished and only the idea of the movement remains.—However, I do not sit down again ; I have a confused feeling that something remains to be done. This particular standing still, therefore, is not the same as any other standing still; in the position which I take up the act to be performed is as it were prefigured, so that I have only to keep this position, to study it, or rather to feel it intimately, in order to recover the idea which had vanished for a moment. Hence, this idea must have tinged with a certain particular colouring the mental image of the intended movement and the position taken up, and this colouring, without doubt, would not have been the same if the end to be attained had been different. Nevertheless

This erroneous tendency aided by language. Illustration.

---

[1] Fouillée, *La Liberté et le Déterminisme.*

language would have still expressed the movement and the position in the same way; and
associationism would have distinguished the two
cases by saying that with the idea of the same
movement there was associated this time the idea
of a new end : as if the mere newness of the end
to be attained did not alter in some degree the
idea of the movement to be performed, even though
the movement itself remained the same! We
should thus say, not that the image of a certain
position can be connected in consciousness with
images of different ends to be attained, but rather
that positions geometrically identical outside look
different to consciousness from the inside, according to the end contemplated. The mistake of
associationism is that it first did away with the
qualitative element in the act to be peformed and
retained only the geometrical and impersonal
element : with the idea of this act, thus rendered
colourless, it was then necessary to associate some
specific difference to distinguish it from many
other acts. But this association is the work of
the associationist philosopher who is studying my
mind, rather than of my mind itself.

I smell a rose and immediately confused recollections of childhood come back to my memory.
Illustration
from " associ- In truth, these recollections have not
ations " of been called up by the perfume of the
smell. rose : I breathe them in with the very
scent ; it means all that to me. To others it will
smell differently.—It is always the same scent,

you will say, but associated with different ideas.—
I am quite willing that you should express yourself in this way ; but do not forget that you have
first removed the personal element from the different impressions which the rose makes on each one
of us ; you have retained only the objective aspect,
that part of the scent of the rose which is public
property and thereby belongs to space.   Only thus
was it possible to give a name to the rose and its
perfume.   You then found it necessary, in order
to distinguish our personal impressions from one
another, to add specific characteristics to the
general idea of rose-scent.   And you now say
that our different impressions, our personal impressions, result from the fact that we associate different recollections with rose-scent.   But the association of which you speak hardly exists except
for you, and as a method of explanation.   It is
in this way that, by setting side by side certain
letters of an alphabet common to a number of
known languages, we may imitate fairly well such
and such a characteristic sound belonging to a
new one ; but not with any of these letters, nor
with all of them, has the sound itself been built up.

We are thus brought back to the distinction
which we set up above between the multiplicity

Associationism fails to distinguish between the multiplicity of juxtaposition and that of fusion.

of juxtaposition and that of fusion or
interpenetration.   Such and such a feeling, such and such an idea, contains an
indefinite plurality of conscious states :
but the plurality will not be observed

unless it is, as it were, spread out in this homogeneous medium which some call duration, but which is
in reality space. We shall then perceive terms
external to one another, and these terms will no
longer be the states of consciousness themselves,
but their symbols, or, speaking more exactly, the
words which express them. There is, as we have
pointed out, a close connexion between the faculty
of conceiving a homogeneous medium, such as
space, and that of thinking by means of general
ideas. As soon as we try to give an account of a
conscious state, to analyse it, this state, which is
above all personal, will be resolved into impersonal elements external to one another, each of
which calls up the idea of a genus and is expressed
by a word. But because our reason, equipped
with the idea of space and the power of creating
symbols, draws these multiple elements out of the
whole, it does not follow that they were contained in it. For within the whole they did not
occupy space and did not care to express themselves by means of symbols; they permeated
and melted into one another. Associationism
thus makes the mistake of constantly replacing
the concrete phenomenon which takes place in
the mind by the artificial reconstruction of it
given by philosophy, and of thus confusing the
explanation of the fact with the fact itself. We
shall perceive this more clearly as we consider
deeper and more comprehensive psychic states.

The self comes into contact with the external

world at its surface ; and as this surface retains
the imprint of objects, the self will
associate by contiguity terms which it
has perceived in juxtaposition : it is
connexions of this kind, connexions
of quite simple and so to speak impersonal sensations, that the associationist theory fits. But,
just in proportion as we dig below the surface and
get down to the real self, do its states of consciousness cease to stand in juxtaposition and begin to
permeate and melt into one another, and each to be
tinged with the colouring of all the others. Thus
each of us has his own way of loving and hating ;
and this love or this hatred reflects his whole
personality. Language, however, denotes these
states by the same words in every case : so that
it has been able to fix only the objective and
impersonal aspect of love, hate, and the thousand
emotions which stir the soul. We estimate the
talent of a novelist by the power with which he
lifts out of the common domain, to which language
had thus brought them down, feelings and ideas
to which he strives to restore, by adding detail to
detail, their original and living individuality.
But just as we can go on inserting points between
two positions of a moving body without ever filling
up the space traversed, in the same way, by the
mere fact that we associate states with states and
that these states are set side by side instead of
permeating one another, we fail to translate
completely what our soul experiences : there

Failure of as-
sociationism
to explain the
deeper states
of the self.

is no common measure between mind and language.

Therefore, it is only an inaccurate psychology, misled by language, which will show us the soul determined by sympathy, aversion, or hate as though by so many forces pressing upon it. These feelings, provided that they go deep enough, each make up the whole soul, since the whole content of the soul is reflected in each of them. To say that the soul is determined under the influence of any one of these feelings is thus to recognize that it is self-determined. The associationist reduces the self to an aggregate of conscious states : sensations, feelings, and ideas. But if he sees in these various states no more than is expressed in their name, if he retains only their impersonal aspect, he may set them side by side for ever without getting anything but a phantom self, the shadow of the ego projecting itself into space. If, on the contrary, he takes these psychic states with the particular colouring which they assume in the case of a definite person, and which comes to each of them by reflection from all the others, then there is no need to associate a number of conscious states in order to rebuild the person, for the whole personality is in a single one of them, provided that we know how to choose it. And the outward manifestation of this inner state will be just what is called a free act, since the self alone will have been the author

The self is not an aggregate of conscious states. Freedom is self-expression, admitting of degrees, and may be curtailed by education.

of it, and since it will express the whole of the self. Freedom, thus understood, is not *absolute*, as a radically libertarian philosophy would have it ; it admits of degrees. For it is by no means the case that all conscious states blend with one another as raindrops with the water of a lake. The self, in so far as it has to do with a homogeneous space, develops on a kind of surface, and on this surface independent growths may form and float. Thus a suggestion received in the hypnotic state is not incorporated in the mass of conscious states, but, endowed with a life of its own, it will usurp the whole personality when its time comes. A violent anger roused by some accidental circumstance, an hereditary vice suddenly emerging from the obscure depths of the organism to the surface of consciousness, will act almost like a hypnotic suggestion. Alongside these independent elements there may be found more complex series, the terms of which do permeate one another, but which never succeed in blending perfectly with the whole mass of the self. Such is the system of feelings and ideas which are the result of an education not properly assimilated, an education which appeals to the memory rather than to the judgment. Here will be found, within the fundamental self, a parasitic self which continually encroaches upon the other. Many live this kind of life, and die without having known true freedom. But suggestion would become persuasion if the entire self assimilated it ; passion, even sudden passion, would no longer bear the stamp of fatality if the whole history of the person were reflected in it, as in the indignation of Alceste ; [1] and the most authoritative education would not curtail any of our freedom if it only imparted to us ideas and feelings capable of impregnating the whole soul. It is the whole soul, in fact, which gives rise to the free decision : and the act will be so much the freer the more the dynamic series with which it is connected tends to be the fundamental self.

Thus understood, free acts are exceptional, even on the part of those who are most given to controlling and reasoning out what they do. It has been pointed out that we generally perceive our own self by refraction through space, that our conscious states crystallize into words, and that our living and concrete self thus gets covered with an outer crust of clean-cut psychic states, which are separated from one another and consequently fixed. We added that, for the convenience of language and the promotion of social relations, we have everything to gain by not breaking through this crust and by assuming it to give an exact outline of the form of the object which it covers. It should now be added that our daily actions are called forth not so much by our feelings themselves, which are constantly

Our every-day acts obey the laws of association. At great crises our decisions are really free as expressing the fundamental self.

---

[1] In Molière's comedy *Le Misanthrope*, (*Tr.*).

changing, as by the unchanging images with which these feelings are bound up. In the morning, when the hour strikes at which I am accustomed to rise, I might receive this impression σὺν ὅλη τῇ ψυχῇ, as Plato says ; I might let it blend with the confused mass of impressions which fill my mind ; perhaps in that case it would not determine me to act. But generally this impression, instead of disturbing my whole consciousness like a stone which falls into the water of a pond, merely stirs up an idea which is, so to speak, solidified on the surface, the idea of rising and attending to my usual occupations. This impression and this idea have in the end become tied up with one another, so that the act follows the impression without the self interfering with it. In this instance I am a conscious automaton, and I am so because I have everything to gain by being so. It will be found that the majority of our daily actions are performed in this way and that, owing to the solidification in memory of such and such sensations, feelings, or ideas, impressions from the outside call forth movements on our part which, though conscious and even intelligent, have many points of resemblance with reflex acts. It is to these acts, which are very numerous but for the most part insignificant, that the associationist theory is applicable. They are, taken all together, the substratum of our free activity, and with respect to this activity they play the same part as our organic functions in relation to the whole of our conscious life. Moreover we will grant to determinism that we often resign our freedom in more serious circumstances, and that, by sluggishness or indolence, we allow this same local process to run its course when our whole personality ought, so to speak, to vibrate. When our most trustworthy friends agree in advising us to take some important step, the sentiments which they utter with so much insistence lodge on the surface of our ego and there get solidified in the same way as the ideas of which we spoke just now. Little by little they will form a thick crust which will cover up our own sentiments ; we shall believe that we are acting freely, and it is only by looking back to the past, later on, that we shall see how much we were mistaken. But then, at the very minute when the act is going to be performed, *something* may revolt against it. It is the deep-seated self rushing up to the surface. It is the outer crust bursting, suddenly giving way to an irresistible thrust. Hence in the depths of the self, below this most reasonable pondering over most reasonable pieces of advice, something else was going on—a gradual heating and a sudden boiling over of feelings and ideas, not unperceived, but rather unnoticed. If we turn back to them and carefully scrutinize our memory, we shall see that we had ourselves shaped these ideas, ourselves lived these feelings, but that, through some strange reluctance to exercise our will, we had thrust them back into the darkest depths of our soul whenever they came up to the surface. And this is why we seek in vain to explain our sudden change of mind by the visible circumstances which preceded it. We wish to know the reason why we have made up our mind, and we find that we have decided without any reason, and perhaps even against every reason. But, in certain cases, that is the best of reasons. For the action which has been performed does not then express some superficial idea, almost external to ourselves, distinct and easy to account for : it agrees with the whole of our most intimate feelings, thoughts and aspirations, with that particular conception of life which is the equivalent of all our past experience, in a word, with our personal idea of happiness and of honour. Hence it has been a mistake to look for examples in the ordinary and even indifferent circumstances of life in order to prove that man is capable of choosing without a motive. It might easily be shown that these insignificant actions are bound up with some determining reason. It is at the great and solemn crisis, decisive of our reputation with others, and yet more with ourselves, that we choose in defiance of what is conventionally called a motive, and this absence of any tangible reason is the more striking the deeper our freedom goes.

But the determinist, even when he refrains from regarding the more serious emotions or deep-seated psychic states as forces, nevertheless distinguishes them from one another and is thus led to a mechanical conception of the self.   He

Determinism
sets on the
one side the
ego, always
self-identical,
and on the
other con-
trary feelings.
But this is mere
symbolism. will show us this self hesitating between two contrary feelings, passing from one to the other and finally deciding in favour of one of them.   The self and the feelings which stir it are thus treated as well defined objects, which remain identical during the whole of the process.   But if it is always the same self which deliberates, and if the two opposite feelings by which it is moved do not change, how, in virtue of this very principle of causality which determinism appeals to, will the self ever come to a decision ?   The truth is that the self, by the mere fact of experiencing the first feeling, has already changed to a slight extent when the second supervenes : all the time that the deliberation is going on, the self is changing and is consequently modifying the two feelings which agitate it.   A dynamic series of states is thus formed which permeate and strengthen one another, and which will lead by a natural evolution to a free act.   But determinism, ever craving for symbolical representation, cannot help substituting words for the opposite feelings which share the ego between them, as well as for the ego itself.   By giving first the person and then the feelings by which he is moved a fixed form by means of sharply defined words, it deprives them in advance of every kind of living activity.   It will then see on the one side an ego always self-identical, and on the other contrary feelings, also

self-identical, which dispute for its possession ;
victory will necessarily belong to the stronger.
But this mechanism, to which we have condemned
ourselves in advance, has no value beyond that
of a symbolical representation : it cannot hold
good against the witness of an attentive consciousness, which shows us inner dynamism as a fact.

In short, we are free when our acts spring from
our whole personality, when they express it, when
they have that indefinable resemblance
to it which one sometimes finds between
the artist and his work. It is no use
asserting that we are then yielding to
the all-powerful influence of our char-
acter. Our character is still ourselves ; and because
we are pleased to split the person into two parts so
that by an effort of abstraction we may consider
in turn the self which feels or thinks and the self
which acts, it would be very strange to conclude
that one of the two selves is coercing the other.
Those who ask whether we are free to alter our
character lay themselves open to the same objection. Certainly our character is altering imperceptibly every day, and our freedom would suffer
if these new acquisitions were grafted on to our
self and not blended with it. But, as soon as
this blending takes place, it must be admitted that
the change which has supervened in our character
belongs to us, that we have appropriated it. In
a word, if it is agreed to call every act free which
springs from the self and from the self alone, the

(marginal note) Freedom and character. The determinist next asks, could our act have been different or can it be foretold ?

act which bears the mark of our personality is truly free, for our self alone will lay claim to its paternity. It would thus be recognized that free will is a fact, if it were agreed to look for it in a certain characteristic of the decision which is taken, in the free act itself. But the determinist feeling that he cannot retain his hold on this position, takes refuge in the past or the future. Sometimes he transfers himself in thought to some earlier period and asserts the necessary determination, from this very moment, of the act which is to come ; sometimes, assuming in advance that the act is already performed, he claims that it could not have taken place in any other way. The opponents of determinism themselves willingly follow it on to this new ground and agree to introduce into their definition of our free act —perhaps not without some risk—the anticipation of what we might do and the recollection of some other decision which we might have taken. It is advisable, then, that we should place ourselves at this new point of view, and, setting aside all translation into words, all symbolism in space, attend to what pure consciousness alone shows us about an action that has come to pass or an action which is still to come. The original error of determinism and the mistake of its opponents will thus be grasped on another side, in so far as they bear explicitly on a certain misconception of duration.

"To be conscious of free will," says Stuart

Mill, " must mean to be conscious, before I have
Determinist
and libertarian
doctrines of
"possible
acts." decided, that I am able to decide either
way." [1] This is really the way in which
the defenders of free will understand it ;
and they assert that when we perform an action
freely, some other action would have been "equally
possible." On this point they appeal to the testimony of consciousness, which shows us, beyond
the act itself, the power of deciding in favour of
the opposite course. Inversely, determinism claims
that, given certain antecedents, only one resultant
action was possible. " When we think of ourselves hypothetically," Stuart Mill goes on, " as
having acted otherwise than we did, we always
suppose a difference in the antecedents. We picture ourselves as having known something that
we did not know, or not known something that
we did know." [2] And, faithful to his principle,
the English philosopher assigns consciousness the
rôle of informing us about what is, not about what
might be. We shall not insist for the moment on
this last point : we reserve the question in what
sense the ego perceives itself as a determining
cause. But beside this psychological question
there is another, belonging rather to metaphysics,
which the determinists and their opponents solve
a priori along opposite lines. The argument of

---

[1] *Examination of Sir W. Hamilton's Philosophy.* 5th ed.,
(1878), p. 580.
  [2] *Ibid.* p. 583.

the former implies that there is only one possible
act corresponding to given antecedents : the
believers in free will assume, on the other hand,
that the same series could issue in several different
acts, equally possible. It is on this question of
the equal possibility of two contrary actions or
volitions that we shall first dwell : perhaps we
shall thus gather some indication as to the nature
of the operation by which the will makes its choice.

I hesitate between two possible actions X and
Y, and I go in turn from one to the other.   This
means that I pass through a series of
Geometrical
(and thereby states, and that these states can be
deceptive)
representation divided into two groups according as I
of the process
of coming to a incline more towards X or in the contrary
decision.
direction.   Indeed, these opposite inclinations alone have a real existence, and X and Y
are two symbols by which I represent at their
arrival- or termination-points, so to speak, two
different tendencies of my personality at successive moments of duration. Let us then rather
denote the tendencies themselves by X and Y ;
will this new notation give a more faithful image
of the concrete reality ?   It must be noticed, as
we said above, that the self grows, expands, and
changes as it passes through the two contrary
states : if not, how would it ever come to a decision ?   Hence there are not exactly two contrary
states, but a large number of successive and different states within which I distinguish, by an effort

of imagination, two opposite directions. Thus we shall get still nearer the reality by agreeing to use the invariable signs X and Y to denote, not these tendencies or states themselves, since they are constantly changing, but the two different directions which our imagination ascribes to them for the greater convenience of language. It will also be understood that these are symbolical representations, that in reality there are not two tendencies, or even two directions, but a self which lives and develops by means of its very hesitations, until the free action drops from it like an over-ripe fruit.

But this conception of voluntary activity does not satisfy common sense, because, being essentially a devotee of mechanism, it loves clear-cut distinctions, those which are expressed by sharply defined words or by different positions in space. Hence it will picture a self which, after having traversed a series M O of conscious states, when it reaches the point O finds before it two directions O X and O Y, equally open. These directions thus become *things*, real paths into which the highroad of consciousness leads, and it depends only on the self which of them is entered upon. In short, the continuous and living activity of this self, in which we have dis-

The only reality is the living developing self, in which we distinguish by abstraction two opposite tendencies or directions.

tinguished, by abstraction only, two opposite directions, is replaced by these directions themselves, transformed into indifferent inert things awaiting our choice.   But then we must certainly transfer the activity of the self somewhere or other.   We will put it, according to this hypothesis, at the point O : we will say that the self, when it reaches O and finds two courses open to it, hesitates, deliberates and finally decides in favour of one of them.   As we find it difficult to picture the double direction of the conscious activity in all the phases of its continuous development, we separate off these two tendencies on the one hand and the activity of the self on the other : we thus get an impartially active ego hesitating between two inert and, as it were, solidified courses of action.   Now, if it decides in favour of O X, the line O Y will nevertheless remain ; if it chooses O Y, the path O X will remain open, waiting in case the self retraces its steps in order to make use of it.   It is in this sense that we say, when speaking of a free act, that the contrary action was equally possible.   And, even if we do not draw a geometrical figure on paper, we involuntarily and almost unconsciously think of it as soon as we distinguish in the free act a number of successive phases, the *conception* of opposite motives, *hesitation* and *choice*—thus hiding the geometrical symbolism under a kind of verbal crystallization.   Now it is easy to see that this really mechanical conception of freedom issues naturally and logically in the most unbending determinism.

The living activity of the self, in which we distinguish by abstraction two opposite tend-encies, will finally issue either at X or Y. Now, since it is agreed to localize the double activity of the self at the point O, there is no reason to separate this activity from the act in which it will issue and which forms part and parcel of it. And if experience shows that the decision has been in favour of X, it is not a neutral activity which should be placed at the point O, but an activity tending in advance in the direction O X, in spite of apparent hesitations. If, on the contrary, observation proves that the decision has been in favour of Y, we must infer that the activity localized by us at the point O was bent in this second direction in spite of some oscillations towards the first. To assert that the self, when it reaches the point O, chooses indifferently between X and Y, is to stop half way in the course of our geometrical symbolism ; it is to separate off at the point O only a part of this continuous activity in which we undoubtedly distinguished two different directions, but which in addition has gone on to X or Y : why not take this last fact into account as well as the other two ? Why not assign it the place that belongs to it in the symbolical figure which we have just constructed ? But if the self, when it reaches the point O, is already

If this symbolism represents the facts, the activity of the self has always tended in one direction, and determinism results.

determined in one direction, there is no use in the
other way remaining open, the self cannot take it.
And the same rough symbolism which was meant
to show the contingency of the action performed,
ends, by a natural extension, in proving its absolute necessity.

In short, defenders and opponents of free will
agree in holding that the action is preceded by a
Libertarians kind of mechanical oscillation between
ignore the fact
that one path the two points X and Y. If I decide
has been cho-
sen, and not in favour of X, the former will tell me :
the other. you hesitated and deliberated, therefore
Y was possible. The others will answer : you
chose X, therefore you had some reason for doing
so, and those who declare that Y was equally
possible forget this reason : they leave aside one
of the conditions of the problem. Now, if I dig
deeper underneath these two opposite solutions,
I discover a common postulate : both take up
their position after the action X has been performed, and represent the process of my voluntary
activity by a path M O which branches off at the
point O, the lines O X and O Y symbolizing the
two directions which abstraction distinguishes
within the continuous activity of which X is the
goal. But while the determinists take account
of all that they know, and note that the path
M O X has been traversed, their opponents mean
to ignore one of the data with which they have
constructed the figure, and after having traced
out the lines O X and O Y, which should together

represent the progress of the activity of the self, they bring back the self to the point O to oscillate there until further orders.

It should not be forgotten, indeed, that the figure, which is really a splitting of our psychic activity in space, is purely symbolical, and, as such, cannot be constructed unless we adopt the hypothesis that our deliberation is finished and our mind made up. If you trace it beforehand, you assume that you have reached the end and are present in imagination at the final act. In short this figure does not show me the deed in the doing but the deed already done. Do not ask me then whether the self, having traversed the path M O and decided in favour of X, could or could not choose Y : I should answer that the question is meaningless, because there is no line M O, no point O, no path O X, no direction O Y. To ask such a question is to admit the possibility of adequately representing time by space and a succession by a simultaneity. It is to ascribe to the figure we have traced the value of a description, and not merely of a symbol ; it is to believe that it is possible to follow the process of psychic activity on this figure like the march of an army on a map. We have been present at the deliberation of the self in all its phases until the act was performed: then, recapitulating the terms of the series, we perceive succession under the form of simultaneity, we project

But the figure merely gives the stereotyped memory of the process, and not the dynamic progress which issued in the act.

time into space, and we base our reasoning, con-
sciously or unconsciously, on this geometrical
figure. But this figure represents a *thing* and not
a *progress* ; it corresponds, in its inertness, to a
kind of stereotyped memory of the whole process
of deliberation and the final decision arrived at :
how could it give us the least idea of the concrete
movement, the dynamic progress by which the
deliberation issued in the act ? And yet, once
the figure is constructed, we go back in imagination into the past and will have it that our psychic
activity has followed exactly the path traced out
by the figure. We thus fall into the mistake which
has been pointed out above : we give a mechanical
explanation of a fact, and then substitute the
explanation for the fact itself. Hence we encounter insuperable difficulties from the very beginning : if the two courses were equally possible, how
have we made our choice ? If only one of them
was possible, why did we believe ourselves free ?
And we do not see that both questions come back
to this : Is time space ?

If I glance over a road marked on the map
and follow it up to a certain point, there is
Fundamental nothing to prevent my turning back and
error is con-
fusion of time trying to find out whether it branches
and space.
The self infal- off anywhere. But time is not a line
lible in affirm-
ing immedi- along which one can pass again. Cer-
ate experience
of freedom, tainly, once it has elapsed, we are justi-
but cannot ex-
plain it. fied in picturing the successive moments
as external to one another and in thus thinking

of a line traversing space ; but it must then be understood that this line does not symbolize the time which is passing but the time which has passed. Defenders and opponents of free will alike forget this—the former when they assert, and the latter when they deny the possibility of acting differently from what we have done. The former reason thus : " The path is not yet traced out, therefore it may take any direction whatever." To which the answer is : " You forget that it is not possible to speak of a path till the action is performed : but then it will have been traced out." The latter say : " The path has been traced out in such and such a way : therefore its possible direction was not any direction whatever, but only this one direction." To which the answer is : " Before the path was traced out there was no direction, either possible or impossible, for the very simple reason that there could not yet be any question of a path." Get rid of this clumsy symbolism, the idea of which besets you without your knowing it ; you will see that the argument of the determinists assumes this puerile form : " The act, once performed, is performed," and that their opponents reply : " The act, before being performed, was not yet performed." In other words, the question of freedom remains after this discussion exactly where it was to begin with ; nor must we be surprised at it, since freedom must be sought in a certain shade or quality of the action itself and not in the relation of this act to what it is not or to what it might have been. All the difficulty arises from the fact that both parties picture the deliberation under the form of an oscillation in space, while it really consists in a dynamic progress in which the self and its motives, like real living beings, are in a constant state of becoming. The self, infallible when it affirms its immediate experiences, feels itself free and says so ; but, as soon as it tries to explain its freedom to itself, it no longer perceives itself except by a kind of refraction through space. Hence a symbolism of a mechanical kind, equally incapable of proving, disproving, or illustrating free will.

But determinism will not admit itself beaten, and, putting the question in a new form, it will say : " Let us leave aside actions already performed : let us consider only actions that are to come. The question is whether, knowing from now onwards all the future antecedents, some higher intelligence would not be able to predict with absolute certainty the decision which will result." —We gladly agree to the question being put in these terms : it will give us a chance of stating our own theory with greater precision. But we shall first draw a distinction between those who think that the knowledge of antecedents would enable us to state a *probable* conclusion and those who speak of an *infallible* foresight. To say that

Is prediction of an act possible ? Probable and infallible conclusions.

a certain friend, under certain circumstances, will very probably act in a certain way, is not so much to predict the future conduct of our friend as to pass a judgment on his present character, that is to say, on his past. Although our feelings, our ideas, our character, are constantly altering, a sudden change is seldom observed ; and it is still more seldom that we cannot say of a person whom we know that certain actions seem to accord fairly well with his nature and that certain others are absolutely inconsistent with it. All philosophers will agree on this point ; for to say that a given action is consistent or inconsistent with the present character of a person whom one knows is not to bind the future to the present. But the determinist goes much further : he asserts that our solution is provisional simply because we never know all the conditions of the problem ; that our forecast would gain in probability in proportion as we were provided with a larger number of these conditions ; that, therefore, complete and perfect knowledge of all the antecedents without any exception would make our forecast infallibly true. Such, then, is the hypothesis which we have to examine.

For the sake of greater definiteness, let us imagine a person called upon to make a seemingly free decision under serious circumstances; we shall call him Peter. The question is whether a philosopher Paul, living at the same period as Peter, or, if you

To know *completely* the antecedents and conditions of an action is to be actually performing it.

prefer, a few centuries before, would have been able, knowing *all* the conditions under which Peter acts, to foretell with certainty the choice which Peter made.

There are several ways of picturing the mental condition of a person at a given moment. We try to do it when e.g. we read a novel ; but whatever care the author may have taken in depicting the feelings of his hero, and even in tracing back his history, the end, foreseen or unforeseen, will add something to the idea which we had formed of the character : the character, therefore, was only imperfectly known to us. In truth, the deeper psychic states, those which are translated by free acts, express and sum up the whole of our past history : if Paul knows all the conditions under which Peter acts, we must suppose that no detail of Peter's life escapes him, and that his imagination reconstructs and even lives over again Peter's history. But we must here make a vital distinction. When I myself pass through a certain psychic state, I know exactly the intensity of this state and its importance in relation to the others, not by measurement or comparison, but because the intensity of e.g. a deep-seated feeling is nothing else than the feeling itself. On the other hand, if I try to give you an account of this psychic state, I shall be unable to make you realize its intensity except by some definite sign of a mathematical kind : I shall have to measure its importance, compare it with what goes before and

what follows, in short determine the part which
it plays in the final act.   And I shall say that it
is more or less intense, more or less important,
according as the final act is explained by it or
apart from it.   On the other hand, for my own
consciousness, which perceived this inner state,
there was no need of a comparison of this kind :
the intensity was given to it as an inexpressible
quality of the state itself.   In other words, the
intensity of a psychic state is not given to consciousness as a special sign accompanying this
state and denoting its power, like an exponent in
algebra ; we have shown above that it expresses
rather its shade, its characteristic colouring, and
that, if it is a question of a feeling, for example, its
intensity consists in being felt.   Hence we have
to distinguish two ways of assimilating the conscious states of other people : the one dynamic,
which consists in experiencing them oneself ; the
other static, which consists in substituting for the
consciousness of these states their image or rather
their intellectual symbol, their idea.   In this case
the conscious states are *imagined* instead of being
reproduced ; but, then, to the image of the psychic
states themselves some indication of their *intensity*
should be added, since they no longer act on the
person in whose mind they are pictured and the
latter has no longer any chance of experiencing
their force by actually feeling them.   Now, this
indication itself will necessarily assume a quantitative character : it will be pointed out, for

example, that a certain feeling has more strength than another feeling, that it is necessary to take more account of it, that it has played a greater part ; and how could this be known unless the later history of the person were known in advance, with the precise actions in which this multiplicity of states or inclinations has issued ?   Therefore, if Paul is to have an adequate idea of Peter's state at any moment of his history, there are only two courses open ; either, like a novelist who knows whither he is conducting his characters, Paul must already know Peter's final act, and must thus be able to supplement his mental image of the successive states through which Peter is going to pass by some indication of their value in relation to the whole of Peter's history ; or he must make up his mind to pass through these different states, not in imagination, but in reality. The former hypothesis must be put on one side since the very point at issue is whether, the antecedents *alone* being given, Paul will be able to foresee the final act. We find ourselves compelled, therefore, to alter radically the idea which we had formed of Paul : he is not, as we had thought at first, a spectator whose eyes pierce the future, but an actor who plays Peter's part in advance. And notice that you cannot exempt him from any detail of this part, for the most common-place events have their importance in a life-story ; and even supposing that they have not, you cannot decide that they are insignificant except in relation to the final act, which, by hypothesis, is not given. Neither have you the right to cut short—were it only by a second—the different states of consciousness through which Paul is going to pass before Peter ; for the effects of the same feeling, for example, go on accumulating at every moment of duration, and the sum total of these effects could not be realized all at once unless one knew the importance of the feeling, taken in its totality, in relation to the final act, which is the very thing that is supposed to remain unknown. But if Peter and Paul have experienced the same feelings in the same order, if their minds have the same history, how will you distinguish one from the other ? Will it be by the body in which they dwell ? They would then always differ in some respect, viz., that at no moment of their history would they have a mental picture of the same body. Will it be by the place which they occupy in time ? In that case they would no longer be present at the same events : now, by hypothesis, they have the same past and the same present, having the same experience. You must now make up your mind about it : Peter and Paul are one and the same person, whom you call Peter when he acts and Paul when you recapitulate his history. The more complete you made the sum of the conditions which, when known, would have enabled you to predict Peter's future action, the closer became your grasp of his existence and the nearer you came to living his life over again down to its smallest details : you thus reached the very moment when, the action taking place, there was no longer anything to be foreseen, but only something to be done. Here again any attempt to reconstruct ideally an act really *willed* ends in the mere witnessing of the act whilst it is being performed or when it is already done.

Hence it is a question devoid of meaning to ask : Could or could not the act be foreseen, given the sum total of its antecedents ? For there are two ways of assimilating these antecedents, the one dynamic the other static. In the first case we shall be led by imperceptible steps to identify ourselves with the person we are dealing with, to pass through the same series of states, and thus to get back to the very moment at which the act is performed ; hence there can no longer be any question of foreseeing it. In the second case, we presuppose the final act by the mere fact of annexing to the qualitative description of the previous states the quantitative appreciation of their importance. Here again the one party is led merely to realize that the act is not yet performed when it is to be performed, and the other, that when performed it is performed. This, like the previous discussion, leaves the question of freedom exactly where it was to begin with.

By going deeper into this twofold argument, we

Hence meaningless to ask whether an act can be foreseen when all its antecedents are given.

shall find, at its very root, the two fundamental illusions of the reflective consciousness.

The first consists in regarding intensity as a mathematical property of psychic states and not, as we said at the beginning of this essay, as a special quality, as a particular shade of these various states. The second consists in substituting for the concrete reality or dynamic progress, which consciousness perceives, the material symbol of this progress when it has already reached its end, that is to say, of the act already accomplished together with the series of its antecedents. Certainly, once the final act is completed, I can ascribe to all the antecedents their proper value, and picture the interplay of these various elements as a conflict or a composition of forces. But to ask whether, the antecedents being known as well as their value, one could foretell the final act, is to beg the question ; it is to forget that we cannot know the value of the antecedents without knowing the final act, which is the very thing that is not yet known ; it is to suppose wrongly that the symbolical diagram which we draw in our own way for representing the action *when completed* has been drawn by the action itself *whilst progressing*, and drawn by it in an automatic manner.

Now, in these two illusions themselves a third one is involved, and you will see that the question whether the act could or could not be foreseen always comes back to this : Is time space ?

The note printed in the left margin:

The two fallacies involved: (1) regarding intensity as a magnitude, not a quality; (2) substituting material symbol for dynamic process.

You begin by setting side by side in some ideal

space the conscious states which succeed one another in Peter's mind, and
you perceive his life as a kind of path
M O X Y traced out by a moving body M
in space. You then blot out in thought
the part O X Y of this curve, and you inquire
whether, knowing M O, you would have been able
to determine the portion O X of the curve which
the moving body describes beyond O. Such is,
in the main, the question which you put when you

bring in a philo-
sopher Paul, who
lives before Peter
and has to picture to himself the conditions under
which Peter will act. You thus materialize these
conditions ; you make the time to come into a
road already marked out across the plain, which
we can contemplate from the top of the mountain,
even if we have not traversed it and are never to
do so. But, now, you soon notice that the knowledge of the part M O of the curve would not be
enough, unless you were shown the position of the
points of this line, not only in relation to one
another, but also in relation to the points of the
whole line M O X Y ; which would amount to being
given in advance the very elements which have
to be determined. So you then alter your hypothesis ; you realize that time does not require to
be seen, but to be lived ; and hence you conclude
that, if your knowledge of the line M O was not

a sufficient datum, the reason must have been that you looked at it from the outside instead of identifying yourself with the point M, which describes not only M O but also the whole curve, and thus making its movement your own. Therefore, you persuade Paul to come and coincide with Peter ; and naturally, then, it is the line M O X Y which Paul traces out in space, since, by hypothesis, Peter describes this line. But in no wise do you prove thus that Paul foresaw Peter's action ; you only show that Peter acted in the way he did, since Paul became Peter. It is true that you then come back, unwittingly, to your former hypothesis, because you continually confuse the line M O X Y in its tracing with the line M O X Y already traced, that is to say, time with space. After causing Paul to come down and identify himself with Peter as long as was required, you let him go up again and resume his former post of observation. No wonder if he then perceives the line M O X Y complete : he himself has just been completing it.

What makes the confusion a natural and almost an unavoidable one is that science seems to point to many cases where we do anticipate the future. Do we not determine beforehand the conjunctions of heavenly bodies, solar and lunar eclipses, in short the greater number of astronomical phenomena ? Does not, then, the human intellect embrace in the present moment immense intervals of duration still to come ? No doubt it does ; but an anticipation of this kind has not the slightest resemblance to the anticipation of a voluntary act. Indeed, as we shall see, the reasons which render it possible to foretell an astronomical phenomenon are the very ones which prevent us from determining in advance an act which springs from our free activity. For the future of the material universe, although contemporaneous with the future of a conscious being, has no analogy to it.

In order to put our finger on this vital difference, let us assume for a moment that some mischievous genius, more powerful still than the mischievous genius conjured up by Descartes, decreed that all the movements of the universe should go twice as fast. There would be no change in astronomical phenomena, or at any rate in the equations which enable us to foresee them, for in these equations the symbol *t* does not stand for a duration, but for a relation between two durations, for a certain number of units of time, in short, for a certain number of *simultaneities*: these simultaneities, these coincidences would still take place in equal number : only the intervals which separate them would have diminished, but these intervals never make their appearance in our calculations. Now these intervals are just duration *lived*, duration which our consciousness perceives, and our consciousness would soon inform us of a shortening of the day if we had not experienced the usual amount of duration between sunrise and

Illustration from hypothetical acceleration of physical movements.

sunset. No doubt it would not measure this shortening, and perhaps it would not even perceive it immediately as a change of quantity ; but it would realize in some way or other a decline in the usual storing up of experience, a change in the progress usually accomplished between sunrise and sunset.

Now, when an astronomer foretells e.g. a lunar eclipse, he merely exercises in his own way the power which we have ascribed to our mischievous genius. He decrees that time shall go ten times, a hundred times, a thousand times as fast, and he has a right to do so, since all that he thus changes is the nature of the conscious intervals, and since these intervals, by hypothesis, do not enter into the calculations. Therefore, into a psychological duration of a few seconds he may put several years, even several centuries of astronomical time : that is his procedure when he traces in advance the path of a heavenly body or represents it by an equation. What he does is nothing but establishing a series of relations of position between this body and other given bodies, a series of simultaneities and coincidences, a series of numerical relations : as for duration properly so called, it remains outside the calculation and could only be perceived by a consciousness capable of living through the intervals and, in fact, living the intervals themselves, instead of merely perceiving their extremities. Indeed it is even conceivable that this

Astronomical prophecy such an acceleration.

consciousness could live so slow and lazy a life as
to take in the whole path of the heavenly body
in a single perception, just as we do when we perceive the successive positions of a shooting star
as one line of fire. Such a consciousness would
find itself really in the same conditions in which
the astronomer places himself ideally ; it would
see in the present what the astronomer perceives
in the future. In truth, if the latter foresees a
future phenomenon, it is only on condition of
making it to a certain extent a present phenomenon, or at least of enormously reducing the
interval which separates us from it. In short, the
time of which we speak in astronomy is a number,
and the nature of the units of this number cannot
be specified in our calculations ; we may therefore
assume them to be as small as we please, provided
that the same hypothesis is extended to the whole
series of operations, and that the successive relations of position in space are thus preserved. We
shall then be present in imagination at the phenomenon we wish to foretell ; we shall know exactly at what point in space and after how many
units of time this phenomenon takes place ; if we
then restore to these units their psychical nature,
we shall thrust the event again into the future and
say that we have foreseen it, when in reality we
have seen it.

But these units of time which make up living
duration, and which the astronomer can dispose
of as he pleases because they give no handle to

science, are just what concern the psychologist,
for psychology deals with the intervals
themselves and not with their extremities.   Certainly pure consciousness does
not perceive time as a sum of units of
duration : left to itself, it has no means

In dealing with states of consciousness we cannot vary their duration without altering their nature.

and even no reason to measure time ; but a feeling
which lasted only half the number of days, for
example, would no longer be the same feeling
for it ; it would lack thousands of impressions
which gradually thickened its substance and
altered its colour.   True, when we give this feeling
a certain name, when we treat it as a thing, we
believe that we can diminish its duration by half,
for example, and also halve the duration of all the
rest of our history : it seems that it would still
be the same life, only on a reduced scale.   But we
forget that states of consciousness are processes,
and not things ; that if we denote them each by a
single word, it is for the convenience of language ;
that they are alive and therefore constantly changing ; that, in consequence, it is impossible to cut
off a moment from them without making them
poorer by the loss of some impression, and thus
altering their quality.   I quite understand that
the orbit of a planet might be perceived all at
once or in a very short time, because its successive
positions or the *results* of its movement are the
only things that matter, and not the duration of
the equal intervals which separate them.   But
when we have to do with a feeling, it has no precise

result except its having been felt ; and, to estimate this result adequately, it would be necessary to have gone through all the phases of the feeling itself and to have taken up the same duration. Even if this feeling has finally issued in some definite action, which might be compared to the definite position of a planet in space, the knowledge of this act will hardly enable us to estimate the influence of the feeling on the whole of a lifestory, and it is this very influence which we want to know. All foreseeing is in reality seeing, and this seeing takes place when we can reduce as much as we please an interval of future time while preserving the relation of its parts to one another, as happens in the case of astronomical predictions. But what does reducing an interval of time mean, except emptying or impoverishing the conscious states which fill it ?   And does not the very possibility of seeing an astronomical period in miniature thus imply the impossibility of modifying a psychological series in the same way, since it is only by taking this psychological series as an invariable basis that we shall be able to make an astronomical period vary arbitrarily as regards the unit of duration ?

Thus, when we ask whether a future action could have been foreseen, we unwittingly identify that time with which we have to do in the exact sciences, and which is reducible to a number, with real duration, whose so-called quantity is really a quality,

Difference between past and future duration in this respect.

and which we cannot curtail by an instant without
altering the nature of the facts which fill it.   No
doubt the identification is made easier by the fact
that in a large number of cases we are justified in
dealing with real duration as with astronomical
time.   Thus, when we call to mind the past, i.e.
a series of deeds done, we always shorten it, without however distorting the nature of the event
which interests us.   The reason is that we know
it already ; for the psychic state, when it reaches
the end of the *progress* which constitutes its very
existence, becomes a *thing* which one can picture
to oneself all at once.   Here we find ourselves
in the same position as the astronomer, when he
takes in at a glance the orbit which a planet
will need several years to traverse.   In fact,
astronomical prediction should be compared with
the recollection of the past state of consciousness,
not with the anticipation of the future one. But
when we have to determine a future state of consciousness, however superficial it may be, we can
no longer view the antecedents in a static condition
as things ; we must view them in a   dynamic
condition as processes, since we are   concerned
with their influence alone.   Now their duration
is this very influence.   Therefore it will no longer
do to shorten future duration in order to picture
its parts beforehand ; one is bound to *live* this
duration whilst it is unfolding. As far as
deep-seated psychic states are concerned, there
is no perceptible difference between foreseeing,
seeing, and acting.

Only one course will remain open to the determinist. He will probably give up asserting the possibility of foreseeing a certain future act or state of consciousness, but will maintain that every act is determined by its psychic antecedents, or, in other words, that the facts of consciousness, like the phenomena of nature, are subject to laws. This way of arguing means, at bottom, that he will leave out the particular features of the concrete psychic states, lest he find himself confronted by phenomena which defy all symbolical representation and therefore all anticipation. The particular nature of these phenomena is thus thrust out of sight, but it is asserted that, being phenomena, they must remain subject to the law of causality. Now, it is argued, this law means that every phenomenon is determined by its conditions, or, in other words, that the same causes produce the same effects. Either, then, the act is inseparably bound to its antecedents, or the principle of causality admits of an incomprehensible exception.

The determinist argument that psychic phenomena are subject to the law "same antecedents, same consequent."

This last form of the determinist argument differs less than might be thought from all the others which have been examined above. To say that the same inner causes will reproduce the same effects is to assume that the same cause can appear a second time on the stage of consciousness. Now, if duration is what we say, deep-

But as regards inner states the same antecedents will never recur.

seated psychic states are radically heterogeneous
to each other, and it is impossible that any two of
them should be quite alike, since they are two
different moments of a life-story. While the
external object does not bear the mark of the time
that has elapsed and thus, in spite of the difference of time, the physicist can again encounter
identical elementary conditions, duration is something real for the consciousness which preserves
the trace of it, and we cannot here speak of identical conditions, because the same moment does
not occur twice. It is no use arguing that, even
if there are no two deep-seated psychic states
which are altogether alike, yet analysis would
resolve these different states into more general
and homogeneous elements which might be compared with each other. This would be to forget
that even the simplest psychic elements possess
a personality and a life of their own, however
superficial they may be ; they are in a constant
state of becoming, and the same feeling, by
the mere fact of being repeated, is a new feeling.
Indeed, we have no reason for calling it by its
former name save that it corresponds to the same
external cause or projects itself outwardly into
similar attitudes : hence it would simply be beg-
ging the question to deduce from the so-called
likeness of two conscious states that the same cause
produces the same effect. In short, if the causal
relation still holds good in the realm of inner states,
it cannot resemble in any way what we call

causality in nature. For the physicist, the same
cause always produces the same effect : for a
psychologist who does not let himself be misled
by merely apparent analogies, a deep-seated inner
cause produces its effect once for all and will
never reproduce it. And if it is now asserted that
this effect was inseparably bound up with this
particular cause, such an assertion will mean one
of two things : either that, the antecedents being
given, the future action might have been foreseen ;
or that, the action having once been performed,
any other action is seen, under the given conditions,
to have been impossible. Now we saw that both
these assertions were equally meaningless, and that
they also involved a false conception of duration.

Nevertheless it will be worth while to dwell on
this latter form of the determinist argument, even
though it be only to explain from our
point of view the meaning of the two
words " determination " and " causality." In vain do we argue that there
cannot be any question either of foreseeing a future action in the way that an astronomical phenomenon is foreseen, or of asserting,
when once an action is done, that any other action
would have been impossible under the given conditions. In vain do we add that, even when it
takes this form : " The same causes produce the
same effects," the principle of universal determination loses every shred of meaning in the inner world
of conscious states. The determinist will perhaps

Analysis of the
conception of
cause, which
underlies the
whole deter-
minist argu-
ment.

yield to our arguments on each of these three points in particular, will admit that in the psychical field one cannot ascribe any of these three meanings to the word determination, will probably fail to discover a fourth meaning, and yet will go on repeating that the act is inseparably bound up with its antecedents. We thus find ourselves here confronted by so deep-seated a misapprehension and so obstinate a prejudice that we cannot get the better of them without attacking them at their root, which is the principle of causality. By analysing the concept of cause, we shall show the ambiguity which it involves, and, though not aiming at a formal definition of freedom, we shall perhaps get beyond the purely negative idea of it which we have framed up to the present.

We perceive physical phenomena, and these phenomena obey laws. This means : (1) that phenomena *a, b, c, d*, previously perceived, can occur again in the same shape ; (2) that a certain phenomenon *P*, which appeared after the conditions *a, b, c, d*, and after these conditions only, will not fail to recur as soon as the

Causality as " regular succession " does not apply to conscious states and cannot disprove free will.

same conditions are again present. If the principle of causality told us nothing more, as the empiricists claim, we should willingly grant these philosophers that their principle is derived from experience ; but it would no longer prove anything against our freedom. For it would then be understood that definite antecedents give rise to a definite consequent *wherever* experience shows us this regular succession ; but the question is whether this regularity is found in the domain of consciousness too, and that is the whole problem of free will. We grant you for a moment that the principle of causality is nothing but the summing up of the uniform and unconditional successions observed in the past : by what right, then, do you apply it to those deep-seated states of consciousness in which no regular succession has yet been discovered, since the attempt to foresee them ever fails ? And how can you base on this principle your argument to prove the determinism of inner states, when, according to you, the determinism of observed facts is the sole source of the principle itself ? In truth, when the empiricists make use of the principle of causality to disprove human freedom, they take the word cause in a new meaning, which is the very meaning given to it by common sense.

To assert the regular succession of two phenomena is, indeed, to recognize that, the first being given, we already catch sight of the second. But this wholly subjective connexion between two ideas is not enough for common sense. It seems to common .sense that, if the idea of the second phenomenon is already implied in that of the first, the second phenomenon itself must exist objectively, in some way or other, within the first phenomenon. And common sense was bound to come to this conclusion, because to distinguish exactly between an objective connexion of phenomena and a subjective association between their ideas presupposes a fairly high degree of philosophical culture. We thus pass imperceptibly from the first meaning to the second, and we picture the causal relation as a kind of prefiguring of the future phenomenon in its present conditions. Now this prefiguring can be understood in two very different ways, and it is just here that the ambiguity begins.

In the first place, mathematics furnishes us with *one* type of this kind of prefiguring. The very movement by which we draw the circumference of a circle on a sheet of paper generates all the mathematical properties of this figure : in this sense an unlimited number of theorems can be said to pre-exist within the definition, although they will be spread out in duration for the mathematician who deduces them. It is true that we are here in the realm of pure quantity and that, as geometrical properties can be expressed in the form of equations, it is easy to understand how the original equation, expressing the fundamental property of the figure, is transformed into an unlimited number of new ones, all virtually contained in the first. On the contrary, physical phenomena, which succeed one another and are perceived by our senses, are distinguished by quality not less than by quantity, so that there would be some difficulty in at once declaring them

Causality, as the prefiguring of the future phenomenon in its present conditions, in one form destroys concrete phenomena.

equivalent to one another.   But, just because
they are perceived through our sense-organs, we
seem justified in ascribing their qualitative differences to the impression which they make on us and
in assuming, behind the heterogeneity of our sensations, a homogeneous physical universe.   Thus,
we shall strip matter of the concrete qualities
with which our senses clothe it, colour, heat, resistance, even weight, and we shall finally find
ourselves confronted with homogeneous extensity,
space without body.   The only step then remaining will be to describe figures in space, to make
them move according to mathematically formulated laws, and to explain the apparent qualities
of matter by the shape, position, and motion of
these geometrical figures.   Now, position is given
by a system of fixed magnitudes and motion is
expressed by a law, i.e. by a constant relation
between variable magnitudes ; but shape is a
mental image, and, however tenuous, however
transparent we assume it to be, it still constitutes,
in so far as our imagination has, so to speak, the
visual perception of it, a concrete and therefore
irreducible quality of matter.   It will therefore
be necessary to make a clean sweep of this image
itself and replace it by the abstract formula of the
movement which gives rise to the figure.   Picture then algebraical relations getting entangled
in one another, becoming objective by this very
entanglement, and producing, by the mere effect
of their complexity, concrete, visible, and tangible

reality,—you will be merely drawing the consequences of the principle of causality, understood
in the sense of an actual prefiguring of the future
in the present. The scientists of our time do not
seem, indeed, to have carried abstraction so far,
except perhaps Lord Kelvin. This acute and profound physicist assumed that space is filled with
a homogeneous and incompressible fluid in which
vortices move, thus producing the properties of
matter : these vortices are the constituent elements of bodies ; the atom thus becomes a movement, and physical phenomena are reduced to
regular movements taking place within an incompressible fluid. But, if you will notice that this
fluid is perfectly homogeneous, that between its
parts there is neither an empty interval which
separates them nor any difference whatever by
which they can be distinguished, you will see that
all movement taking place within this fluid is
really equivalent to absolute immobility, since
before, during, and after the movement nothing
changes and nothing has changed in the whole.
The movement which is here spoken of is thus not
a movement which actually takes place, but only
a movement which is pictured mentally : it is a
relation between relations. It is implicitly supposed, though perhaps not actually realized, that
motion has something to do with consciousness,
that in space there are only simultaneities, and
that the business of the physicist is to provide
us with the means of calculating these relations

of simultaneity for any moment of our duration. Nowhere has mechanism been carried further than in this system, since the very shape of the ultimate elements of matter is here reduced to a movement. But the Cartesian physics already anticipated this interpretation ; for if matter is nothing, as Descartes claimed, but homogeneous extensity, the movements of the parts of this extensity can be conceived through the abstract law which governs them or through an algebraical equation between variable magnitudes, but cannot be represented under the concrete form of an image. And it would not be difficult to prove that the more the progress of mechanical explanations enables us to develop this conception of causality and therefore to relieve the atom of the weight of its sensible qualities, the more the concrete existence of the phenomena of nature tends to vanish into algebraical smoke.

Thus understood, the relation of causality is a necessary relation in the sense that it will indefinitely approach the relation of identity, as a curve approaches its asymptote. The principle of identity is the absolute law of our consciousness : it asserts that what is thought is thought at the moment when we think it : and what gives this principle its absolute necessity is that it does not bind the future to the present, but only the present to the present : it expresses the unshakable confidence that consciousness feels in

It thus leads to Descartes' physics and Spinoza's metaphysics, but cannot bind future to present without neglecting duration.

itself, so long as, faithful to its duty, it confines itself to declaring the apparent present state of the mind. But the principle of causality, in so far as it is supposed to bind the future to the present, could never take the form of a necessary principle ; for the successive moments of real time are not bound up with one another, and no effort of logic will succeed in proving that what has been will be or will continue to be, that the same antecedents will always give rise to identical consequents. Descartes understood this so well that he attributed the regularity of the physical world and the continuation of the same effects to the constantly renewed grace of Providence ; he built up, as it were, an instantaneous physics, intended for a universe the whole duration of which might as well be confined to the present moment. And Spinoza maintained that the indefinite series of phenomena, which takes for us the form of a succession in time, was equivalent, in the absolute, to the divine unity : he thus assumed, on the one hand, that the relation of apparent causality between phenomena melted away into a relation of identity in the absolute, and, on the other, that the indefinite duration of things was all contained in a single moment, which is eternity. In short, whether we study Cartesian physics, Spinozistic metaphysics, or the scientific theories of our own time, we shall find everywhere the same anxiety to establish a relation of logical necessity between cause and effect, and we shall see that this anxiety shows itself in a tendency to transform relations of succession into relations of inherence, to do away with active duration, and to substitute for apparent causality a fundamental identity.

Now, if the development of the notion of causality, understood in the sense of necessary connexion, leads to the Spinozistic or Cartesian conception of nature, inversely, all relation of necessary determination established between successive phenomena may be supposed to arise from our perceiving, in a confused form, some mathematical mechanism behind their heterogeneity. We do not claim that common sense has any intuition of the kinetic theories of matter, still less perhaps of a Spinozistic mechanism ; but it will be seen that the more the effect seems necessarily bound up with the cause, the more we tend to put it in the cause itself, as a mathematical consequence in its principle, and thus to cancel the effect of duration. That under the influence of the same external conditions I do not behave to-day as I behaved yesterday is not at all surprising, because I *change*, because I *endure*. But things considered apart from our perception do not seem to endure ; and the more thoroughly we examine this idea, the more absurd it seems to us to suppose that the same cause should not produce to-day the effect which it produced yesterday. We certainly feel, it is true, that although things do not

The necessary determination of phenomena implies non-duration ; but we endure and are therefore free.

endure as we do ourselves, nevertheless there must be some reason why phenomena are seen to *succeed* one another instead of being set out all at once. And this is why the notion of causality, although it gets indefinitely near that of identity, will never seem to us to coincide with it, unless we conceive clearly the idea of a mathematical mechanism or unless some subtle metaphysics removes our very legitimate scruples on the point. It is no less obvious that our belief in the necessary determination of phenomena by one another becomes stronger in proportion as we are more inclined to regard duration as a subjective form of our consciousness. In other words, the more we tend to set up the causal relation as a relation of necessary determination, the more we assert thereby that things do not *endure* like ourselves. This amounts to saying that the more we strengthen the principle of causality, the more we emphasize the difference between a physical series and a psychical one. Whence, finally, it would result (however paradoxical the opinion may seem) that the assumption of a relation of mathematical inherence between external phenomena ought to bring with it, as a natural or at least as a plausible consequence, the belief in human free will. But this last consequence will not concern us for the moment : we are merely trying here to trace out the first meaning of the word causality, and we think we have shown that the prefiguring of the future in the present is easily conceived under a mathematical form, thanks to a certain conception of duration which, without seeming to be so, is fairly familiar to common sense.

But there is a prefiguring of another kind, still more familiar to our mind, because immediate consciousness gives us the type of it. We go, in fact, through successive states of consciousness, and although the later was not contained in the earlier, we had before us at the time a more or less confused idea of it.   The actual realization of this idea, however, did not appear as certain but merely as possible.   Yet, between the idea and the action, some hardly perceptible intermediate processes come in, the whole mass of which takes for us a form *sui generis*, which is called the feeling of effort.   And from the idea to the effort, from the effort to the act, the progress has been so continuous that we cannot say where the idea and the effort end, and where the act begins.   Hence we see that in a certain sense we may still say here that the future was prefigured in the present ; but it must be added that this prefiguring is very imperfect, since the future action of which we have the present idea is conceived as realizable but not as realized, and since, even when we plan the effort necessary to accomplish it, we feel that there is still time to stop.   If, then, we decide to picture the causal relation in this second form, we can assert *a priori* that there will no longer be a relation of necessary determination between the cause and

Prefiguring, as having an idea of a future act which we cannot realize without effort, does not involve necessary determination.

the effect, for the effect will no longer be given in the cause. It will be there only in the state of pure possibility and as a vague idea which perhaps will not be followed by the corresponding action. But we shall not be surprised that this approximation is enough for common sense if we think of the readiness with which children and primitive people accept the idea of a whimsical Nature, in which caprice plays a part no less important than necessity. Nay, this way of conceiving causality will be more easily understood by the general run of people, since it does not demand any effort of abstraction and only implies a certain analogy between the outer and the inner world, between the succession of objective phenomena and that of our subjective states.

In truth, this second way of conceiving the relation of cause to effect is more natural than the first This second in that it immediately satisfies the need conception of of a mental image. If we look for the causality leads phenomenon B within the phenomenon to Leibniz as the first led phenomenon B within the phenomenon to Spinoza. A, which regularly precedes it, the reason is that the habit of associating the two images ends in giving us the idea of the second phenomenon wrapped up, as it were, in that of the first. It is natural, then, that we should push this objectification to its furthest limit and that we should make the phenomenon A itself into a psychic state, in which the phenomenon B is supposed to be contained as a very vague idea. We simply suppose, thereby, that the objective connexion of the two phenomena resembles the subjective association which suggested the idea of it to us. The qualities of things are thus set up as actual *states*, somewhat analogous to those of our own self ; the material universe is credited with a vague personality which is diffused through space and which, although not exactly endowed with a conscious will, is led on from one state to another by an inner impulse, a kind of effort. Such was ancient hylozoism, a half-hearted and even contradictory hypothesis, which left matter its extensity although attributing to it real conscious states, and which spread the qualities of matter throughout extensity while treating these qualities as inner i.e. simple states.   It was reserved for Leibniz to do away with this contradiction and to show that, if the succession of external qualities or phenomena is understood as the succession of our own ideas, these qualities must be regarded as simple states or perceptions, and the matter which supports them as an unextended monad, analogous to our soul.   But, if such be the case, the successive states of matter cannot be perceived from the outside any more than our own psychic states ; the hypothesis of pre-established harmony must be introduced in order to explain how these inner states are representative of one another.   Thus, with our second conception of the relation of causality we reach Leibniz, as with the first we reached Spinoza.   And in both cases we merely push to their extreme limit or formulate with greater precision two half-hearted and confused ideas of common sense.

Now it is obvious that the relation of causality, understood in this second way, does not involve the necessary determination of the effect by the cause. History indeed proves it.

We see that ancient hylozoism, the first outcome of this conception of causality, explained the regular succession of causes and effects by a real *deus ex machina* : sometimes it was a Necessity external to things and hovering over them, sometimes an inner Reason acting by rules somewhat similar to those which govern our own conduct. Nor do the perceptions of Leibniz's monad necessitate one another ; God has to regulate their order in advance. In fact, Leibniz's determinism does not spring from his conception of the monad, but from the fact that he builds up the universe with monads only. Having denied all mechanical influence of substances on one another, he had to explain how it happens that their states correspond. Hence a determinism which arises from the necessity of positing a pre-established harmony, and not at all from the dynamic conception of the relation of causality. But let us leave history aside. Consciousness itself testifies that the abstract idea of force is that of indeterminate effort, that of an effort which has not yet issued in an act and in which the act is still only at the stage of an idea. In other words, the dynamic conception of the causal relation ascribes to things a duration absolutely like our own, whatever may be the nature of this duration ; to picture in this way the relation of cause to effect is to assume that the future is not more closely bound up with the present in the external world than it is in our own inner life.

It follows from this twofold analysis that the principle of causality involves two contradictory conceptions of duration, two mutually exclusive ways of prefiguring the future in the present. Sometimes all phenomena, physical or psychical, are pictured as *enduring* in the same way, and therefore in the way that *we* do : in this case the future will exist in the present only as an idea, and the passing from the present to the future will take the form of an effort which does not always lead to the realization of the idea conceived. Sometimes, on the other hand, duration is regarded as the characteristic form of conscious states ; in this case, things are no longer supposed to *endure* as we do, and a mathematical pre-existence of their future in their present is admitted. Now, each of these two hypotheses, when taken by itself, safeguards human freedom; for the first would lead to the result that even the phenomena of nature were contingent, and the second, by attributing the necessary determination of physical phenomena to the fact that things do not *endure* as we do, invites us to regard the self which is subject to duration

Each of these contradictory interpretations of causality and duration by itself safeguards freedom ; taken together they destroy it.

as a free force. Therefore, every clear conception of causality, where we know our own
meaning, leads to the idea of human freedom
as a natural consequence. Unfortunately, the
habit has grown up of taking the principle of causality in both senses at the same time, because the
one is more flattering to our imagination and the
other is more favourable to mathematical reasoning. Sometimes we think particularly of the
regular *succession* of physical phenomena and of
the kind of inner effort by which one *becomes*
another ; sometimes we fix our mind on the absolute
regularity of these phenomena, and from the idea
of regularity we pass by imperceptible steps to
that of mathematical necessity, which excludes
duration understood in the first way. And we
do not see any harm in letting these two conceptions blend into one another, and in assigning
greater importance to the one or the other according as we are more or less concerned with the
interests of science. But to apply the principle
of causality, in this ambiguous form, to the succession of conscious states, is uselessly and wan-
tonly to run into inextricable difficulties. The
idea of force, which really excludes that of necessary determination, has got into the habit, so to
speak, of amalgamating with that of necessity, in
consequence of the very use which we make of
the principle of causality in nature. On the one
hand, we know force only through the witness of
consciousness, and consciousness does not assert,

does not even understand, the absolute determination, now, of actions that are still to come : that is all that experience teaches us, and if we hold by experience we should say that we feel ourselves free, that we perceive force, rightly or wrongly, as a free spontaneity. But, on the other hand, this idea of force, carried over into nature, travelling there side by side with the idea of necessity, has got corrupted before it returns from the journey. It returns impregnated with the idea of necessity : and in the light of the rôle which we have made it play in the external world, we regard force as determining with strict necessity the effects which flow from it. Here again the mistake made by consciousness arises from the fact that it looks at the self, not directly, but by a kind of refraction through the forms which it has lent to external perception, and which the latter does not give back without having left its mark on them. A compromise, as it were, has been brought about between the idea of force and that of necessary determination. The wholly mechanical determination of two external phenomena by one another now assumes in our eyes the same form as the dynamic relation of our exertion of force to the act which springs from it : but, in return, this latter relation takes the form of a mathematical derivation, the human action being supposed to issue mechanically, and therefore necessarily, from the force which produces it. There is no doubt that this mingling of two different and almost opposite ideas offers advantages to common sense, since it enables us to picture in the same way, and denote by one and the same word, both the relation which exists between two moments of our life and that which binds together the successive moments of the external world. We have seen that, though our deepest conscious states exclude numerical multiplicity, yet we break them up into parts external to one another ; that though the elements of concrete duration permeate one another, duration expressing itself in extensity exhibits moments as distinct as the bodies scattered in space. Is it surprising, then, that between the moments of our life, when it has been, so to speak, objectified, we set up a relation analogous to the objective relation of causality, and that an exchange, which again may be compared to the phenomenon of endosmosis, takes place between the dynamic idea of free effort and the mathematical concept of necessary determination ?

But the sundering of these two ideas is an accomplished fact in the natural sciences. The physicist *Though united in popular thought, the ideas of free effort and necessary determination are kept apart by physical science.* may speak of *forces,* and even picture their mode of action by analogy with an inner effort, but he will never introduce this hypothesis into a scientific explanation. Even those who, with Faraday, replace the extended atoms by dynamic points, will treat the centres of force and the lines of force mathematically, without troubling about force itself considered as an activity or an effort. It thus comes to be understood that the relation of external causality is purely mathematical, and has no resemblance to the relation between psychical force and the act which springs from it.

It is now time to add that the relation of inner causality is purely dynamic, and has no analogy

They should be kept apart, too, by psychology.

with the relation of two external phenomena which condition one another. For, as the latter are capable of recurring in a homogeneous space, their relation can be expressed in terms of a law, whereas deep-seated psychic states occur once in consciousness and will never occur again. A careful analysis of the psychological phenomenon led us to this conclusion in the beginning : the study of the notions of causality and duration, viewed in themselves, has merely confirmed it.

We can now formulate our conception of freedom. Freedom is the relation of the concrete

Freedom real but indefinable.

self to the act which it performs. This relation is indefinable, just because we *are* free. For we can analyse a thing, but not a process; we can break up extensity, but not duration. Or, if we persist in analysing it, we unconsciously transform the process into a thing and duration into extensity. By the very fact of breaking up concrete time we set out its moments in homogeneous space ; in place of the doing we put the already done ; and, as we have begun by, so to speak, stereotyping the activity of the self, we see spontaneity settle down into inertia and freedom into necessity. Thus, any positive definition of freedom will ensure the victory of determinism.

Shall we define the free act by saying of this act, when it is once done, that it might have been left undone ? But this assertion, as also its opposite, implies the idea of an absolute equivalence between concrete duration and its spatial symbol : and as soon as we admit this equivalence, we are led on, by the very development of the formula which we have just set forth, to the most rigid determinism.

Shall we define the free act as " that which could not be foreseen, even when all the conditions were known in advance ? " But to conceive all the conditions as given, is, when dealing with concrete duration, to place oneself at the very moment at which the act is being performed. Or else it is admitted that the matter of psychic duration can be pictured symbolically in advance, which amounts, as we said, to treating time as a homogeneous medium, and to reasserting in new words the absolute equivalence of duration with its symbol. A closer study of this second definition of freedom will thus bring us once more to determinism.

Shall we finally define the free act by saying that it is not necessarily determined by its cause ? But either these words lose their meaning or we understand by them that the same inner causes will not always call forth the same effects. We admit, then, that the psychic antecedents of a free act can be repeated, that freedom is displayed in a duration whose moments resemble one another, and that time is a homogeneous medium, like space. We shall thus be brought back to the idea of an equivalence between duration and its spatial symbol ; and by pressing the definition of freedom which we have laid down, we shall once more get determinism out of it.

To sum up ; every demand for explanation in regard to freedom comes back, without our suspecting it, to the following question : " Can time be adequately represented by space ? " To which we answer : Yes, if you are dealing with time flown ; No, if you speak of time flowing. Now, the free act takes place in time which is flowing and not in time which has already flown. Freedom is therefore a fact, and among the facts which we observe there is none clearer. All the difficulties of the problem, and the problem itself, arise from the desire to endow duration with the same attributes as extensity, to interpret a succession by a simultaneity, and to express the idea of freedom in a language into which it is obviously untranslatable.

CONCLUSION

To sum up the foregoing discussion, we shall put aside for the present Kant's terminology and also his doctrine, to which we shall return

later, and we shall take the point of view of common sense. Modern psychology seems to us particularly concerned to prove that we perceive things through the medium of certain forms, borrowed from our own constitution. This tendency has become more and more marked since Kant : while the German philosopher drew a sharp line of separation between time and space, the extensive and the intensive, and, as we should say to-day, consciousness and external perception, the empirical school, carrying analysis still further, tries to reconstruct the extensive out of the intensive, space out of duration, and externality out of inner states. Physics, moreover, comes in to complete the work of psychology in this respect :. it shows that, if we wish to forecast phenomena, we must make a clean sweep of the impression which they produce on consciousness and treat sensations as signs of reality, not as reality itself.

It seemed to us that there was good reason to set ourselves the opposite problem and to ask

But are not the states of the self per- ceived through forms bor- rowed from the external world ? whether the most obvious states of the ego itself, which we believe that we grasp directly, are not mostly per- ceived through the medium of certain forms borrowed from the external world, which thus gives us back what we have lent it. *A priori* it seems fairly probable that this is what happens. For, assuming that the forms alluded to, into which we fit matter, come entirely from the mind, it seems difficult to apply them con- stantly to objects without the latter soon leaving a mark on them : by then using these forms to gain a knowledge of our own person we run the risk of mistaking for the colouring of the self the reflection of the frame in which we place it, i.e. the external world. But one can go further still and assert that forms applicable to things cannot be entirely our own work, that they must result from a compromise between matter and mind, that if we give much to matter we probably receive something from it, and that thus, when we try to grasp ourselves after an excursion into the external world, we no longer have our hands free.

Now just as, in order to ascertain the real relations of physical phenomena to one another, we abstract whatever obviously clashes with them in our way of perceiving and thinking, so, in order to view the self in its original purity, psychology ought to eliminate or correct certain forms which bear the obvious mark of the external world. What are these forms? When isolated from one another and regarded as so many distinct units, psychic states seem to be more or less *intense*. Next, looked at in their multiplicity, they unfold in time and constitute *duration*. Finally, in their relations to one another, and in so far as a certain unity is preserved throughout their multiplicity, they seem to *determine* one another. Intensity, duration, voluntary determination, these are the three ideas which had to be clarified by ridding them of all that they owe to the intrusion of the sensible world and, in a word, to the obsession of the idea of space.

To understand the intensity, duration and voluntary determination of psychic states, we must eliminate the idea of space.

Examining the first of these ideas, we found that psychic phenomena were in themselves pure quality or qualitative multiplicity, and that, on the other hand, their cause situated in space was quantity. In so far as this quality becomes the sign of the quantity and we suspect the presence of the latter behind the former, we call it intensity. The intensity of a simple state, therefore, is not quantity but its qualitative sign. You will find that it arises from a compromise between

Intensity is quality and not quantity or magnitude.

pure quality, which is the state of consciousness, and pure quantity, which is necessarily space. Now you give up this compromise without the least scruple when you study external things, since you then leave aside the forces themselves, assuming that they exist, and consider only their measurable and extended effects. Why, then, do you keep to this hybrid concept when you analyse in its turn the state of consciousness ? If magnitude, outside you, is never intensive, intensity, within you, is never magnitude. It is through having overlooked this that philosophers have been compelled to distinguish two kinds of quantity, the one extensive, the other intensive, without ever succeeding in explaining what they had in common or how the same words " increase " and " decrease " could be used for things so unlike. In the same way they are responsible for the exaggerations of psychophysics, for as soon as the power of increasing in magnitude is attributed to sensation in any other than a metaphorical sense, we are invited to find out by how much it increases. And, although consciousness does not measure intensive quantity, it does not follow that science may not succeed indirectly in doing so, if it be a magnitude. Hence, either a psychophysical formula is possible or the intensity of a simple psychic state is pure quality.

Turning then to the concept of multiplicity, we saw that to construct a number we must first have the intuition of a homogeneous medium,

viz. space, in which terms distinct from one
Our conscious another could be set out in line, and,
states not a
discrete mul- secondly, a process of permeation and or-
tiplicity. ganization by which these units are dynamically added together and form what we called
a qualitative multiplicity. It is owing to this
dynamic process that the units *get added*, but it is
because of their presence in space that they remain *distinct*. Hence number or discrete multiplicity also results from a compromise. Now,
when we consider material objects in themselves,
we give up this compromise, since we regard them
as impenetrable and divisible, i.e. endlessly distinct
from one another. Therefore, we must give it
up, too, when we study our own selves. It is
through having failed to do so that associationism
has made many mistakes, such as trying to reconstruct a psychic state by the addition of distinct
states of consciousness, thus substituting the
symbol of the ego for the ego itself.

These preliminary considerations enabled us to
approach the principal object of this work, the
analysis of the ideas of duration and voluntary
determination.

What is duration within us? A qualitative
multiplicity, with no likeness to number; an
Inner dura- organic evolution which is yet not an
tion is a
qualitative increasing quantity; a pure hetero-
multiplicity. geneity within which there are no distinct
qualities. In a word, the moments of inner
duration are not external to one another.

What duration is there existing outside us?
The present only, or, if we prefer the expression,
In the exter- simultaneity. No doubt external things
nal world we
find not dura- change, but their moments do not
tion but sim-
ultaneity. *succeed* one another, if we retain the
ordinary meaning of the word, except for a consciousness which keeps them in mind. We observe outside us at a given moment a whole
system of simultaneous positions ; of the simultaneities which have preceded them nothing
remains. To put duration in space is really to
contradict oneself and place succession within
simultaneity. Hence we must not say that external things *endure,* but rather that there is in them
some inexpressible reason in virtue of which we
cannot examine them at successive moments of our
own duration without observing that they have
changed. But this change does not involve succession unless the word is taken in a new meaning :
on this point we have noted the agreement of
science and common sense.

Thus in consciousness we find states which
succeed, without being distinguished from one
another ; and in space simultaneities which,
without succeeding, are distinguished from one
another, in the sense that one has ceased to exist
when the other appears. Outside us, mutual
externality without succession ; within us, succession without mutual externality.

Here again a compromise comes in. To the
simultaneities, which constitute the external

world, and, although distinct, succeed one an-

The idea of a measurable time arises from com-promise be-tween ideas of succession and externality. other *for our consciousness*, we attribute succession *in themselves*. Hence the idea that things *endure* as we do our-selves and that time may be brought within space. But while our consciousness thus introduces succession into external things, inversely these things themselves externalize the successive moments of our inner duration in relation to one another. The simultaneities of physical phenomena, absolutely distinct in the sense that the one has ceased to be when the other takes place, cut up into portions, which are also distinct and external to one another, an inner life in which succession implies interpenetration, just as the pendulum of a clock cuts up into distinct fragments and spreads out, so to speak, length-wise, the dynamic and undivided tension of the spring. Thus, by a real process of endosmosis we get the mixed idea of a measurable time, which is space in so far as it is homogeneity, and duration in so far as it is succession, that is to say, at bottom, the contradictory idea of succes-sion in simultaneity.

Now, these two elements, extensity and dura-tion, science tears asunder when it undertakes *As science eliminates du-ration from the outer, phil-osophy must eliminate space from the inner world.* the close study of external things. For we have pointed out that science retains nothing of duration but simul-taneity, and nothing of motion itself but the position of the moving body, i.e. immobility. A very sharp separation is here made and space gets the best of it.

Therefore the same separation will have to be made again, but this time to the advantage of duration, when inner phenomena are studied, —not inner phenomena once developed, to be sure, or after the discursive reason has separated them and set them out in a homogeneous medium in order to understand them, but inner phenomena in their developing, and in so far as they make up, by their interpenetration, the continuous evolution of a free person. Duration, thus restored to its original purity, will appear as a wholly qualitative multiplicity, an absolute heterogeneity of elements which pass over into one another.

Now it is because they have neglected to make this necessary separation that one party has been **The neglect to** led to deny freedom and the other to **separate extensity and** define it, and thereby, involuntarily, **duration leads** to deny it too. They ask in fact **one party to** **deny freedom** whether the act could or could not be **and the other** **to define it.** foreseen, the whole of its conditions being given ; and whether they assert it or deny it, they admit that this totality of conditions could be conceived as given in advance : which amounts, as we have shown, to treating duration as a homogeneous thing and intensities as magnitudes. They will either say that the act is *determined* by its conditions, without perceiving that they are playing on the double sense of the word causality, and that they are thus giving to duration at the same time two forms which are mutually exclusive. Or else they will appeal to the principle of the conservation of energy, without asking whether this principle is equally applicable to the moments of the external world, which are equivalent to one another, and to the moments of a living and conscious being, which acquire a richer and richer content. In whatever way, in a word, freedom is viewed, it cannot be denied except on condition of identifying time with space; it cannot be defined except on condition of demanding that space should adequately represent time; it cannot be argued about in one sense or the other except on condition of previously confusing succession and simultaneity. All determinism will thus be refuted by experience, but every attempt to define freedom will open the way to determinism.

Inquiring then why this separation of duration and extensity, which science carries out so naturally in the external world, demands such an effort and rouses so much repugnance when it is a question of inner states, we were not long in perceiving the reason. The main object of science is to forecast and measure: now we cannot forecast physical phenomena except on condition that we assume that they do not *endure* as we do; and, on the other hand, the only thing we are able to measure is space. Hence the breach here comes about of itself between quality and quantity, between true

This separation favourable to physical science, but against the interests of language and social life.

duration and pure extensity. But when we turn
to our conscious states, we have everything to
gain by keeping up the illusion through which
we make them share in the reciprocal externality
of outer things, because this distinctness, and at
the same time this solidification, enables us to
give them fixed names in spite of their instability,
and distinct ones in spite of their interpenetration.
It enables us to objectify them, to throw them
out into the current of social life.

Hence there are finally two different selves,
one of which is, as it were, the external projection
of the other, its spatial and, so to speak,
social representation. We reach the
former by deep introspection, which
leads us to grasp our inner states as
living things, constantly *becoming*, as
states not amenable to measure, which
permeate one another and of which the succession
in duration has nothing in·common with juxtaposition in homogeneous space. But the moments at which we thus grasp ourselves are rare,
and that is just why we are rarely free. The
greater part of the time we live outside ourselves,
hardly perceiving anything of ourselves but
our own ghost, a colourless shadow which pure
duration projects into homogeneous space. Hence
our life unfolds in space rather than in time ;
we live for the external world rather than for
ourselves ; we speak rather than think ; we
"are acted " rather than act ourselves. To act

Hence two dif-
ferent selves :
(1) the funda-
mental self :
(2) its spatial
and social re-
presentation :
only the former
is free.

freely is to recover possession of oneself, and to get back into pure duration.

Kant's great mistake was to take time as a homogeneous medium. He did not notice that

Kant clung to freedom, but put the self which is free outside both space and time. real duration is made up of moments inside one another, and that when it seems to assume the form of a homogeneous whole, it is because it gets expressed in space. Thus the very distinction which he makes between space and time amounts at bottom to confusing time with space, and the symbolical representation of the ego with the ego itself. He thought that consciousness was incapable of perceiving psychic states otherwise than by juxtaposition, forgetting that a medium in which these states are set side by side and distinguished from one another is of course space, and not duration. He was thereby led to believe that the same states can recur in the depths of consciousness, just as the same physical phenomena are repeated in space ; this at least is what he implicitly admitted when he ascribed to the causal relation the same meaning and the same function in the inner as in the outer world. Thus freedom was made into an incomprehensible fact. And yet, owing to his unlimited though unconscious confidence in this inner perception whose scope he tried to restrict, his belief in freedom remained unshakable. He therefore raised it to the sphere of noumena ; and as he had

confused duration with space, he made this
genuine free self, which is indeed outside space,
into a self which is supposed to be outside duration
too, and therefore out of the reach of our faculty of
knowledge. But the truth is that we perceive this
self whenever, by a strenuous effort of reflection,
we turn our eyes from the shadow which follows us
and retire into ourselves. Though we generally
live and act outside our own person, in space
rather than in duration, and though by this
means we give a handle to the law of causality,
which binds the same effects to the same causes, we
can nevertheless always get back into pure duration, of which the moments are internal and heterogeneous to one another, and in which a cause
cannot repeat its effect since it will never repeat
itself.

In this very confusion of true duration with
its symbol both the strength and the weakness
Kant regarded of Kantianism reside. Kant imagines
both time and on the one side "things in themselves,"
space as ho-
mogeneous. and on the other a homogeneous Time
and Space, through which the "things in themselves," are refracted : thus are supposed to
arise on the one hand the phenomenal self—a self
which consciousness perceives—and, on the other,
external objects. Time and space on this view
would not be any more in us than outside us ;
the very distinction of outside and inside would
be the work of time and space. This doctrine has
the advantage of providing our empirical thought

with a solid foundation, and of guaranteeing that phenomena, as phenomena, are adequately knowable. Indeed, we might set up these phenomena as absolute and do without the incomprehensible "things in themselves," were it not that the Practical Reason, the revealer of duty, came in, like the Platonic reminiscence, to warn us that the "thing in itself" exists, invisible but present. The controlling factor in the whole of this theory is the very sharp distinction between the matter of consciousness and its form, between the homogeneous and the heterogeneous, and this vital distinction would probably never have been made unless time also had been regarded as a medium indifferent to what fills it.

But if time, as immediate consciousness perceives it, were, like space, a homogeneous medium, **But if time, as duration, were homogeneous, science could deal with it.** science would be able to deal with it, as it can with space. Now we have tried to prove that duration, as duration, and motion, as motion, elude the grasp of mathematics : of time everything slips through its fingers but simultaneity, and of movement everything but immobility. This is what the Kantians and even their opponents do not seem to have perceived : in this so-called phenomenal world, which, we are told, is a world cut out for scientific knowledge, all the relations which cannot be translated into simultaneity, i.e. into space, are scientifically unknowable.

In the second place, in a duration assumed to

be homogeneous, the same states could occur over again, causality would imply necessary determination, and all freedom would become incomprehensible. Such, indeed, is the result to which the Critique of Pure Reason leads. But instead of concluding from this that real duration is heterogeneous, which, by clearing up the second difficulty, would have called his attention to the first, Kant preferred to put freedom outside time and to raise an impassable barrier between the world of phenomena, which he hands over root and branch to our understanding, and the world of things in themselves, which he forbids us to enter.

And freedom would be incomprehensible. Kant's solution.

But perhaps this distinction is too sharply drawn and perhaps the barrier is easier to cross than he supposed. For if perchance the moments of real duration, perceived by an attentive consciousness, permeated one another instead of lying side by side, and if these moments formed in relation to one another a heterogeneity within which the idea of necessary determination lost every shred of meaning, then the self grasped by consciousness would be a free cause, we should have absolute knowledge of ourselves, and, on the other hand, just because this absolute constantly commingles with phenomena and, while filling itself with them, permeates them, these phenomena themselves would not be as amenable as is claimed to mathematical reasoning.

How corrected by taking real duration into account.

So we have assumed the existence of a homogeneous Space and, with Kant, distinguished this space from the matter which fills it. With him we have admitted that homogeneous space is a "form of our sensibility" : and we understand by this simply that other minds, e.g. those of animals, although they perceive objects, do not distinguish them so clearly either from one another or from themselves. This intuition of a homogeneous medium, an intuition peculiar to man, enables us to externalize our concepts in relation to one another, reveals to us the objectivity of things, and thus, in two ways, on the one hand by getting everything ready for language, and on the other by showing us an external world, quite distinct from ourselves, in the perception of which all minds have a common share, foreshadows and prepares the way for social life.

With Kant, we assume a homogeneous space, the intuition of which is peculiar to man and prepares the way for social life.

Over against this homogeneous space we have put the self as perceived by an attentive consciousness, a living self, whose states, at once undistinguished and unstable, cannot be separated without changing their nature, and cannot receive a fixed form or be expressed in words without becoming public property. How could this self, which distinguishes external objects so sharply and represents them so easily by means of symbols, withstand the temptation to introduce the same distinctions into its own life and to replace the

But if concrete duration is heterogeneous, the relation of psychic state to act is unique and the act is rightly judged free.

interpenetration of its psychic states, their wholly qualitative multiplicity, by a numerical plurality of terms which are distinguished from one another, set side by side, and expressed by means of words ? In place of a heterogeneous duration whose moments permeate one another, we thus get a homogeneous time whose moments are strung on a spatial line. In place of an inner life whose successive phases, each unique of its kind, cannot be expressed in the fixed terms of language, we get a self which can be artificially reconstructed, and simple psychic states which can be added to and taken from one another just like the letters of the alphabet in forming words. Now, this must not be thought to be a mode of symbolical representation only, for immediate intuition and discursive thought are one in concrete reality, and the very mechanism by which we only meant at first to explain our conduct will end by also controlling it. Our psychic states, separating then from each other, will get solidified ; between our ideas, thus crystallized, and our external movements we shall witness permanent associations being formed ; and little by little, as our consciousness thus imitates the process by which nervous matter procures reflex actions, automatism will cover over freedom.[1] It is just at this point

[1] Renouvier has already spoken of these voluntary acts which may be compared to reflex movements, and he has restricted freedom to moments of crisis. But he does not seem to have noticed that the process of our free activity goes

that the associationists and the determinists come in on the one side, and the Kantians on the other. As they look at only the commonest aspect of our conscious life, they perceive clearly marked states, which can recur in time like physical phenomena, and to which the law of causal determination applies, if we wish, in the same sense as it does to nature. As, on the other hand, the medium in which these psychic states are set side by side exhibits parts external to one another, in which the same facts seem capable of being repeated, they do not hesitate to make time a homogeneous medium and treat it as space. Henceforth all difference between duration and extensity, succession and simultaneity, is abolished : the only thing left is to turn freedom out of doors, or, if you cannot entirely throw off your traditional respect for it, to escort it with all due ceremony up to the supratemporal domain of " things in themselves," whose mysterious threshold your consciousness cannot cross. But, in our view, there is a third course which might be taken, namely, to carry

on, as it were, unknown to ourselves, in the obscure depths of our consciousness at every moment of duration, that the very feeling of duration comes from this source, and that without this heterogeneous and continuous duration, in which our self evolves, there would be no moral crisis. The study, even the close study, of a given free action will thus not settle the problem of freedom. The whole series of our heterogeneous states of consciousness must be taken into consideration. In other words, it is in a close analysis of the idea of duration that the key to the problem must be sought.

ourselves back in thought to those moments of our
life when we made some serious decision, moments
unique of their kind, which will never be repeated
—any more than the past phases in the history of a
nation will ever come back again. We should see
that if these past states cannot be adequately
expressed in words or artificially reconstructed
by a juxtaposition of simpler states, it is because
in their dynamic unity and wholly qualitative
multiplicity they are phases of our real and concrete duration, a heterogeneous duration and a
living one. We should see that, if our action
was pronounced by us to be free, it is because
the relation of this action to the state from which
it issued could not be expressed by a law, this
psychic state being unique of its kind and unable
ever to occur again. We should see, finally, that
the very idea of necessary determination here
loses every shred of meaning, that there cannot be
any question either of foreseeing the act before
it is performed or of reasoning about the possibility
of the contrary action once the deed is done, for
to have all the conditions given is, in concrete
duration, to place oneself at the very moment of
the act and not to foresee it. But we should also
understand the illusion which makes the one party
think that they are compelled to deny freedom,
and the others that they must define it. It is
because the transition is made by imperceptible
steps from concrete duration, whose elements permeate one another, to symbolical duration, whose

moments are set side by side, and consequently from free activity to conscious automatism. It is because, although we are free whenever we are willing to get back into ourselves, it seldom happens that we are willing. It is because, finally, even in the cases where the action is freely performed, we cannot reason about it without setting out its conditions externally to one another, therefore in space and no longer in pure duration. The problem of freedom has thus sprung from a misunderstanding : it has been to the moderns what the paradoxes of the Eleatics were to the ancients, and, like these paradoxes, it has its origin in the illusion through which we confuse succession and simultaneity, duration and extensity, quality and quantity.

BIBLIOGRAPHY

I. WORKS BY BERGSON.

(a) *Books.*

Quid Aristoteles de loco senserit, (Thesis), Paris, 1889.

Essai sur les données immédiates de la conscience, Paris, 1889, 1910.[7]

Matière et Mémoire, Essai sur la relation du corps avec l'esprit, Paris, 1896, 1910.[6]

Le Rire, Essai sur la signification du comique, Paris, 1900, 1910.[6] (First published in the *Revue de Paris*, 1900, Vol. I., pp. 512–545 and 759–791.)

L'Évolution créatrice, Paris, 1907, 1910.[6]

(b) *Articles.*

La Spécialité. (Address at the distribution of prizes at the lycée of Angers, Aug. 1882.)

De la simulation inconsciente dans l'état d'hypnotisme. *Revue philosophique*, Vol. 22, 1886, pp. 525–531.

Le bon sens et les études classiques. (Address at the distribution of prizes at the " Concours général des lycées et collèges," 1895.)

Mémoire et reconnaissance. (*Revue philos.* Mar., Apr. 1896, pp. 225–248 and 380–399. Republished in *Matière et Mémoire.*)

Perception et matière. (*Rev. de Mét. et de Mor.* May 1896, pp. 257–277. Republished in *Matière et Mémoire.*)

Note sur les origines psychologiques de notre croyance à la loi de causalité. (Lecture at the Philosophical Congress in Paris, 1900, published in the *Bibliothèque du Congrès International de Philosophie;* cf. *Revue de Métaphysique et de Morale*, Sept. 1900, p. 655.)

Le Rêve. (Lecture at the *Institut psychologique international*: published in the *Bulletin de l'Institut psych. intern.* May 1901 ; cf. *Revue scientifique*, 4ᵉ S., Vol. 15, June 8, 1901, pp. 705–713, and *Revue de Philosophie*, 1901, pp. 486–489.)

Le Parallélisme psycho-physique et la métaphysique positive. *Bulletin de la Société française de Philosophie,*
June 1901.

L'Effort intellectuel. *Revue philosophique,* Jan. 1902.

Introduction à la métaphysique. *Revue de Mét. et de Mor.*
Jan. 1903.

Le Paralogisme psycho-physiologique. (Lecture at the
Philosophical Congress in Geneva, 1904, published in the
Revue de Mét. et de Mor. Nov. 1904, pp. 895–908; see
also pp. 1027–1036.

L'Idée de néant, *Rev. philos.* Nov. 1906, pp. 449–466.
(Part of Chap. 4 of *L'Évolution créatrice*).

Notice sur la vie et les oeuvres de M. Félix Ravaisson-
Mollien. (Lecture before the Académie des Sciences
morales et politiques : published in the *Proceedings* of
the 'Academy, Vol. 25, pp. 1 ff. Paris, 1907.)

Le Souvenir du présent et la fausse reconnaissance. *Rev.
philos.* Dec. 1908, pp. 561–593.

(c) *Miscellaneous.*

Lucrèce : Extraits . . . avec une étude sur la poésie, la
philosophie, la physique, le texte et la langue de Lucrèce.
Paris, 1884.

Principes de métaphysique et de psychologie d'après
M. Paul Janet. *Revue philos.,* Vol. 44, Nov. 1897, pp.
525–551.

Sur sa relation à W. James, *Revue philosophique,* Vol. 60,
1905, p. 229 f.

Sur sa théorie de la perception, *Bulletin de la Soc. fr. de
Philos.* Mar. 1905, pp. 94 ff.

Rapport sur le concours pour le prix Bordin, 1905, ayant
pour sujet Maine de Biran. (*Mémoires de l'Académie
des Sciences morales et politiques,* Vol. 25, pp. 809 ff.
Paris, 1907).

Rapport sur le concours pour le prix Le Dissez de Penanrun,
1907. (*Mémoires de l'Académie des Sciences morales et
politiques,* Vol. 26, pp. 771 ff. Paris, 1909.)

Sur *l'Évolution créatrice, Revue du Mois.* Sept. 1907, p. 351.

A propos de l'évolution de l'intelligence géométrique,
Revue de Mét. et de Mor. Jan. 1908, pp. 28–33.

Sur l'influence de sa philosophie sur les élèves des lycées, *Bulletin de la Soc. fr. de Philos.*, Jan. 1908, p. 21 ; cf. *L'Année psychologique*, 1908, pp. 229–231.
Note súr le mot " immédiat," *Bulletin de la Soc. fr. de Philos.* Aug. 1908, p. 341.
Préface à un volume de la collection *Les grands philosophes*, (*G. Tarde*, par ses fils). Paris. Michaud, 1909.)
Remarques à propos d'une thèse soutenue par M. Dwelshauvers " L'inconscient dans la vie mentale." *Bulletin, de la Soc. fr. de Phil.*, Feb. 1910.

II. Select List of Books and Articles dealing in Whole or in Part with Bergson and his Philosophy.

(Arranged alphabetically under each language.)

S. Alexander, Matière et Mémoire, (*Mind*, Oct. 1897, pp. 572–3).
B. H. Bode, L'Évolution créatrice, (*Philosophical Review*, 1908, pp. 84–89).
W. Boyd, L'Évolution créatrice, (*Review of Theology and Philosophy*, Oct., 1907. pp. 249–251).
H. Wildon Carr, Bergson's Theory of Knowledge, (*Proceedings of the Aristotelian Society*, London, 1909. New Series, Vol. IX, pp. 41–60).
H. Wildon Carr, Bergson's Theory of Instinct, (*Proceedings of the Aristotelian Society*, London, 1910, New Series, Vol. X.).
H. Wildon Carr, The Philosophy of Bergson, (*Hibbert Journal*, July 1910, pp. 873–883).
H. N. Gardiner, Mémoire et reconnaissance, (*Psychological Review*, 1896, pp. 578–580).
T. E. Hulme, The New Philosophy, (*New Age*, July 1, 29, 1909).
William James, A Pluralistic Universe, London, 1909, pp. 225–273.
William James, The Philosophy of Bergson, (*Hibbert Journal*, April 1909, pp. 562–577. Reprinted in *A Pluralistic Universe ;* see above).

William James, Bradley or Bergson ? (*Journal of Philosophy, Psychology and Scientific Methods*, Vol. VII, No. 2, Jan. 20, 1910, pp. 29–33).

A. Lalande, Philosophy in France, 1907, (*Philosophical Review*, May, 1908).

T. Loveday, L'Évolution créatrice, (*Mind*, July 1908, pp. 402–8).

A. O. Lovejoy, The Metaphysician of the Life-Force, (*Nation*, New York, Sept. 30, 1909).

A. Mitchell, L'Évolution créatrice, (*Journal of Philosophy, Psychology and Scientific Methods*, Vol. V, No. 22, Oct. 22, 1908, pp. 603–612).

W. Scott Palmer, Presence and Omnipresence, (*Contemporary Review*, June 1908, pp. 734–742).

W. Scott Palmer, Thought and Instinct, (*Nation*, June 5, 1909).

W. Scott Palmer, Life and the Brain, (*Contemporary Review*, Oct., 1909. pp. 474–484).

W. B. Pitkin, James and Bergson ; or, Who is against Intellect ? (*Journal of Philosophy, Psychology and Scientific Methods*, Apr. 28, 1910.)

G. R. T. Ross, A New Theory of Laughter, (*Nation*, Nov. 28, 1908).

G. R. T. Ross, The Philosophy of Vitalism, (*Nation*, Mar. 13, 1909).

G. M. Sauvage, The New Philosophy in France, (*Catholic University Bulletin*, Washington, Apr. 1906, Mar. 1908).

Norman Smith, Subjectivism and Realism in Modern Philosophy, (*Philosophical Review*, Vol. XVII, 1908, pp. 138–148).

G. F. Stout, Free Will and Determinism, (*Speaker*, London, May 10, 1890).

J. H. Tufts, Humor, (*Psychological Review*, 1901, pp. 98–99).

G. Tyrrell, Creative Evolution, (*Hibbert Journal*, Jan. 1908, pp. 435–442).

T. Whittaker, Essai sur les données immédiates de la conscience, (*Mind*, Apr. 1890, pp. 292–3).

G. *Aimel*, Individualisme et philosophie bergsonienne, (*Revue de Philos.*, June, 1908).

Balthasar, Le problème de Dieu d'après la philosophie nouvelle, (*Revue néo-scolastique*, Nov. 1907).

G. *Belot*, Une théorie nouvelle de la liberté, (*Revue philosophique*, Vol. XXX, 1890, pp. 360–392).

G. *Belot*, Un nouveau spiritualisme, *Matière et Mémoire*, (*Rev. Philos.* Vol. XLIV, 1897, pp. 183–199).

Jean Blum, La philosophie de M. Bergson et la poésie symboliste, (*Mercure de France*, Sept. 15, 1906).

C. *Bouglé*, Syndicalistes et Bergsoniens, (*Revue du Mois*, Apr. 1909, pp. 403–416).

L. *Brunschvicg*, L'Idéalisme contemporain, Paris, 1905.

G. *Cantecor*, La philosophie nouvelle et la vie de l'esprit, (*Rev. philos.* Mar. 1903, pp. 252–277).

A. *Chaumeix*, La philosophie de Bergson, (*Journal des Débats*, May 24, 1908. Reprinted in *Pragmatisme et Modernisme*, Paris, Alcan, 1909).

A. *Chaumeix*, Les critiques du rationalisme, (*Revue Hebdomadaire*, Paris, Jan. 1, 1910, pp. 1–33).

A. *Chide*, Le mobilisme moderne, Paris, Alcan, 1908. (See also *Revue philos.*, Apr. 1908, Dec. 1909.)

C. *Coignet*, Kant et Bergson, (*Revue Chrétienne*, July, 1904).

L. *Constant*, Cours de M. Bergson sur l'histoire de l'idée de temps, (*Revue de Philos.* Jan. 1904, pp. 105–111. Summary of lectures).

P. L. *Couchoud*, La métaphysique nouvelle, à propos de *Matière et Mémoire* de M. Bergson, (*Revue de Métaphysique et de Morale*, Mar. 1902, pp. 225–243).

L. *Couturat*, La théorie du temps de Bergson, (*Rev. de Mét. et de Mor.* 1896).

Léon Cristiani, Le problème de Dieu et le pragmatisme, Paris, Bloud et Cie., 1908.

F. *Le Dantec*, L'Évolution créatrice, (*Revue du Mois*, Aug. 1907 Reprinted in *Science et Conscience*, Paris, Flammarion, 1908).

L. *Dauriac*, Le Rire, (*Revue philos.* Dec. 1900, pp. 665–670).

V. *Delbos*, Matière et Mémoire, (*Rev. de Mét. et de Mor.* May 1897, pp. 353–389).

G. L. Duprat, La spatialité des faits psychiques, (*Rev. philos.*, May 1907, pp. 492–501).

G. Dwelshauvers, Raison et Intuition, Étude sur la philosophie de M. Bergson, (*La Belgique artistique et littéraire*, Nov. Dec. 1905, Apr. 1906).

G. Dwelshauvers, M. Bergson et la méthode intuitive, (*Revue du Mois*, Sept. 1907, pp. 336–350).

G. Dwelshauvers, De l'intuition dans l'acte de l'esprit, (*Rev. de Mét. et de Mor.* Jan. 1908).

A. Farges, Le problème de la contingence d'après M. Bergson, (*Revue pratique d'apologétique*, Apr. 15, 1909).

A. Farges, L'erreur fondamentale de la philosophie nouvelle, (*Revue thomiste*, May–June, 1909).

A. Farges, Théorie fondamentale de l'acte, avec la critique de la philosophie nouvelle de M. Bergson, Paris, Berche et Tralin, 1909.

Alfred Fouillée, Le mouvement idéaliste et la réaction contre la science positive, Paris, Alcan, 1896, pp. 198–206.

Fr. Garrigou-Lagrange, Le sens commun, la philosophie de l'être et les formules dogmatiques, Paris, Beauchesne, 1909.

René Gillouin, Henri Bergson, Paris, 1910. (A volume in the series *Les grands philosophes*).

A. Joussain, Romantisme et Religion, Paris, Alcan, 1910.

P. Landormy, Remarques sur la philosophie nouvelle et sur ses rapports avec l'intellectualisme, (*Rev. de Mét. et de Mor.* July, 1901).

Legendre, M. Bergson et son *Évolution créatrice*, (*Bulletin de la Semaine*, May 6, 1908).

Lenoble, L'*Évolution créatrice*, (*Revue du Clergé français*, Jan., 1908).

E. Le Roy, Science et Philosophie, (A series of articles in the *Rev. de Mét. et de Mor.* 1899 and 1900).

L. Lévy-Bruhl, L'*Essai sur les données immédiates de la conscience*, (*Rev. philos.*, Vol. 29, 1890, pp. 519–538).

G. H. Luquet, Idées générales de psychologie, Paris, Alcan.

J. Lux, Nos philosophes, M. Henri Bergson, (*Revue Bleue*, Dec. 1, 1906).

X. Moisant, La notion de multiplicité dans la philosophie de M. Bergson, (*Revue de Philos.*, June, 1902).

X. *Moisant*, Dieu dans la philosophie de M. Bergson, (*Revue de Philos.*, May, 1905).

D. *Parodi*, Le Rire, par H. Bergson, (*Rev. de Mét. et de Mor.* Mar. 1901, pp. 224–236).

T. M. *Pègues*, L'Évolution créatrice, (*Revue thomiste*, May–June, 1908, pp. 137–163).

C. *Piat*, De l'insuffisance des philosophies de l'intuition, Paris, 1908.

G. *Rageot*, L'Évolution créatrice, (*Rev. philos.*, July, 1907). Reprinted and enlarged in Les savants et la philosophie, Paris, Alcan, 1907.

F. *Rauh*, La conscience du devenir, (*Rev. de Mét. et de Mor.* Nov. 1897, pp. 659 ff. and Jan. 1898).

F. *Rauh*, Sur la position du libre arbitre, (*Rev. de Mét. et de Mor.* Nov., 1904).

P. P. *Raymond*, La philosophie de l'intuition et la philosophie du concept, (*Études françaises*, June, 1909).

E. *Seillière*, L'Allemagne et la philosophie bergsonienne, (*L'Opinion*, July 3, 1909).

G. *Sorel*, L'Évolution créatrice, (*Le Mouvement socialiste*, Oct. Dec. 1907, Jan. Mar. Apr. 1908).

T. *Steeg*, Henri Bergson : Notice biographique avec portrait, (*Revue universelle*, Jan. 1902, pp. 15–16).

J. *de Tonquébec*, La notion de la vérité dans la philosophie nouvelle, Paris, 1908.

J. *de Tonquébec*, Comment interpréter l'ordre du monde à propos du dernier ouvrage de M. Bergson, Paris, Beauchesne, 1908.

H. *Trouche*, L'Évolution créatrice, (*Revue de Philos.* Nov., 1908).

H. *Villassère*, L'Évolution créatrice, (*Bulletin critique*, pp. 392–411).

L. *Weber*, L'Évolution créatrice, (*Rev. de Mét. et de Mor.* Sept. 1907.

I. *Benrubi*, Henri Bergson, (*Die Zukunft*, June 4, 1910).

K. *Bornhausen*, Die Philosophie Henri Bergsons und ihre Bedeutung für den Religionsbegriff, (*Zeitschrift für Theologie und Kirche*, Tübingen, Jahrg. XX, Heft 1, 1910, pp. 39–77.

O. Braun, Materie und Gedächtnis, (Archiv für die gesamte
Psychologie, Vol. 15, 1909, Heft 4, pp. 13-15).

Hans Driesch, H. Bergson, der biologische Philosoph,
(Zeitschrift für den Ausbau der Entwickelungslehre, Jahrg.
II, Heft 1/2, Stuttgart, 1908).

V. Eschbach, Henri Bergson, (Kölnische Volkszeitung, Jan.
20, 1910).

Giessler, Le Rêve, (Zeitschrift für Psychologie und Physiologie der Sinnesorgane, Vol. 29, 1902, p. 231).

Giessler, L'Effort intellectuel, (Zeitsch. f. Psychol. u. Physiol.
d. Sinnesorgane, Vol. 32, 1903, pp. 128–9).

J. Goldstein, Henri Bergson und der Zeitlosigkeitsidealismus,
(Frankfurter Zeitung, May 2, 1909).

A. Gurewitsch, Die französische Metaphysik der Gegenwart
(Archiv für system. Philos. IX, pp. 463 ff.).

Heymans, Le Rire, (Zeitsch. f. Psychol. u. Physiol. d. Sinnesorgane, Vol. 25, 1901, pp. 155–6).

K. Joël, Neues Denken, (Neue Rundschau, Apr. 1910, pp.
549–558).

H. von Keyserling, Bergson, (Allgemeine Zeitung, München,
Nov. 28, 1908).

R. Kroner, Henri Bergson, (Logos, Bd. I, Heft 1, Tübingen
1910).

A Lasson, Henri Bergson, (Deutsche Literatur-Zeitung, May
28, 1910).

R. Müller-Freienfels, Materie und Gedächtnis, (Zeitsch. f. Psychol. u. Physiol. d. Sinnesorgane, May 1910, Vol. 56, Heft
1/2, pp. 126–129).

A. Pilzecker, Mémoire et reconnaissance, (Zeitschrift für
Psychologie und Physiologie der Sinnesorgane, Vol. 13,
1897, pp. 229–232).

G. Seliber, Der Pragmatismus und seine Gegner, (Archiv für
system. Philos. 1909, pp. 287–298).

A. Steenbergen, Henri Bergsons Intuitive Philosophie,
Jena, 1909.

W. Windelband, Preface to Materie und Gedächtnis, Jena,
1908, pp. I–XV.

Th. Ziehen, Matière et Mémoire, (Zeitschrift für Philosophie
und philos. Kritik, Dec. 1898, pp. 295–299).

Roberto Ardigò, Una pretesa pregiudiziale contro il positivismo, (*Rivista di Filosofia e Scienze affini*, Jan.–Feb., Mar.–Apr. 1908. Reprinted in Vol. 10 of his Collected Works).

A. Crespi, La metafisica di H. Bergson, (*Coenobium*, July–Aug. 1908).

L. Ferri, Essai sur les données immédiates de la conscience, (*Rivista Italiana di Filosofia*, Mar.–Apr. 1890, pp. 248–9).

A. Levi, Sulle ultime forme dell' indeterminismo francese, Firenze, Civelli, 1903.

A. Levi, L'Indeterminismo nella filosofia francese contemporanea, Firenze, Seeber, 1905.

F. Masci, L'idealismo indeterminista, Napoli, 1899.

E. Morselli, Un nuovo idealismo, (H. Bergson), Udine, Tosolini, 1900.

I. Petrone, Sui limiti del determinismo scientifico, Modena, 1900 ; Roma, 1903.

G. Prezzolini, Del linguaggio come causa di errore, (H. Bergson), Firenze, Spinelli, 1904.

G. Prezzolini, La filosofia di H. Bergson, (in *La Teoria Sindicalista*, Napoli, Perrella, 1909, pp. 283–335).

F. de Sarlo, Le correnti filosofiche del secolo XIX, (*Flegrea*, III, 6 ; Sept. 20, 1901, pp. 531–554).

G. Tarozzi, Della necessità nel fatto naturale ed umano, Torino, Loescher, 1896–97.

B. Varisco, La Creazione, (*Rivista filosofica*, Mar.–Apr. 1908, pp. 149–180).

C. Antoniade, Filosofia lui Henri Bergson, (*Studii filosofice*, Bucarest, 1908, Vol. II, pp. 161–192 and 259–278).

F. Garcia Calderón, Dos filosofos franceses, Bergson y Boutroux, (*El Comercio*, Lima, May 5, 1907).

E. Duprat, Estudios de Filosofia contemporanea : la Filosofia de H. Bergson, (*Cultura Española*, Madrid, 1908, pp. 185–202 and 567–584).

Silberstein, L'Evolution créatrice, (*Przeglad Filozoficzny*, 1908).

Michal Sobeski, H. Bergson, (*Kurier Warszawski*, 20 stycznia, 1910).

INDEX

Absolute, reality of space, 91 ; freedom not, 166 ; law of consciousness, 207 ; Spinoza and, 208 ; knowledge of ourselves, 235.

Abstraction, implies homogeneous medium, 97 ; breaks up elements of idea, 134 ; and diagram of process of reaching a decision, 177 f. ; and Lord Kelvin's theory of matter, 206.

Acceleration, hypothetical, of motions of universe, 116 f., 193 ff.

Achilles, and tortoise, 73 f.

Act, not divisible like object, 112 ; free acts, 165 ff. ; " possible acts," 174 ff.

Act, of mind : all unity due to, 80 f. ; neglected in empirical theory of space, 93 f. ; nature of, 95.

Addition, of sensation - differences, 64, 65 ; process of, 80, 123, 226 ; implies multiplicity of parts, 85.

Advice, relation of, to freedom, 169.

Aeolus, cave of, 20.

Aesthetic, Kant's *Transcendental*, 92, 93.

Aesthetic feelings, 11 ff. ; suggested, not caused, 17 ; stages in, 17.

Alceste, indignation of, 167.

Algebra, deals with results not processes, 119.

Analysis, already visible in mental image, 84 ; distorts feelings, 132 f. ; of a thing, not of a process, 219.

Anger, psychic element in, 29 ; and organic disturbance, 30.

Animals, ability to find their way through space, 96 ; space not so homogeneous for, 97 ; perceive duration as quality, 127 ; do not picture distinct external world, 138, 236.

Antecedents, same, and same consequents, 199, 208.

Architecture, compared with rhythm, 15.

Aristotle, distinguishes potential and actual, 121.

Arithmetic, splits up units, 84.

Art, and beauty, 14 ; object of, 14 ; and hypnotism, 14 ; the plastic arts, 15 ; suggesting, not expressing feelings, 16 ; merit of work of, 17 ; yielding only sensations, 17 ; aim and method of artist, 18.

Artificial, reconstruction of concrete phenomenon, 163.

Aspect, twofold, of terms in a series, 124, 226 ; of the self, 128 ff. ; of conscious states, 129 ff. ; 137 ff.

Association, by contiguity, 136, 164 ; self cannot be constituted by, 139, 165, 226 ; associationist determinism, 148, 155, 159 ; of ideas in interrupted conversation, 156 ; illustration from hypnotism, 157 ; illustration from deliberation, 158 ; involves defective conception of self, 159 ff., 165, 226 ; of end and movement, 160 f. ; associations of smell, 161 ; its mistakes, 161 ff. ; fits simple sensations, 164 ; cannot explain deeper states of self, 164 ; everyday acts obey laws of, 167 ff., 238.

Astronomy, measurement of time in, 107 ; prediction of celestial phenomena, 117, 192 ff., 198.

Attention, and muscular tension, 27 ; Fechner on, 27 ; Ribot on, 27 ; and psychic tension, 28 ; and formation of number, 82, 84.

Bain, on nervous energy, 21 ; on theory of space, 93 ; on conflict of motives, 159.

Beauty, feeling of, 14 ff. ; in nature and art, 14 ff.

Beliefs, adopted without reason, 135 ; compared to cell in organism, 135 ; some not properly assimilated, 136.

Blix, experiments on temperature sense, 46.

Body, movements of, as suggesting psychic state, 18 ; inclination of, in comparing pleasures, 38.

Causality, law of, 199, 201 ; as regular succession, 202 f. ; common sense and meaning of, 203 ; as prefiguring of future phenomenon in present conditions, 204 ff. ; not a necessary principle, 208 ; Spinoza on, 208 ; identity and, 209, 210 ; as necessary determination of phenomena means human freedom, 210 ; and second type of prefiguring, 211 f. ; this leads to Leibniz, 213 , this does not involve determinism, 214 ; involves two

251

conceptions of duration, 215 ; confusion of these two senses, 216 ; relation of external, as mathematical, 219 ; relation of inner, as dynamic, 219 ; Kant ascribed same meaning to, in inner and outer world, 232.

Cause, external, and intensity, 4 f., 20, 42 ff., 72 ; introduced into effect, 42, 47, 54, 68 ; external, and separation of sensations, 109, 125 ; series of associations sometimes effect rather than, 156 ff. ; in inner states no recurrence of same, 154, 199 f., 233 ; assertion that effect bound up with, 201 ; analysis of concept of, 201 ; self as free, 235.

Cell, in organism, beliefs compared to, 135.

Change, but not duration, attributed to external things, 227.

Character, freedom and, 172 f. ; and prediction of future actions, 184.

Clocks, measurement of time by, 108 f. ; perception of strokes of without expressly counting, 127.

Co-existence, number and relations of, 75 n. ; can space result from relations of, 94 ; of past and present only in consciousness, 112.

Cold, perception of, 46.

Colour, changes of hue and invariable colours, 51 white, grey and black, 53 f. ; degrees of saturation, 54 ; intensity of, 54 ; colours of spectrum, 51, 54, 57 ; changes in sensation of, 57 ; can there be equidistant tints, 58.

Compromise, see also Endosmosis : between idea of free force and necessity, 217 ; forms of perception result of, 223 ; intensity as compromise between quality and quantity, 225 ; number results from a, 226 ; idea of measurable time results from a, 228.

Consciousness, compared to invisible musician, 147 ; as epiphenomenon, 152 ; Kant separates external perception and, 222 ; succession without distinction in, 227 ; matter and form of, 234.

Conservation, of energy, see Energy ; of motion, 151 ; of vis viva, 151 ; conservative systems not the only ones possible, 152.

Continuity, of number when formed, 82 f.

Contradiction, law of non-, 89, 150, 207 ; reconciliation of apparent at deeper level, 136.

Counting, units must be identical, 76 ;

also distinct, 77 ; flock of sheep, 76 f. ; battalion of soldiers, 76 ; implies intuition of space, 77 ff. ; material objects, 85 ; conscious states, 86, 89 ; strokes of a bell, 86 ; moments of duration, 104 ; oscillations of a pendulum, 104 f. ; two sides of the process of, 123 ; strokes of a clock by qualitative effect, 127.

Crisis, freedom shown at, 170, 239.

Critique of Pure Reason, result of, 235.

Critique philosophique, article in, 75 n.

Dancer, and feeling of grace, 12.

Darwin, on rage, 29 ; on violent emotions and reflex movements, 30 ; on pain and reactions, 37.

Definition, of equality of sensation-differences, 64 ; of addition of sensation-differences, 64, 65 ; of number, 75 ; of subjective and objective, 83 ; of space, 95, 98 ; none of right and left, 97 ; of simultaneity, 110 ; of equal intervals of time, 115 ; of velocity, 117 f. ; of inertia of matter, 142 ; of freedom, leads to determinism, 220 f., 230, 239.

Delbœuf, his measurement of luminous sensation, 52, 56 ff., 67 ff. ; his underlying postulate, 60.

Deliberation, process of, 158, 171 ; wrongly pictured as oscillation in space, 183.

Depth, of æsthetic feeling, 17 f. ; of emotional states, 31.

Descartes, and conservation of motion, 151 ; his mischievous genius, 193 ; his view of matter, 207 ; Cartesian physics, 207 ; and regularity of physical world, 208.

Desire, progress of a, 8 ; conceived as a distinct thing, 159.

Determinism, two kinds of, 142 ; physical, 143 ff. ; psychological, 155 ff. ; rests on misconception of duration, 143, 173 ; and molecular theory of matter, 143 f., 147 ; of psychic states does not follow from that of cerebral states, 146 f. ; associationist, 148, 155, 159 ; and hypnotism, 157 ; self-determination, 165, 172 ; its mechanical conception of self, 171 ; could act have been different ? 173, 201, 220, 239 ; can act be predicted ? 173, 183 ff., 201, 220, 239 ; and "possible acts," 174 ; and character, 184 ff., 172 ; and astronomical prediction, 192 ff. ; and law of causality, 199 ff. ; misunderstanding of causality underlies all, 201 ff. ; of phenomena as involving human freedom, 210, 215 ff. ; not involved in second type of prefiguring, 211 f., 215 f. ; Leibniz's, 214 ; as compromise between idea of free effort and necessity, 217 ; attempt to define freedom leads to, 220, 230, 239 ; all, refuted by experience, 230 ; meaningless if duration heterogeneous, 235, 239.

Diagrams, geometrical, 176, 191.

Differentials, expressing Fechner's Law, 62, 65 ; dealing with motion, 119.

Dimension, time as fourth, 109.

Discontinuity, of number, 82 f.

Disgust, Richet's description of, 36.

Distinction, two meanings of, 75 n., 121 ; succession without, 101 ; of psychic states, leads to mechanical conception of self, 171 ; Kant's, between matter and form of consciousness, 234.

Donaldson, experiments on temperature sense, 46.

Dreams, freshness in, 8 ; charm in, 10 ; superficial psychic states removed in, 126 ; overlying images in, 136.

Duration, moments counted by means of points in space, 78 f., 87 ; differs from homogeneous time in having nothing to do with space, 91 ; empirical attempts to build up space from, 99 f., 222 ; conception of pure, 100, 104 ff., 229 ; expressed in terms of space, 101, 103, 232 ; order of succession in, 101 f. ; any homogeneity in, implies space, 104, 115 ; as interpenetration of conscious states, 104, 107, 108, 110, 128, 218, 226, 232 ff., 235 ; pure, is wholly qualitative, 106, 126 f., 229 ; not measurable, 107 ff. ; not measured by clocks, 108 f. ; as heterogeneous and with no relation to number, 109, 110, 120, 226, 229, 235, 239 ; how mistaken idea of homogeneity arises, 109 ; and motion, 110, 114, 124 ; eliminated from time by science, 115, 116, 228 ; and simultaneity, 115 f. ; and astronomical prediction, 117, 192 ff. ; cannot be represented by mathematical formulae, 119 ; as mental synthesis, 120 ; none in space, 120, 227 ; as quality, 127, 193, 197, 226 ; felt as quality in sleep, 126 ; perceived as quality by animals, 127 ; homogeneous, as symbolical representation derived from space, 128, 219, 239, 240 ; its

two forms, 128 ; constituted by deep-seated conscious states, 137, 224 ; determinism rests on inaccurate conception of, 143, 153, 173, 209, 215 f., 220, 235, 239 ; acts like a cause in realm of life, 153 ; heterogeneity of, precludes return to former state, 154, 200, 219, 232, 233, 239 ; real, and prediction, 183 ff. ; of conscious states unalterable, 196 f. ; difference between past and future, 198 ; applicable to persons, not to external things, 200, 209 f., 215, 227 ; as contained in single moment, 208 ; real, as leading to free will, 210, 215 f. ; attributed to things, 215, 228 ; two conceptions of, in causality, 215 ; separated from extensity by science, 228 f., 230 ; must similarly be separated by philosophy, 229 f. ; Kant put self outside, 233 ; possible to get back into pure, 233 ; Kant confused with space, 233 ; science cannot deal with, 234 ; if homogeneous, no freedom, 235 ; origin of feeling of, 238 n. ; no moral crisis without, 238 n. ; key to problem of free will, 238 n.

Dynamism, as system of nature, 140 ; and relation between facts and laws, 140 f. ; its view of simplicity, 141 ; inner, 172.

Eclipse, prediction of, 117, 194.

Education, not properly assimilated, 166 ; may curtail freedom, 167.

Effort, intensity of, 7, 24, 25, 26 ; muscular, 20 ff. ; apparently quantitative, 21 ; feeling of, 21 ff., 211 ; experimental investigation of, 22 ff. ; superficial, 26 ; in estimating intensity and pitch of sound, 45 f. ; in second type of prefiguring, 211 ; force and, 214 ; ideas of free, and necessity to be kept apart, 217, 218.

Eleatics, their paradoxes, 74, 240 ; arise from confusion between motion and space, 112 ff. ; Achilles and tortoise, 113 f.

Elevation, of aesthetic feeling, 17.

Emotions, violent, intensity of, 28 ff.

Empiricist, theory of space, 93 f. ; derivation of extensive from inextensive, 94, 222.

Endosmosis, see also Compromise :— between succession and externality, 109, 228 ; between mobility and space, 112 ; between free effort and necessary determination, 218.

Energy, kinetic and potential, 152 ; may be new kind of, 152.

Energy, conservation of: incompatible with freedom, 142, 144; and determination of physiological and nervous phenomena, 145; does not involve determinism of conscious states, 146 f.; is it universal? 150, 154; in the natural sciences, 150; implies return of system to former state, 152; conscious force or free will may escape law of, 154; illegitimate extension of, 155, 230.

English philosophers, on extensity and succession, 99. [152.

Epiphenomenon, consciousness as,

Equations, expressing Fechner's Law, 62; express something finished, 119; transformability of, 204.

Évellin, on space, time and motion, 114.

Experiments, and experimental observations: Wundt on paralytic, 21; Vulpian on hemiplegia, 22; Ferrier on feeling of effort, 22 f.; James on feeling of effort, 23; clenching the fist, 24; compressing the lips, 25; lifting a weight, 25, 48 f.; Féré on muscular force, 41; pin pricks, 42; on temperature sense, 46; Helmholtz on colour and intensity, 51; photometric, 52 ff.; Lehmann and Neiglick's, 52; Delbœuf's on measurement of luminous sensation, 52 ff., 56 ff.

Explanation, confused with fact, 163, 181.

Extensity, implies relation of container to contained, 3; no point of contact between extended and unextended, 70; as aspect of physical qualities, 92; Kant on, 92, 148; attempted derivation of, from the unextended, 93 f., 99 f., 222; homogeneous, as result of stripping matter of concrete qualities, 205; Descartes' view of matter as homogeneous, 207; hylozoism and qualities of matter, 213; confusion with duration raises problem of freedom, 221, 240; separated from duration by science, 228, 230.

Externality, of things in space, 99; exists outside the ego, 108, 227; endosmosis between succession and, 109, 228; of things, helps to cut up psychic life, 109, 125 f., 130, 228; animals have not same tendency to picture, 138; empirical school attempts to build up, from inner states, 222; external things subject to change but not duration, 227; external world distinct from ourselves, 236.

Fact, relation between law and, 140 f.; explanation confused with, 163, 181.

Faraday, and centres of force, 218.

Fear, Spencer on, 30; conceived as distinct state, 159.

Fechner, on attention and tension, 27; his psychophysics, 56, 60 ff.; his formulae, 61, 62; his law, 61; his logarithmic law, 62 n.; method of minimum differences, 64, 69.

Feeling, intensity of, 7, 185; deep-seated, 7 ff.; aesthetic, 11 ff.; of grace, 11 f.; of beauty, 14 f.; richness of aesthetic, 17 f.; moral, 18 f.; and physical symptoms, 20 ff.; of effort, 21 ff., 211; distorted by analysis, 132 f.; something living and developing, 133; leads to resolution, 133, 171; whole soul reflected in each, 165; change in duration of, means change in nature, 197 f.

Féré, C., on sensation and muscular force, 41.

Ferrier, on feeling of effort, 16.

Figure, see Diagram.

Flavour, changing, solidified by language, 131.

Force, alleged psychic, 20 f., 25; muscular, 21; nervous, 21; sensation of, 21; conscious states not forces, 165, 170; idea of, as indeterminate effort, 214; self as a free, 216; idea of, and necessity, 216, 217; as free spontaneity, 217; ideas of free force and necessity separated by science, 218.

"Form of Sensibility," Kant's theory of, 94; homogeneous space as, 236.

Forms, borrowed from external world in perception of self, 154, 167, 183, 217, 223; borrowed from self in perception of things, 222; of perception, result of compromise, 223; elimination of those borrowed from external world, 224; Kant's distinction between matter and, 93, 234.

Formulae, Weber's, 61; Fechner's, 62; dealing with velocity, 118.

Fouillée, on freedom as a motive, 160.

Fourth dimension, time as, 109.

Freedom, Free Will, see also Determinism: origin of problem, 74, 139, 221, 240; cause of conflict between mechanism and dynamism, 140; twofold objection to, 142; and molecular theory of matter, 143 f.; and conservation of energy, 145 ff.; strictly limited if principle of conservation universal, 149 f. ; as conscious force, exempt from law of conservation, 154; defenders of, mistakenly agree that conscious states are distinct things, 159 ; Fouillée on, 160 ; as self-expression, 165, 172 ; not absolute, but admits of degrees, 166 ; many live without realizing, 166 ; may be curtailed by education, 167 ; free acts rare, 167, 231, 240 ; free decision springs from whole or fundamental self, 167, 172, 231, 240 ; covered over by automatism, 168, 231, 237 ; sometimes resigned through indolence, 169 ; shown in times of crisis, 170, 239 ; and character, 172 ; to be sought in characteristic of the decision or act, 173, 182 f. ; Mill on, 174 ; and "possible acts," 174 ; free action compared to over-ripe fruit, 176 ; distinction of successive phases in, leads to determinism, 177 ff. ; the self infallible in affirming its, 183 ; not disproved by causality as regular succession, 202 f. ; safe-guarded by different conceptions of causality taken by themselves, 215 f. ; self as free cause, 216, 235 ; real but indefinable, 219 ff., 230, 239 f. ; why denied and defined, 229 ; Kant on, 232, 233, 235, 238 ; incomprehensible if duration homogeneous, 235 ; key to problem of, 238 n. ; follows from uniqueness of relation of psychic state to act, 239.

Fusion, see Interpenetration.
Future, see Prediction.

Ghost, time as ghost of space, 99.
Goldscheider, experiments on temperature sense, 46.
Grace, feeling of, 11 f.

Hamilton, Mill on, quoted, 159, 174.
Harmony, Leibniz on pre-established, 147, 213, 214.
Heat, sensation of, 46 f. ; mechanical theory of, 151.
Helmholtz, on effort of volition, 23 ; on colour and intensity, 51.
Hemiplegia, Vulpian on, 22.
Heterogeneity, qualitative, interpreted as extensive homogeneity, 95 ; of pure duration, 109, 110, 120, 128, 226, 229, 235, 239 ; of deep-seated psychic states, 200 ; homogeneous universe assumed behind, 205 ; Kant's distinction between homogeneity and, 234.
Homogeneity, of time, 90, 98, 107,

124, 234, 237 ; of space, 95 f., 98, 120, 236 ; is all homogeneity space ? 98 ; supposed two forms of, 98 ; none in duration, 104, 115 ; none in motion, 110, 115 ; how introduced into duration, 124 f., 128 ; connection between, and general ideas, 163 ; assumed behind heterogeneity, 205 ; Kant's distinction between heterogeneity and, 234.
Hope, why pleasurable, 9 f.
Hylozoism, ancient, 213, 214.
Hypnotism, and art, 14 ; and aesthetic feeling, 17 ; illustrating association of ideas, 157 ; non-incorporation of idea received during, 166.

Ideas, analysis of, 134 ; interpenetration of, 135 ; unreasoning adherence to, 135 ; some not incorporated, 135 ; associationism fits superficial, 136 ; reconciliation of, at deeper level, 136 ; association of, in interrupted conversation, 156 ; general, and perception of homogeneous medium, 163.
Identity, principle of, 207 ; attempt to replace causality by, 209 ; causality does not coincide with, 210.
Illusion, as to psychic states possessing magnitude, 21 ; reflective consciousness has two fundamental, 190 ; of attributing mutual externality to conscious states, 231 ; leading to difficulties about free will, 240.
Immobility, movement cannot be made from, 115 ; all that science retains of motion is, 119, 229, 234.
Impenetrability, of matter, 88 f
Inertia, of organism, and pleasure, 38 ; vis inertiae, 38 ; dynamism derives, from voluntary activity, 140 ; idea of spontaneity simpler than, 141 ; spontaneity settling down into, 220.
Instinct, perception of duration in sleep compared to, 127 ; of the intellect, 135.
Intensity, of psychic states, 1 ff., 224 f. ; of sensations, 1 ff., 7, 20, 32, 40, 42, 47, 172 f. ; alleged intensive magnitude, 2, 3 f., 71 f., 106, 225 ; no point of contact with extensive, 3, 70 ; estimated by external causes, 4 f., 20, 32 f., 42, 72 ; estimated by atomic movements, 6 ; different kinds of, 7 ; of deep-seated psychic states, 8, 26 ; of a growing desire, 8 f. ; of joy, 10

of sorrow, 11 ; of aesthetic feelings, 11 ff., 17 f., of moral feelings, pity, 18 f. ; of feeling of effort, 24 f. ; of superficial effort, 26 ; of intermediate states, 27 ; of violent emotions, 28 f., 31 ; as multiplicity of simple states, 31, 73 ; of affective sensations, 32 f., 34 f., 47, 73 ; and organic disturbance, 32 ; of pain, 35 ff. ; of disgust, 36 ; of representative sensations, 39 ff., 72 ; as quality, 42, 90, 190, 224 ; of sensation of sound, 43 f. ; of heat and cold, 46 f. ; of sensation of weight, 48 ; of sensation of light, 50 ff. ; of a colour, 54 ; two factors contributing to, 73 ; as qualitative sign of quantity, 90, 224 ; of deep-seated feeling, nothing but the feeling, 185 ; how others made to realize, 185 f. ; as compromise between quality and quantity, 225.

Interpenetration, multiplicity of, 75 *n.*, 162 ; of conscious states, 99, 100 f., 132 f., 163, 164, 231, 237 ; in pure duration, 104, 107, 108, 110, 128, 218, 235 ; of states of deep-seated self, 125, 137, 164 ; of strong feelings, 132 f. ; of ideas, 135 ; of apparently contradictory ideas at deeper level, 136 ; in process of addition, 226 ; replaced by plurality, 237.

Introspection, as leading to fundamental self, 231.

Intuition, of space necessary to idea of number, 77 ff., 84, 225 ; of homogeneous medium, perhaps peculiar to man, 95 f., 236 ; of motion and duration, 114 ; of homogeneous space as step towards social life, 138, 163, 236 ; immediate, and discursive thought, 237.

James, W. on feeling of effort, 22, 23, 24 ; on rage, 29.

Joy, feeling of, 10.

Juxtaposition, see also Interpenetration : inapplicable to inner states, 8 f. ; multiplicity of, 75 *n.*, 162 ; implies intuition of space, 77 f. ; number as a, 85, 89 ; of conscious states, 101, 232 ; in homogeneous time, 121 ; of lifeless states, replaces a feeling, 133.

Kant, theory of space, 92 f. ; Transcendental Aesthetic, 92, 93 ; distinguished matter and form of representation, 93 ; "form of sensibility," 94, 236 ; separated time and space, 222, 232 ; mistake

about time, 232 ; gave causality same meaning in inner and outer world, 232 ; clung to freedom but made it noumenal, 232, 238 ; put free self outside space and time, 233, 235 ; on "things in themselves," 233 f. ; made time and space homogeneous, 233 ; and the Practical Reason, 234 ; distinguished matter and form of consciousness, 234 ; result of Critique of Pure Reason, 235 ; raised barrier between phenomena and things in themselves, 235 ; distinguished space from matter, 236.

Kelvin, Lord, his theory of matter, 206.

Lange, on materialism and determinism, 144.

Language, unequal to psychological analysis, 9, 13, 160, 196, 237 ; foreign, sounds louder, 41 ; dominates thought, 70, 231 ; perhaps implies intuition of space, 97, 163, 236 ; uses terms borrowed from space, 122 ; favours separation of states of self, 128, 137, 139, 167, 231 ; solidifying influence of, on impressions, 129 f. ; gives fixed form to fleeting sensations, 131 f. ; description distorts the feelings, 132 ff. ; only ideas which least belong to us can be expressed by, 136, 164 ; and social life, 137, 167, 231, 236 ; same impulse to picture externality as to speak, 138 ; second self formed, whose states expressed by, 138 ; illustration of inadequacy of, 160 f. ; general ideas and intuition of space, 163 ; fixes only impersonal aspect of emotions, 164 ; psychology misled by, 165 ; how determinism aided by, 171 ; why same feeling, when repeated, called by same name, 200 ; favoured by avoiding separation of duration and extensity, 230 f.

La Rochefoucauld, on sympathy, 19.

Law, Weber's, 60 ; Fechner's, 62 ; Fechner's logarithmic, 62 *n.* ; of non-contradiction, 89, 150, 207 ; of Nature, mechanism and dynamism on, 140 f. ; relation between facts and, 140 f. ; "same antecedents, same consequents," 199, 208 ; of causality, 199 ff. ; physical phenomena obey, 202, 219 ; principle of identity as absolute, 207 ; relation of psychic state to act cannot be expressed by, 239.

Lehmann, his photometric experiments, 52.

Leibniz, on pre-established harmony, 147, 213, 214 ; and conservation of *vis viva*, 151; on qualities of matter, 213 ; on matter as monad, 213, 214 ; conception of causality as leading to, 213; and determinism, 214.

Light, sensation of, 50 ff.

Line, succession symbolized as a, 103 ; motion not a, 120 ; time not a, 181.

"Local signs," 49, 95 ; Lotze on, 93.

Lotze, theory of local signs, 93.

Magnitude, quantitative differences applicable to, 2 ff. ; alleged intensive, 2, 3 f., 71 f., 106, 225 ; two species of, 3 f. ; of growing desire, 9 ; and muscular effort, 20 f. ; of sensations, 31 ff., 72 ; intensity of pain as a, 37 ; pleasure as a, 38 ; of representative sensations, 47 ; interval between colours as, 57 f. ; interval between sensations as, 66, 68 f. ; intensity not a, 225.

Mathematics, represents results, not processes, 119, 234 ; exemplifies one type of prefiguring, 204 f.

Matter, impenetrability · of, 88 ; molecular theory of, and determinism, 143 f., 209 ; atomic theory of, still hypothetical, 145 ; has no apparent duration, 153 ; stripped of concrete qualities, 205 ; shape as quality of, 205 ; Lord Kelvin's vortex theory of, 206 ; Descartes' view of, 207 ; hylozoism and qualities of, 213 ; Leibniz and qualities of, 213 ; distinguished from form, 223, 234 ; distinguished from space, 236.

Mean gradations, method of, 56, 59, 67, 69.

Mechanics, treatment of time and duration in, 115 ; and notion of velocity, 117 ; deals with equations, 119.

Mechanism, as system of nature, 140 ; and relation between facts and laws, 140 f. ; its view of simplicity, 141 ; its influence on determinism, 148, 209 ; makes consciousness an epiphenomenon, 152 ; and Lord Kelvin's theory of matter, 207 ; Spinozistic, 209 ; and coincidence of causality with identity, 210 ; meant to explain conduct, will control it, 237.

Metaphor, see Symbolical Representation.

Method, of mean gradations, 56, 59, 67, 69 ; of minimum differences, 64 f., 69.

Mill, on Hamilton, 159 *n.*, 174 *n.* ; on distinct states of self, 159 ; on free will, 174.

Mind, act of, see Act.

Mind, articles in, quoted, 29 *n.*, 46 *n.*

Minimum differences, method of, 64 f., 69.

Mobility, and motion, 111 f. ; eliminated by science, 115, 228.

Molière, *Le Misanthrope* quoted, 167.

Monad, Leibniz on matter as, 213, 214.

Motion, see also Movement : analysis of concept of, 110 f. ; real only for conscious spectator, 111 ; as mental synthesis, 111, 120 ; mobility and, 111 ; of shooting star, 111 ; confused with space in Eleatic paradox, 113 f. ; intuition of, 114 ; not derivable from immobilities, 115 ; no homogeneous element in, 115 ; science eliminates mobility from, 115, 228, 234 ; hypothetical acceleration of cosmic, 116 f., 193 ff. ; cannot be represented by mathematical formulae, 119 f., 234 ; helps to form idea of homogeneous duration, 124 ; Descartes and conservation of, 151 ; and Lord Kelvin's theory of matter, 206.

Motives, actions explained by, 148 ; and process of deliberation, 158 ; act not determined by, 158 ; Bain on conflict of, 159 ; Fouillée on freedom as a, 160 ; choice without, shown at crisis, 170.

Movement, see also Motion : atomic, and intensity, 6 ; molecular, and sensation, 33, 34 ; automatic and free, 33, 35 ; in estimating sensation of weight, 49 f. ; measurement of velocity of, 107, 117.

Müller, Johann, nativistic theory of space, 93.

Multiplicity, inner, 73 ; of conscious states, 75 ff., 90 f. ; of juxtaposition, 75 *n.*, 162 ; of interpenetration, 75 *n.*, 162 ; implied in number, 76, 80 f. ; implied in addition. 85 ; two kinds of 85 f., 91, 121, 128, 129 ; discrete, 90, 91, 120 f., 226 ; of number and of conscious states, 91, 121 ; continuous or qualitative, 105, 121, 128, 224, 226, 229, 239 ; determinism rests on inaccurate conception of, 143, 173 ; associationism confuses the two kinds of, 162 f. ; of psychic states as constituting duration, 224 ; duration as qualitative, 226, 229.

Music, and suggestion, 15, 44 ; duration and musical rhythm, 100 ; increase of stimulus compared to musical phrase, 106 ; organization of sensations compared to melodic phrase, 111 ; strokes of clock compared to musical phrase, 127 ; consciousness compared to invisible musician, 147.

Nativist theory of space, 93.
Nature beauty in, 14 ; compared with art, 16 ; profoundly utilitarian, 33 ; view taken by mechanism and dynamism, 140 f. ; concrete phenomena of, abolished, 207 ; view of, as whimsical, 212.
Necessity, see also Determinism : mechanism cannot escape, 140 ; as *deus ex machina* in ancient hylozoism, 214 ; and idea of force, 216 ff.
Neiglick, his photometric experiments, 52
Noël, G., article on number and space, 75 *n.*
Notes, why classified as higher and lower, 45 f.
Noumenon, freedom as, 232.
Novelist, how effects produced, 133, 164, 185.
Number, natural series, 2, 80 ; definition of, 75 ; article on space and, 75 *n.* ; units of, identical, 76 ; units of, distinct, 77, 226 ; implies intuition of space, 77 ff., 83 f., 225 ; both unit and synthesis of units, 80 f. ; discontinuity of, 82 ; process of forming a, 82 f. ; why divisible at will, 83 ; subjective and objective in, 84 ; thought of as a juxtaposition, 85 ; inapplicable to multiplicity of conscious states, 87 ; and impenetrability of matter, 89 ; those in daily use have emotional equivalents, 123 ; time as a, 195, 197 ; results from a compromise, 226.

Objective, definition of, 83.
Objectivity, of things, 236.
Objects, contrasted with progress, 111, 112, 219 ; can be analysed, 112 ; help to cut up our psychic life, 124 f. ; seem to live and grow old, 130 ; tend to fix changing feelings, 130 ; in human soul processes, not, 131.
Order, of succession, implies space, 101 f.

Pain, and pity, 18 f. ; as sign of future reaction, 33 ; intensity of, 35 f. ; Darwin on, 37 ; conceived as distinct thing, 159.
Paradox, the Eleatic, 74, 112 f., 240.
Parallelism, of physical and psychical series, 146 f.

Paralysis, and feeling of effort, 21, 22.
Past, no recurrence of, 154, 200 f., 219, 232, 233, 239.
Paul, his prediction of Peter's action, 184 ff.
Pendulum, counting oscillations of, 104 f. ; what do oscillations of, measure, 107 ff ; oscillations of, help to cut up our psychic life, 109 ; spreads out undivided tension of spring, 228.
Permeation, see Interpenetration.
Peter, Paul's prediction of his action, 184 ff.
Photometric experiments, 52 ff.
Physics, and sound-vibrations, 46 ; and degrees of luminous intensity, 52 f. ; interested in external cause, 71 ; physical phenomena and law, 202 ; Cartesian, 207, 208 ; Descartes' instantaneous, 208 ; and forecasting of phenomena, 222, 230.
Pillon, F., article on number and space, 75 *n.*
Pitch, of a sound, 44 f.
Plateau, his method of measuring luminous sensations, 56.
Plato, quoted, 168 ; Platonic reminiscence, 234.
Pleasure, as sign of future reaction, 33 f. ; and bodily inclination, 38 ; keenness of, as inertia of organism, 38 ; conceived as distinct thing, 159.
Poetry, how effects produced, 15.
" Possible acts," 174 f., 239.
Postulate, Delbœuf's, 60 ; Fechner's, 60 ; fundamental, of psychophysics, 65, 70 ; underlying geometrical representation of voluntary activity, 179.
Prediction, astronomical, 117, 192 ff., 198 ; determinism and, 173, 183 ff., 220 ; real duration and, 183 ff. ; of future actions, 183 ff., 229, 239 ; probable and infallible, 183 f., and character, 184, 172 ; hypothetical case of Peter and Paul, 184 ff. ; all foreseeing as seeing, 195, 197, 198 ; of phenomena, and physics, 222, 230.
Prefiguring, of future phenomenon in present conditions, 204 ff., 210 ; two kinds of, 204 ff., 215 ; as in mathematics, 204 f. ; as having idea of possible future act, 211 f.
Pressure, sensation of, 47 f.
Process, motion as a, 111 ; conscious states not things but, 131, 196 ; misleading to substitute material symbol for, 190 ; cannot be analysed, 219.
Progress, motion as a, 111 ; not

divisible, 112 ; cannot be represented by geometrical figure, 181 ; misleading to substitute material symbol for, 190 ; psychic state as a, 198 ; from idea to act, 211.

Providence, Descartes and grace of, 208.

Psychology, descriptive, limits of, 139 ; sometimes misled by language, 165 ; deals with intervals of duration and not their extremities, 196 ; modern, and perception through subjective forms, 222.

Psychophysics, and measurement of sensations, 1, 55 ff. ; measurement of intensity of light, 52 ff. ; Delbœuf's experiments, 52, 56, 58 f., 67 f. ; method of mean gradations, 56, 59, 67, 69 ; method of minimum differences, 64 f., 69 ; Delbœuf's postulate, 60 ; Weber's Law, 60 ; all, involved in transition from stimulus to amount of sensation, 61 ; Fechner's Law, 61 f. ; postulate of, 65, 70 ; fallacy of all, 65 f., 70 ; exaggerations of, 225.

Quality, interpreted as quantity or magnitude, 9, 13, 39, 42, 43, 48 f., 51, 58, 69, 70 ; sound as a, 46 ; sensation of increase qualitative, 48 ; intensity of light as a, 50 ; variations in brightness qualitative, 54 ; psychophysics attempts to measure, 63 ; no point of contact with quantity, 70 ; sensation as a, 72, 90 ; confusion with quantity invades whole series of psychic states, 74 ; space devoid of, 95 ; qualitative multiplicity, 105, 121, 128, 224, 226, 229, 239 ; sensation of mobility qualitative, 112 ; qualitative distinctions, 121 f., 204 ; counting as a qualitative progress, 123 ; of quantity, 123 ; strokes of a clock estimated by quality of musical phrase, 127 ; time as, 129 ; deep-seated conscious states as pure, 137 f., 224 ; matter stripped of concrete, 205 ; attempt to explain apparent, of matter, 205 ; shape as, of matter, 205 ; qualities of things set up as states, 213 ; Leibniz and external, 213 ; psychic phenomena as pure, 224 ; intensity as compromise between quantity and, 225.

Quantity, see also Magnitude : as applied to inner states, 1 ff. ; alleged two kinds of, 3 ff., 72, 225 ; quality interpreted as, 9, 13, 39, 42, 43, 48 f., 51, 58, 69, 70 ; and muscular

effort, 20 f., 25 ; of cause, transferred to quality of effect, 42, 70 ; pitch and, 45, 46 ; increase of sensation as, 48 ; difference between hues of a colour as, 60 ; psychophysics makes intervals between sensations into a, 62, 65, 66, 68 f. ; no point of contact between quality and, 70 ; how quantitative relations set up between sensations, 71 ; quantitative distinctions, 121 f., 204 ; without quality, 123 ; time as, 129 ; cause of psychic phenomena as, 224 ; quality as sign of, 224 ; intensity as compromise between quality and, 225.

Rage, Darwin on, 29 ; James on, 29.

Reality, of space, 91 f., 95, 110 ; two kinds of, 97, 110 ; real duration, 110, 125 ff., 154 ; of facts for dynamism, 141 ; of laws for mechanism, 141 ; time as a, 155 ; attempt to produce, from algebraical relations, 205 ; physics treats sensations as signs of, 223.

Reason, beliefs adopted without, 135 ; decisions taken without or against, 170 ; in ancient hylozoism, 214 ; the discursive, 229, 237 ; Kant's doctrine of the Practical, 234 ; Critique of Pure, 235.

Refraction through space, self perceived by, 128, 129, 137, 167, 183, 217, 223 ; of " things in themselves," Kant's view, 233.

Renouvier, on freedom, 237 n.

Representation, see Symbolical Representation.

Resolution, how feeling leads to, 133, 171.

Revue philosophique, referred to, 52 n.

Revue scientifique, Tannery's criticism of Fechner in, 67.

Rhythm, connecting dancer and spectator, 12 ; effect in music, 14 ; in poetry, 15 ; and architecture, 15 ; Nature does not command, 16 ; succession of conscious states compared to, 100.

Ribot, on attention and movements, 27 f.

Richet, on pain, 35 f. ; on disgust, 36.

Rood, on changes of hue, 51.

Saturation, of a colour, 54.

Scale, notes of, why classified as higher and lower, 45 f.

Science, eliminates duration from time and mobility from motion, 115 ff., 228 ; and hypothetical acceleration of motions of universe,

116, 193 ff. ; attempts to do away with duration and causality, 208 f. ; separates ideas of free effort and necessary determination, 218 ; attempts to measure intensive quantity, 225 ; separates extensity and duration, 228, 230 ; main object of, 230 ; could deal with time if homogeneous, 234.

Scottish philosophers, 72.

Sculpture, ancient, 15.

Self, whole, reflected in each conscious state, 98, 165 ; recovery of the fundamental, 100, 128, 129, 231, 233, 236, 240 ; introduces distinctions derived from external objects into its own states, 109, 125, 237 ; superficial, with mutually external states, 125, 128, 136, 138, 167, 237 ; deep-seated, with interpenetrating states, 125, 128, 136, 164, 236 ; many conscious states never blend with whole mass of, 135, 166, 168 ; perceived by refraction through space, 128, 129, 137, 167, 183, 217, 223 ; the two aspects of the, 129 ff., 137, 231 ; tendency to form secondary, 138, 166 ; not an association of terms, 139, 159 ff., 164, 165, 226 ; recourse to living and concrete, necessary to solve problems of causality, freedom, etc., 139 ; activity of, cannot be compared to that of any other force, 143, 216 ; perception of, through forms borrowed from external world, 154, 217, 223 ; self-determination, 165 ; parasitic, as result of education, 166 ; free decisions spring from whole or fundamental, 167, 172, 231, 240 ; covered over with crust of clean-cut psychic states, 167 ; does not intervene in carrying out every-day acts, 168 ; uprush of deep-seated, at moment of crisis, 169 ; distinction of psychic states leads to mechanical conception of, 171 ; constantly changing and growing, 171, 175 f. ; view of, involved in geometrical representation of process of deciding, 176 f. ; infallible in affirming its immediate experiences, 183 ; as a free force, 216, 235 ; Kant put free, outside space and duration, 233 ; Kant and phenomenal, 233 ; as a free cause, 235.

Sensations, intensity of, 1 ff., 7 ff., 20 ff., 40, 42, 47, 72 f. ; art yielding only, 17 ; and external causes, 20 ff. ; peripheral, and muscular effort, 24, 26 ; peripheral, and

violent emotions, 31 ; magnitude of, 31, 32, 47, 72 ; affective and representative : affective, 32 ff., 72 f. ; and organic disturbance, 32 f. ; pleasure and pain, 33 ff. ; affective, and free movements, 33 ; representative, 39 ff., 73, 90 ; medium, 41 ; representative, measured by external causes, 42 ; of sound, 43 f. ; of heat and cold, 46 f., 64 ; of pressure and weight, 47 f. ; increase of, and sensation of increase, 48 ; as quantity or quality, 48 ; of movement, 50 ; of light, 50 ff. ; measurement of luminous, 52 ff. ; psychophysics attempts to measure, 55 ff., 62, 63, 225 ; equal and identical, 57, 62, 63, 64, 69 ; law connecting stimulus and, 60 f. ; as quantities, 62, 65, 66 ; addition of, 64 ; considered as a sum, 65, 67 ; how quantitative differences set up between, 71 f. ; as pure quality, 72 ; and space, 92, 93, 95 ; can space be built up from, 94 ; simultaneous and identical, 95 ; of motion, indivisible, 112 ; influence of language on, 131 ; not objects but processes, 131 ; altered by repetition, 131 ; physics treats, as signs of reality, 223.

Series, natural, of numbers, 2, 80 ; double aspect of each term in a, 124, 226 ; physical and psychical, 210.

" Several," use of, implies space, 122.

Shape, as quality of matter, 205.

Simplicity, different senses of, in dynamism and mechanism, 141.

Simultaneity, implies space, 95 ; measuring duration and counting, 108 f. ; as connecting link between space and duration, 110 ; definition of, 110 ; in measuring velocity, 114, 117 ; used in defining equal intervals of time, 116, 119 ; in space nothing but, 116, 206, 227 ; and astronomical prediction, 116 f., 193 ff. ; dealt with by mathematics, 119 ; attempted representation of succession by, 180, 221 ; all relations not translatable into, are scientifically unknowable, 234.

Sleep, and perception of duration, 126.

Smell, illustration from associations of, 161 f.

Social life, self with well-defined states better adapted to, 128, 137, 139, 167, 231 ; more important than our inner life, 130 ; intuition of homogeneous medium as step towards, 138, 163, 236.

Solidification, of an act, in space, 112 ; of changing feelings, promoted by language and external objects, 129 f. ; of sensations owing to language, 131 ; of ideas on surface of consciousness, 135, 166, 168 ; of conscious states, promotes social life, 231 ; of conscious states, how brought about, 237.

Sorrow, an increasing, 11.

Sound, sensations of, 43 ff. ; intensity of, 43 ff. ; pitch of, 45 ; why classified as higher and lower, 45 f.

Space, and magnitude, 2 ; introduced into perception of duration, 74 ; article on number and, 75 n. ; intuition of, implied in counting, 77 ff., 83 f., 225 ; material objects counted in, 85 f. ; conscious states not countable unless symbolically represented in, 86 f., 89, 90 ; idea of impenetrability shows interconnexion of number and, 89 ; projection of psychic states into, 90, 101, 106, 231 ; time, but not duration, as spatial, 90 f. ; reality of, 91 f., 95, 110 ; as common element in certain sensations, 92 ; Kant's theory of, 92, 93 ; nativistic and empirical theories of, 93 ; Müller's theory, 93 ; Lotze's theory, 93 ; Bain's theory, 93 ; Wundt's theory, 93 ; attempt to build up, from inextensive sensations, 93 f., 99 f., 222 ; definition of, 95, 98 ; as a homogeneous medium without quality, 95 ff., 98 ; not so homogeneous for animals, 96 ; intuition of homogeneous, peculiar to man, 97, 236 ; intuition of, necessary to counting, abstraction and speech, 97 ; is time, as homogeneous medium, reducible to, 98 f. ; time as ghost of, 99 ; duration expressed in terms of, 101, 110 ; order of succession implies, 101 f. ; symbolical representation of succession as line implies, 103 ; time as fourth dimension of, 109 ; simultaneity as connecting link between time and, 110 ; and motion, 110 ff. ; projection of act into, 112, 181 ; infinitely divisible, 113, 114 ; as homogeneous element in motion, 115 ; the only measurable element in motion, 116, 118, 119 ; nothing but simultaneities in, 116, 206, 227 ; alone homogeneous, 120 ;

no duration or succession in, 120 227 ; self perceived by refraction through, 128, 129, 137, 167, 183, 217, 223 ; intuition of homogeneous, as step towards social life, 138, 163, 236 ; connexion between perception of, and general ideas, 163 ; is time space ? 181, 190, 221 ; time confused with, in prediction, 191 ff. ; as result of stripping matter of concrete qualities, 205 ; separated from time by Kant, 222 ; must be eliminated in studying inner phenomena, 229 ; Kant confused time with, 232 ; Kant put the free self outside, 233 ; we usually live and act in, not in duration, 233 ; Kant on time and, 233 ; existence of homogeneous, assumed, 236 ; as a "form of sensibility," 236 ; intuition of, what it accomplishes, 236.

Spectrum, colours of the, 51, 54, 57.

Spencer, H., on gracefulness, 13 ; on expression of fear, 30.

Spinoza, on modes of thought and modes of extension, 147 ; on causality and apparent succession in time, 208 ; conception of causality which leads to, 208, 213 ; Spinozistic mechanism, 209.

Spontaneity, idea of, simpler than that of inertia, 141 ; force as a free, 217 ; settling down into inertia, 220.

Stimulus, law connecting sensation with, 60 ff. ; effect of slight but continuous, 106.

Subjective, definition of, 83.

Succession, attempt to derive extensity from, 99 f., 222 ; of conscious states compared to rhythm of tune, 100 ; without distinction, 101 ; order of, implies distinction and therefore space, 101 f. ; cannot be symbolized as a line without idea of space, 103 f. ; within the ego succession, without, only externality, 108, 227 ; exists only for conscious spectator, 108, 120, 227 ; endosmosis between externality and, 109, 228 ; none in space, 120, 227 ; attempt to represent by simultaneity, 180, 221 ; causality as regular, 202 f. ; no regular, in deep-seated psychic states, 203 ; attempt to transform into inherence, 209 ; apparent, of phenomena, 201, 227 ; of phenomena and conscious states, 212, 216 ; Leibniz and, 213 ; attributed to things, 228 ; idea of measurable time arises from compromise between simultaneity and, 228.

Suggestion, in art, 14 ff.; in music, 15, 44.

Symbolical Representation, necessary to counting of conscious states, 86 f., 89, 90; of a line, implies idea of space, 103; pure duration cannot be measured without, 105; of duration, derived from space, 110; of time as homogeneous medium, 124 f.; of elements of a conscious state, 163; of the self and its feelings, given by determinism, 171; of process of coming to a decision, 175 ff.; leads to determinism, 178; of time as a line, 182; cannot be substituted for dynamic process, 190; of ego, confused by Kant with ego itself, 232.

Sympathy, physical, and grace, 13; with Nature, 16; with misfortune, 19.

Tannery, J., as critic of Fechner, 67.

Taste, as changeable, 131.

" Things in themselves," Kant and, 233, 234, 238.

Time, sounds not counted in, 87, 91; as homogeneous medium in which conscious states are ranged, 90, 121; as homogeneous medium, nothing but space, 91, 98; distinct from pure duration, 91, 98; is it unbounded medium distinct from space? 98 f.; as ghost of space, 99; attempt to derive extensity from succession in, 99 f.; two possible conceptions of, 100; is it measurable? 107 f.; apparently homogeneous, 107; as dealt with by the astronomer and physicist, 107, 192 ff.; as measured by clocks, 108 f.; as fourth dimension of space, 109; concrete and abstract, 114; science eliminates duration from, 115 f.; definition of equal intervals of, 115; how it comes to be represented as homogeneous, 124 f., 237; as symbolical image of duration, 125 f.; as quality and quantity, 129; confusion of, with concrete duration, 155; is time space? 181, 190, 221; not a line, 181; confused with

space, 181 f., 191 f., 232; as a number, 195, 197; separated from space by Kant, 222, 232; idea of measurable, arises from compromise, 228; Kant's mistake about, 232; Kant on space and, 233; science could deal with, if homogeneous, 234; Kant put freedom outside, 235; heterogeneous duration replaced by homogeneous, 237.

Tortoise, and Achilles, 113 f.

Town, objects in, seem to live and grow old, 129 f.

Tradesmen, their avoidance of round numbers, 123.

Transcendental Aesthetic, Kant's theory of space in his, 92, 93.

Units, those forming a number identical, 76; also distinct, 77; space implied in counting, 79; every number both unit and synthesis of, 80; two kinds, ultimate and provisional, 80 f.; if divisible, then extended, 82; split up by arithmetic, 84; regarded by common sense as indivisible, 84.

Unity, attaching to number, 76; all, due to simple act of the mind, 80 f.; of act and of object, 81, 83; Spinoza and the divine, 208.

Universe, hypothetical acceleration of motions of, 116, 193 ff.; molecular theory of, 143; vague personality ascribed to, 213.

Velocity, measurement of, 107, 114; notion of, analysed, 117; uniform and variable, 117 f.

Vis inertiae, 38; vis viva, 151.

Vulpian, on hemiplegia, 22.

Weber, his law, 60 f.

Weight, sensation of, 25 f.; 47 ff.

Will, see also Free Will: willing for willing's sake, 157, 158.

Words, see language.

Wundt, on paralytic's sensation of force, 21; on connexions of vocal and auditory nervous filaments, 44; theory of space, 93.

Zeno, on Achilles and tortoise, 113.

Selected titles: revised December, 1966

harper 🔥 torchbooks

HUMANITIES AND SOCIAL SCIENCES

American Studies: General

CARL N. DEGLER, Ed.: Pivotal Interpretations of American History   TB/1240, TB/1241
A. S. EISENSTADT, Ed.: The Craft of American History
Vol. I TB/1255; Vol. II TB/1256
CHARLOTTE P. GILMAN: Women and Economics § TB/3073
JOHN HIGHAM, Ed.: The Reconstruction of American History △   TB/1068
JOHN F. KENNEDY: A Nation of Immigrants △   TB/1118
LEONARD W. LEVY, Ed.: American Constitutional Law
TB/1285
ARNOLD ROSE: The Negro in America   TB/3048

American Studies: Colonial

BERNARD BAILYN, Ed.: The Apologia of Robert Keayne: Self-Portrait of a Puritan Merchant   TB/1201
LAWRENCE HENRY GIPSON: The Coming of the Revolution: 1763-1775. † Illus.   TB/3007
PERRY MILLER & T. H. JOHNSON, Eds.: The Puritans: A Sourcebook   Vol. I TB/1093; Vol. II TB/1094
EDMUND S. MORGAN, Ed.: The Diary of Michael Wigglesworth, 1653-1657   TB/1228
EDMUND S. MORGAN: The Puritan Family   TB/1227
RICHARD B. MORRIS: Government and Labor in Early America   TB/1244
WALLACE NOTESTEIN: The English People on the Eve of Colonization: 1603-1630. † Illus.   TB/3006

American Studies: From the Revolution to 1860

RAY A. BILLINGTON: The Far Western Frontier: 1830-1860. † Illus.   TB/3012
W. R. BROCK: An American Crisis: Congress and Reconstruction, 1865-67 ° △   TB/1283
GEORGE DANGERFIELD: The Awakening of American Nationalism: 1815-1828. † Illus.   TB/3061
RICHARD B. MORRIS, Ed.: The Era of the American Revolution   TB/1180
A. F. TYLER: Freedom's Ferment   TB/1074

American Studies: Since the Civil War

MAX BELOFF, Ed.: The Debate on the American Revolution, 1761-1783: A Sourcebook △   TB/1225
EDMUND BURKE: On the American Revolution. † Edited by Elliot Robert Barkan   TB/3068
WHITNEY R. CROSS: The Burned-Over District: The Social and Intellectual History of Enthusiastic Religion in Western New York, 1800-1850   TB/1242
W. A. DUNNING: Reconstruction, Political and Economic: 1865-1877   TB/1073
FRANCIS GRIERSON: The Valley of Shadows   TB/1246
SIDNEY HOOK: Reason, Social Myths, and Democracy
TB/1237

WILLIAM E. LEUCHTENBURG: Franklin D. Roosevelt and the New Deal: 1932-1940. † Illus.   TB/3025
ARTHUR S. LINK: Woodrow Wilson and the Progressive Era: 1910-1917. † Illus.   TB/3023
JAMES MADISON: The Forging of American Federalism. Edited by Saul K. Padover   TB/1226
ROBERT GREEN MC CLOSKEY: American Conservatism in the Age of Enterprise: 1865-1910   TB/1137
ARTHUR MANN: Yankee Reformers in the Urban Age
TB/1247
GEORGE E. MOWRY: The Era of Theodore Roosevelt and the Birth of Modern America: 1900-1912. †   TB/3022
R. B. NYE: Midwestern Progressive Politics   TB/1202
FRANCIS S. PHILBRICK: The Rise of the West, 1754-1830. † Illus.   TB/3067
WILLIAM PRESTON, JR.: Aliens and Dissenters   TB/1287
JACOB RIIS: The Making of an American ‡   TB/3070
PHILIP SELZNICK: TVA and the Grass Roots: A Study in the Sociology of Formal Organization   TB/1230
TIMOTHY L. SMITH: Revivalism and Social Reform: American Protestantism on the Eve of the Civil War
TB/1229
IDA M. TARBELL: The History of the Standard Oil Company. Briefer Version. ‡ Edited by David M. Chalmers
TB/3071
GEORGE B. TINDALL, Ed.: A Populist Reader ‡   TB/3069
ALBION W. TOURGÉE: A Fool's Errand   TB/3074
VERNON LANE WHARTON: The Negro in Mississippi: 1865-1890   TB/1178

Anthropology

JACQUES BARZUN: Race: A Study in Superstition. Revised Edition   TB/1172
JOSEPH B. CASAGRANDE, Ed.: In the Company of Man: Portraits of Anthropological Informants.   TB/3047
DAVID LANDY: Tropical Childhood: Cultural Transmission and Learning in a Puerto Rican Village ¶ TB/1235
EDWARD BURNETT TYLOR: The Origins of Culture. Part I of "Primitive Culture." § Intro. by Paul Radin TB/33
EDWARD BURNETT TYLOR: Religion in Primitive Culture. Part II of "Primitive Culture" §   TB/34
W. LLOYD WARNER: A Black Civilization: A Study of an Australian Tribe. ¶ Illus.   TB/3056

Art and Art History

EMILE MÂLE: The Gothic Image: Religious Art in France of the Thirteenth Century. § △ 190 illus.   TB/44
ERICH NEUMANN: The Archetypal World of Henry Moore. △ 107 illus.   TB/2020
DORA & ERWIN PANOFSKY: Pandora's Box: The Changing Aspects of a Mythical Symbol   TB/2021

Business, Economics & Economic History

GILBERT BURCK & EDITORS OF FORTUNE: The Computer Age: And Its Potential for Management   TB/1179

---

† The New American Nation Series, edited by Henry Steele Commager and Richard B. Morris.
‡ American Perspectives series, edited by Bernard Wishy and William E. Leuchtenburg.
* The Rise of Modern Europe series, edited by William L. Langer.
¶ Researches in the Social, Cultural, and Behavioral Sciences, edited by Benjamin Nelson.
§ The Library of Religion and Culture, edited by Benjamin Nelson.
Σ Harper Modern Science Series, edited by James R. Newman.
° Not for sale in Canada.
△ Not for sale in the U. K.

THOMAS C. COCHRAN: The American Business System: *A Historical Perspective, 1900-1955* TB/1080
FRANK H. KNIGHT: Risk, Uncertainty and Profit TB/1215
ABBA P. LERNER: Everybody's Business TB/3051
HERBERT SIMON: The Shape of Automation TB/1245
PIERRE URI: Partnership for Progress: *A Program for Transatlantic Action* TB/3036

Historiography & Philosophy of History

JACOB BURCKHARDT: On History and Historians. △ *Intro. by H. R. Trevor-Roper* TB/1216
H. STUART HUGHES: History as Art and as Science: *Twin Vistas on the Past* TB/1207
ARNOLDO MOMIGLIANO: Studies in Historiography TB/1288
GEORGE H. NADEL, Ed.: Studies in the Philosophy of History: *Essays from History and Theory* TB/1208
KARL R. POPPER: The Open Society and Its Enemies △ Vol. I TB/1101; Vol. II TB/1102
KARL R. POPPER: The Poverty of Historicism ° △ TB/1126
G. J. RENIER: History: Its Purpose and Method △ TB/1209
W. H. WALSH: Philosophy of History △ TB/1020

History: General

L. CARRINGTON GOODRICH: A Short History of the Chinese People. △ *Illus.* TB/3015
DAN N. JACOBS & HANS H. BAERWALD: Chinese Communism: *Selected Documents* TB/3031
BERNARD LEWIS: The Arabs in History △ TB/1029
BERNARD LEWIS: Middle East and West ° △ TB/1274

History: Ancient and Medieval

HELEN CAM: England before Elizabeth △ TB/1026
NORMAN COHN: The Pursuit of the Millennium △ TB/1037
CHRISTOPHER DAWSON, Ed.: Mission to Asia △ TB/315
ADOLF ERMAN, Ed.: The Ancient Egyptians TB/1233
F. L. GANSHOF: Feudalism △ TB/1058
DENO GEANAKOPLOS: Byzantine East and Latin West △ TB/1265
DENYS HAY: Europe: Emergence of an Idea TB/1275
DENYS HAY: The Medieval Centuries ° △ TB/1192
SAMUEL NOAH KRAMER: Sumerian Mythology TB/1055
NAPHTALI LEWIS & MEYER REINHOLD, Eds.: Roman Civilization Vol. I TB/1231; Vol. II TB/1232
CHARLES PETIT-DUTAILLIS: The Feudal Monarchy in France and England ° △ TB/1165
HENRI PIRENNE: Early Democracies in the Low Countries TB/1110
STEVEN RUNCIMAN: A History of the Crusades. △ Vol. I TB/1143; Vol. II TB/1243

History: Renaissance & Reformation

JACOB BURCKHARDT: The Civilization of the Renaissance in Italy △ Vol. I TB/40; Vol. II TB/41
JOHN CALVIN & JACOPO SADOLETO: A Reformation Debate. *Edited by John C. Olin* TB/1239
G. CONSTANT: The Reformation in England △ TB/314
G. R. ELTON: Reformation Europe, 1517-1559 ° △ TB/1270
J. H. HEXTER: More's Utopia: *The Biography of an Idea. New Epilogue by the Author* TB/1195
HAJO HOLBORN: Ulrich von Hutten and the German Reformation . TB/1238
JOEL HURSTFIELD, Ed.: The Reformation Crisis △ TB/1267
ULRICH VON HUTTEN et al.: On the Eve of the Reformation. *"Letters of Obscure Men." Introduction by Hajo Holborn* TB/1124
PAUL O. KRISTELLER: Renaissance Thought: *The Classic, Scholastic, and Humanist Strains* TB/1048
ROBERT LATOUCHE: The Birth of Western Economy TB/1290
GARRETT MATTINGLY et al.: Renaissance Profiles. △ *Edited by J. H. Plumb* TB/1162
J. E. NEALE: The Age of Catherine de Medici ° △ TB/1085
ERWIN PANOFSKY: Studies in Iconology △ TB/1077
J. H. PLUMB: The Italian Renaissance △ TB/1161
A. F. POLLARD: Henry VIII ° △ TB/1249
A. F. POLLARD: Wolsey ° △ TB/1248

A. L. ROWSE: The Expansion of Elizabethan England. ° △ *Illus.* TB/1220
G. M. TREVELYAN: England in the Age of Wycliffe, 1368-1520 ° △ TB/1112
VESPASIANO: Renaissance Princes, Popes, and Prelates: *The Vespasiano Memoirs* TB/1111

History: Modern European

MAX BELOFF: The Age of Absolutism, 1660-1815 △ TB/1062
ASA BRIGGS: The Making of Modern England, 1784-1867: *The Age of Improvement* ° △ TB/1203
CRANE BRINTON: A Decade of Revolution, 1789-1799. * *Illus.* TB/3018
D. W. BROGAN: The Development of Modern France. ° △ Vol. I TB/1184; Vol. II TB/1185
J. BRONOWSKI & BRUCE MAZLISH: The Western Intellectual Tradition: *From Leonardo to Hegel* △ TB/3001
ALAN BULLOCK: Hitler, A Study in Tyranny ° △ TB/1123
E. H. CARR: German-Soviet Relations Between the Two World Wars, 1919-1939 TB/1278
E. H. CARR: International Relations Between the Two World Wars, 1919-1939 ° △ TB/1279
E. H. CARR: The Twenty Years' Crisis, 1919-1939 ° △ TB/1122
GORDON A. CRAIG: Bismarck to Adenauer TB/1171
FRANKLIN L. FORD: Robe and Sword: *The Regrouping of the French Aristocracy after Louis XIV* TB/1217
RENÉ FUELOEP-MILLER: The Mind and Face of Bolshevism TB/1188
HANS KOHN, Ed.: The Mind of Modern Russia TB/1065
WALTER LAQUEUR & GEORGE L. MOSSE, Eds.: International Fascism, 1920-1945 ° △ TB/1276
WALTER LAQUEUR & GEORGE L. MOSSE, Eds.: Left-Wing Intelligentsia Between the Two World Wars △ TB/1286
FRANK E. MANUEL: The Prophets of Paris: *Turgot, Condorcet, Saint-Simon, Fourier, and Comte* TB/1218
L. B. NAMIER: Facing East △ TB/1280
L. B. NAMIER: Personalities and Powers △ TB/1186
FRANZ NEUMANN: Behemoth TB/1289
DAVID OGG: Europe of the Ancien Régime, 1715-1783 ° △ TB/1271
PENFIELD ROBERTS: The Quest for Security, 1715-1740. * *Illus.* TB/3016
GEORGE RUDÉ: Revolutionary Europe, 1783-1815 ° △ TB/1272
LOUIS, DUC DE SAINT-SIMON: Versailles, The Court, and Louis XIV △ TB/1250
A. J. P. TAYLOR: From Napoleon to Lenin: *Historical Essays* ° △ TB/1268
A. J. P. TAYLOR: The Habsburg Monarchy, 1809-1918 ° △ TB/1187
G. M. TREVELYAN: British History in the Nineteenth Century and After: *1782-1919* △ TB/1251
H. R. TREVOR-ROPER: Historical Essays ° △ TB/1269
ELIZABETH WISKEMANN: Europe of the Dictators, 1919-1945 ° △ TB/1273

Intellectual History & History of Ideas

ERNST CASSIRER: The Individual and the Cosmos in Renaissance Philosophy. △ *Translated with an Introduction by Mario Domandi* TB/1097
FRANK E. MANUEL: The Prophets of Paris: *Turgot, Condorcet, Saint-Simon, Fourier, and Comte* TB/1218
PHILIP P. WIENER: Evolution and the Founders of Pragmatism. △ *Foreword by John Dewey* TB/1212

Literature, Poetry, The Novel & Criticism

JAMES BOSWELL: The Life of Dr. Johnson & The Journal of a Tour to the Hebrides with Samuel Johnson LL.D.: *Selections* ° △ TB/1254
RICHMOND LATTIMORE: The Poetry of Greek Tragedy △ TB/1257
J. B. LEISHMAN: The Monarch of Wit: *An Analytical and Comparative Study of the Poetry of John Donne* ° △ TB/1258

J. B. LEISHMAN: Themes and Variations in Shakespeare's
   Sonnets ○ △   TB/1259
V. DE S. PINTO: Crisis in English Poetry, 1880-1940 ○ △
                                  TB/1260
C. K. STEAD: The New Poetic: Yeats to Eliot ○ △ TB/1263
BASIL WILLEY: Nineteenth Century Studies: Coleridge to
   Matthew Arnold ○ △   TB/1261
BASIL WILLEY: More Nineteenth Century Studies: A
   Group of Honest Doubters ○ △   TB/1262
RAYMOND WILLIAMS: Culture and Society, 1780-1950 △
                                  TB/1252
RAYMOND WILLIAMS: The Long Revolution △   TB/1253

Philosophy

G. E. M. ANSCOMBE: An Introduction to Wittgenstein's
   Tractatus. ○ △ Second edition, Revised   TB/1210
HENRI BERGSON: Time and Free Will ○ △   TB/1021
FREDERICK COPLESTON: Medieval Philosophy ○ △ TB/376
F. M. CORNFORD: Principium Sapientiae   TB/1213
F. M. CORNFORD: From Religion to Philosophy § TB/20
WILFRID DESAN: The Tragic Finale: An Essay on the
   Philosophy of Jean-Paul Sartre   TB/1030
MARVIN FARBER: The Aims of Phenomenology   TB/1291
PAUL FRIEDLÄNDER: Plato: An Introduction △ TB/2017
W. K. C. GUTHRIE: The Greek Philosophers ○ △ TB/1008
F. H. HEINEMANN: Existentialism and the Modern Pre-
   dicament △   TB/28
EDMUND HUSSERL: Phenomenology and the Crisis of
   Philosophy   TB/1170
IMMANUEL KANT: The Doctrine of Virtue   TB/110
IMMANUEL KANT: Lectures on Ethics § △   TB/105
IMMANUEL KANT: Religion Within the Limits of Reason
   Alone. § Intro. by T. M. Greene & J. Silber TB/67
QUENTIN LAUER: Phenomenology   TB/1169
GABRIEL MARCEL: Being and Having △   TB/310
GEORGE A. MORGAN: What Nietzsche Means   TB/1198
MICHAEL POLANYI: Personal Knowledge △   TB/1158
WILLARD VAN ORMAN QUINE: Elementary Logic. Revised
   Edition   TB/577
WILLARD VAN ORMAN QUINE: From a Logical Point of
   View: Logico-Philosophical Essays   TB/566
BERTRAND RUSSELL et al.: The Philosophy of Bertrand
   Russell   Vol. I TB/1095; Vol. II TB/1096
L. S. STEBBING: A Modern Introduction to Logic △ TB/538
ALFRED NORTH WHITEHEAD: Process and Reality: An
   Essay in Cosmology △   TB/1033
WILHELM WINDELBAND: A History of Philosophy
          Vol. I TB/38; Vol. II TB/39
LUDWIG WITTGENSTEIN: Blue and Brown Books ○ TB/1211

Political Science & Government

KENNETH E. BOULDING: Conflict and Defense TB/3024
CRANE BRINTON: English Political Thought in the Nine-
   teenth Century   TB/1071
F. L. GANSHOF: Feudalism △   TB/1058
SIDNEY HOOK: Reason, Social Myths and Democracy △
                               TB/1237
DAN N. JACOBS, Ed.: The New Communist Manifesto &
   Related Documents. Third edition, Revised TB/1078
DAN N. JACOBS & HANS BAERWALD, Eds.: Chinese Com-
   munism: Selected Documents   TB/3031
HANS KOHN: Political Ideologies of the 20th Century
                               TB/1277
ROBERTO MICHELS: First Lectures in Political Sociology.
   Edited by Alfred de Grazia ¶ ○ △   TB/1224
BARRINGTON MOORE, JR.: Political Power and Social
   Theory: Seven Studies ¶   TB/1221
BARRINGTON MOORE, JR.: Soviet Politics—The Dilemma
   of Power ¶   TB/1222
BARRINGTON MOORE, JR.: Terror and Progress—USSR ¶
                               TB/1266
KARL R. POPPER: The Open Society and Its Enemies △
         Vol. I TB/1101; Vol. II TB/1102
PETER WOLL, Ed.: Public Administration and Policy
                               TB/1284

Psychology

ALFRED ADLER: The Individual Psychology of Alfred
   Adler △   TB/1154
ARTHUR BURTON & ROBERT E. HARRIS, Editors: Clinical
   Studies of Personality
         Vol. I TB/3075; Vol. II TB/3076
HADLEY CANTRIL: Invasion from Mars   TB/1282
SIGMUND FREUD: On Creativity and the Unconscious § △
                                 TB/45
C. G. JUNG: Symbols of Transformation △
         Vol. I: TB/2009; Vol. II TB/2010
JOHN T. MC NEILL: A History of the Cure of Souls TB/126
KARL MENNINGER: Theory of Psychoanalytic Technique
                               TB/1144
MUZAFER SHERIF: The Psychology of Social Norms
                               TB/3072

Sociology

JACQUES BARZUN: Race: A Study in Superstition TB/1172
BERNARD BERELSON, Ed.: The Behavioral Sciences Today
                               TB/1127
ALVIN W. GOULDNER: Wildcat Strike ¶   TB/1176
CLARK KERR: The Uses of the University   TB/1264
R. M. MAC IVER: Social Causation   TB/1153
ROBERT K. MERTON, LEONARD BROOM, LEONARD S. COTTRELL,
   JR., Editors: Sociology Today: Problems and Prospe-
   cts ¶   Vol. I TB/1173; Vol. II TB/1174
ARNOLD ROSE: The Negro in America   TB/3048
PHILIP SELZNICK: TVA and the Grass Roots   TB/1230
GEORG SIMMEL et al.: Essays on Sociology, Philosophy,
   and Aesthetics. ¶ Edited by Kurt H. Wolff TB/1234
HERBERT SIMON: The Shape of Automation △ TB/1245

RELIGION

Ancient & Classical

HENRI FRANKFORT: Ancient Egyptian Religion TB/77
G. RACHEL LEVY: Religious Conceptions of the Stone Age
   and their Influence upon European Thought △ TB/106
MARTIN P. NILSSON: Greek Folk Religion   TB/78
ERWIN ROHDE: Psyche △
         Vol. I TB/140; Vol. II TB/141
H. J. ROSE: Religion in Greece and Rome △   TB/55

Biblical Thought & Literature

W. F. ALBRIGHT: The Biblical Period from Abraham to
   Ezra   TB/102
C. K. BARRETT, Ed.: The New Testament Background:
   Selected Documents △   TB/86
C. H. DODD: The Authority of the Bible △   TB/43
GEORGE ADAM SMITH: Historical Geography of the Holy
   Land   TB/138

The Judaic Tradition

MARTIN BUBER: Eclipse of God △   TB/12
MARTIN BUBER: Hasidism and Modern Man   TB/839
MARTIN BUBER: Moses △   TB/837
MARTIN BUBER: The Origin and Meaning of Hasidism △
                               TB/835
MARTIN BUBER: Pointing the Way △   TB/103
MARTIN BUBER: The Prophetic Faith   TB/73
MARTIN BUBER: Two Types of Faith ○ △   TB/75
SOLOMON GRAYZEL: A History of the Contemporary Jews
                               TB/816
JOSHUA TRACHTENBERG: The Devil and the Jews: The
   Medieval Conception of the Jew and its Relation to
   Modern Anti-Semitism   JP/22

Christianity: Origins & Early Development

AUGUSTINE: An Augustine Synthesis △   TB/335
ADOLF DEISSMANN: Paul   TB/15
EDWARD GIBBON: The Triumph of Christendom in the
   Roman Empire § △ Illus.   TB/46
MAURICE GOGUEL: Jesus and the Origins of Christi-
   anity. ○ △   Vol. I: TB/65; Vol. II: TB/66

EDGAR J. GOODSPEED: A Life of Jesus   TB/1
ROBERT M. GRANT: Gnosticism and Early Christianity △
                                                         TB/136
ORIGEN: On First Principles △   TB/311
SULPICIUS SEVERUS et al.: The Western Fathers △ TB/309

Christianity: The Middle Ages and The Reformation

JOHN CALVIN & JACOPO SADOLETO: A Reformation Debate. Edited by John C. Olin   TB/1239
G. CONSTANT: The Reformation in England △   TB/314

Christianity: The Protestant Tradition

KARL BARTH: Dogmatics in Outline △   TB/56
RUDOLF BULTMANN et al.: Translating Theology into the Modern Age   TB/252
SOREN KIERKEGAARD: On Authority and Revelation TB/139
SOREN KIERKEGAARD: The Journals ° △   TB/52
SOREN KIERKEGAARD: The Present Age § △   TB/94
SOREN KIERKEGAARD: Purity of Heart △   TB/4
SOREN KIERKEGAARD: Repetition △   TB/117
SOREN KIERKEGAARD: Works of Love △   TB/122
JOHN MACQUARRIE: The Scope of Demythologizing: Bultmann and his Critics △   TB/134
JAMES M. ROBINSON et al.: The Bultmann School of Biblical Interpretation: New Directions? TB/251
F. SCHLEIERMACHER: The Christian Faith △
                   Vol. I TB/108; Vol. II TB/109
PAUL TILLICH: Dynamics of Faith △   TB/42

Christianity: The Roman and Eastern Traditions

DOM CUTHBERT BUTLER: Western Mysticism § ° △ TB/312
A. ROBERT CAPONIGRI, Ed.: Modern Catholic Thinkers △
                   Vol. I TB/306; Vol. II TB/307
G. P. FEDOTOV: The Russian Religious Mind: Kievan Christianity, the 10th to the 13th Centuries TB/370
G. P. FEDOTOV, Ed.: A Treasury of Russian Spirituality   TB/303
ÉTIENNE GILSON: The Spirit of Thomism   TB/313
DAVID KNOWLES: The English Mystical Tradition TB/302
GABRIEL MARCEL: Being and Having   TB/310
GABRIEL MARCEL: Homo Viator   TB/397
FRANCIS DE SALES: Introduction to the Devout Life TB/316
GUSTAVE WEIGEL, S. J.: Catholic Theology in Dialogue   TB/301

Oriental Religions: Far Eastern, Near Eastern

TOR ANDRAE: Mohammed § △   TB/62
EDWARD CONZE: Buddhism ° △   TB/58
ANANDA COOMARASWAMY: Buddha and the Gospel of Buddhism. △ Illus.   TB/119
H. G. CREEL: Confucius and the Chinese Way   TB/63
FRANKLIN EDGERTON, Trans. & Ed.: The Bhagavad Gita   TB/115
SWAMI NIKHILANANDA, Trans. & Ed.: The Upanishads: A One-Volume Abridgment △   TB/114

Philosophy of Religion

NICOLAS BERDYAEV: The Beginning and the End § △ TB/14
NICOLAS BERDYAEV: Christian Existentialism △   TB/130
RUDOLF BULTMANN: History and Eschatology °   TB/91
RUDOLF BULTMANN & 5 CRITICS: Kerygma and Myth △
                                                 TB/80
RUDOLF BULTMANN and KARL KUNDSIN: Form Criticism: Two Essays on New Testament Research △ TB/96
MIRCEA ELIADE: The Sacred and the Profane △   TB/81
LUDWIG FEUERBACH: The Essence of Christianity § TB/11
IMMANUEL KANT: Religion Within the Limits of Reason Alone. § Intro. by T. M. Greene & J. Silber TB/67
K. E. KIRK: The Vision of God §   TB/137
JOHN MACQUARRIE: An Existentialist Theology: A Comparison of Heidegger and Bultmann ° △ TB/125
PIERRE TEILHARD DE CHARDIN: Divine Milieu ° △ TB/384
PIERRE TEILHARD DE CHARDIN: Phenomenon of Man ° △
                                                 TB/383
PAUL TILLICH: Morality and Beyond   TB/142

NATURAL SCIENCES AND MATHEMATICS

Biological Sciences

CHARLOTTE AUERBACH: Science of Genetics Σ △   TB/568
LUDWIG VON BERTALANFFY: Modern Theories of Development: An Introduction to Theoretical Biology TB/554
LUDWIG VON BERTALANFFY: Problems of Life △   TB/521
HAROLD F. BLUM: Time's Arrow and Evolution   TB/555
JOHN TYLER BONNER: The Ideas of Biology Σ △   TB/570
R. W. GERARD: Unresting Cells. Illus.   TB/541
ADOLF PORTMANN: Animals as Social Beings ° △   TB/572
O. W. RICHARDS: The Social Insects. △ Illus.   TB/542
P. M. SHEPPARD: Natural Selection and Heredity △ TB/528
EDMUND W. SINNOTT: Cell and Psyche   TB/546
C. H. WADDINGTON: How Animals Develop. △ Illus. TB/553
C. H. WADDINGTON: The Nature of Life △   TB/580

Geography

R. E. COKER: The Great and Wide Sea: An Introduction to Oceanography and Marine Biology. Illus. TB/551
F. K. HARE: The Restless Atmosphere △   TB/560

History of Science

MARIE BOAS: The Scientific Renaissance, 1450-1630 △
                                               TB/583
A. HUNTER DUPREE: Science in the Federal Government: A History of Policies and Activities to 1940 △ TB/573
O. NEUGEBAUER: The Exact Sciences in Antiquity TB/552
STEPHEN TOULMIN & JUNE GOODFIELD: Architecture of Matter ° △   TB/584
STEPHEN TOULMIN & JUNE GOODFIELD: Discovery of Time ° △   TB/585
LANCELOT LAW WHYTE: Essay on Atomism △   TB/565

Mathematics

E. W. BETH: The Foundations of Mathematics △   TB/581
H. DAVENPORT: The Higher Arithmetic △   TB/526
H. G. FORDER: Geometry: An Introduction △   TB/548
D. E. LITTLEWOOD: Skeleton Key of Mathematics: A Simple Account of Complex Algebraic Problems △
                                               TB/525
GEORGE E. OWEN: Fundamentals of Scientific Mathematics   TB/569
WILLARD VAN ORMAN QUINE: Mathematical Logic TB/558
FREDERICK WAISMANN: Introduction to Mathematical Thinking. Foreword by Karl Menger TB/511

Philosophy of Science

R. B. BRAITHWAITE: Scientific Explanation   TB/515
J. BRONOWSKI: Science and Human Values △   TB/505
ALBERT EINSTEIN et al.: Albert Einstein: Philosopher-Scientist   Vol. I TB/502; Vol. II TB/503
WERNER HEISENBERG: Physics and Philosophy △   TB/549
JOHN MAYNARD KEYNES: A Treatise on Probability. ° △ Introduction by N. R. Hanson   TB/557
KARL R. POPPER: Logic of Scientific Discovery △ TB/576
STEPHEN TOULMIN: Foresight and Understanding △ TB/564
G. J. WHITROW: Natural Philosophy of Time ° △ TB/563

Physics and Cosmology

JOHN E. ALLEN: Aerodynamics △   TB/582
STEPHEN TOULMIN & JUNE GOODFIELD: The Fabric of the Heavens: The Development of Astronomy and Dynamics. △ Illus.   TB/579
DAVID BOHM: Causality and Chance in Modern Physics. △ Foreword by Louis de Broglie TB/536
P. W. BRIDGMAN: Nature of Thermodynamics   TB/537
C. V. DURELL: Readable Relativity △   TB/530
ARTHUR EDDINGTON: Space, Time and Gravitation TB/510
GEORGE GAMOW: Biography of Physics Σ △   TB/567
MAX JAMMER: Concepts of Force   TB/550
MAX JAMMER: Concepts of Mass   TB/571
MAX JAMMER: Concepts of Space   TB/533
G. J. WHITROW: The Structure and Evolution of the Universe: An Introduction to Cosmology △ Illus. TB/504

4

The Year with
Grandma Moses

To my grandmothers, Augusta and Minnie

W. N.-L.

ACKNOWLEDGMENTS

I have found in my writing a deep connection between my reading interests and writing projects. This book is no exception. The original idea for this project came while I was reading Jane Kallir's authoritative text, *Grandma Moses: The Artist Behind the Myth*. Kallir's work not only introduced me to many of the paintings found here, but also led me to Grandma Moses's autobiography, *My Life's History,* from which all the memoirs except Grandma Moses's Christmas reflection are taken. I am indebted as well to my agent, Jane Jordan Browne, whose patience and forbearance are quite admirable.

The Year with

Grandma Moses

W. NIKOLA-LISA

With selected writings and paintings by Grandma Moses

Henry Holt and Company

New York

Grandma Moses at Her Painting Table, 1952.

AUTHOR'S NOTE

GRANDMA MOSES WAS BORN ANNA MARY ROBERTSON in 1860 in Greenwich, New York, the third of ten children. As a girl, Anna Mary lived a typical rural life—helping with farm chores, attending a one-room schoolhouse for several months of the year, and then, at the age of twelve, leaving home to earn her living as a hired girl on a neighboring farm.

In her late twenties, Anna Mary met and married Thomas Salmon Moses, also a hired hand. Striking out on their own, they moved to Virginia, where they managed several tenant farms until they could afford to buy one of their own. They returned to upstate New York in 1905 and settled outside the town of Eagle Bridge, not far from Anna Mary's birthplace.

Mother Moses, as she was now called, was a determined, hardworking woman who understood her role as farm wife and mother. She cooked, cleaned, washed, canned, embroidered, even wall-papered. In fact, Mother Moses was an incredibly handy woman all around, not unusual for someone living in the country, where hard work, common sense, and a good bit of ingenuity went a long way.

It was in this setting that Grandma Moses, as she ultimately became known to her extended family and to the world outside, developed her artistic interests, which were apparent in her "fancy work"—her embroidered pictures and decorative sewing. But not until an amateur art collector from New York City, Louis Caldor, stumbled upon her work in a drugstore window in 1938—when Grandma Moses was in her late seventies—did her career take off.

Caldor persuaded Sidney Janis to include three of Grandma Moses's paintings in a members-only exhibition, entitled "Contemporary Unknown American Painters," at the Museum of Modern Art. But, beyond a polite thank-you note, nothing came of it. Then, a year later,

Caldor introduced Otto Kallir, an Austrian immigrant and owner of Galerie St. Etienne, to Grandma Moses's work. Kallir, interested in folk art, agreed to mount Grandma Moses's first one-woman exhibition in October 1940 in his New York City gallery.

The exhibition, entitled "What a Farm Wife Painted," attracted the attention of Gimbel's department store, which invited her to show several paintings in its annual Thanksgiving Festival. Additional exhibitions and press acclaim followed, and Grandma Moses's success began to skyrocket.

By her hundredth birthday on September 7, 1960, named "Grandma Moses Day" by Governor Nelson Rockefeller, Grandma Moses had become not only one of the most well-known and beloved artists of her time, but a true American icon as well. She died in 1961 at the age of 101.

Although I have known of Grandma Moses's work for many years, it was not until I stood at an outdoor book fair in Chicago thumbing through a visual biography of the artist that I truly began to admire her work. Two things struck me instantly: her love of nature, and her appreciation of the people and events around her. But I also realized something else: she painted one small corner of the world—upstate New York—with great detail season by season. This thought, more than anything else, gave me the idea for *The Year with Grandma Moses*.

I see this book operating on several levels. First of all, there are Grandma Moses's paintings, which can be viewed individually or as a sequence of images reflecting the seasonal cycle and its related activities. Next, paired with each painting, there are excerpts from Grandma Moses's memoirs, which reflect her experiences in a more detailed, personal way. Finally, to provide an entry point for young children, there is my read-aloud text, which tries, in as few lines as possible, to capture the "poetry" of Grandma Moses's world.

I, Anna Mary Robertson, was born
back in the green meadows and wild woods
on a farm in Washington County,
in the year of 1860, September 7th,
of Scotch Irish ancestry. . . .
Here I spent the first twelve years of my life
with mother, father and sisters and brothers.
Those were my happy days, free from care or worry,
helping mother, rocking sister's cradle, taking
sewing lessons from mother, sporting with my brothers,
making rafts to float over the mill pond,
roaming the wild woods, gathering flowers,
and building air castles.

When Grandma Moses looks out her window,
she sees a world of spotted cows,
and rolling hills,
and white picket fences.

In my childhood days, on Monday morning,
bright and early, we would get up the wash bench,
two wooden tubs, rubbing board and pounding barrel
and two pails from the cellar, that was our washing machine through
all the years. We carried the water from a spring a long ways
from the house and were thankful to have that. And a large,
snow-white wash would be floating on the wind by
eleven o'clock, if we were not lazy folks.

A world of thunderstorms,
rain-drenched fields,
and hand-washed laundry flapping in the wind.

One summer there was a little girl in the tenant house,
and we got up in the yard or in the orchard and built houses.
We would get a nice spot and pick up the largest stones and build
a room, and that would be surrounded by stones, and finally
we'd have three or four rooms. We would each have a house.
Hers would be a little different than mine. Then we
would get hold of broken dishes, and we would have a pantry
with shelves, and we would set our dishes on them.
All imagination! Then we'd get our dolls and our
sun bonnets and we'd go visiting each other.

Where hired hands plow open fields,
and children play in flowering orchards.

[We] left the Bell Farm to go farther

down the river to the dairy farm near Fort Defiance. . . .

It was 15 miles down to that farm so we baked bread, pies, cake and

meat to take with us the day before, so as to have something to eat

when we got there into an empty house. . . . [We] got up

at 3 o'clock in the morning to get our breakfast and take down

the stove and beds and pack all on two lumber wagons.

The cows, we had but two of them, were to be driven,

the pigs and chickens had been taken the day before.

I had half a barrel of flour, so I tucked a

table cloth down on it, then I packed all of

my tin ware on top of the flour, so as to fill

the barrel, tying a cloth over the barrel

to protect its contents.

Where friends and family gather
on moving day
to help a needy neighbor,

As summer advanced the work grew harder
in-doors and out. After harvest we had to have
thrashers for oats, rye and wheat, wheat principally.
There a gang of about six men would go from farm to farm,
as they were needed, with a threshing machine. Then we would
have to furnish as many more men and the neighbors would furnish
two or three wagons. . . . This summer I only had a few hours to get ready
for them, and as we were 15 miles from a store where we could get dishes,
and I did not know the neighbors, we had to make out with what we had.
On a milk pan we had baked beans, boiled ham, sliced; on another
board we had sliced bread and butter, a pan of mashed potatoes;
on six of the dinner plates we placed the berry pies, we gave
[the men] milk, buttermilk and water in a pail with a dipper.

14

or congregate in hay-filled fields
to celebrate nature's fullness.

[On] a farm the days are nearly all the same,
nothing changes but the seasons. In the early morning,
before the sun was up, I would dress and build the fire,
and put on the tea kettle for hot water, go out to the hen house,
feed and water the chickens, come in and get breakfast, calling
all hands to the table. By this time the men have finished the
milking, and the horses have been curried and fed, ready for work.
Coffee and hot cakes are all ready, now we have breakfast.
Then for five to six long hours in the field and in the house.
Then a good dinner and back to work again till sun down,
then supper and the milking; and . . . then
to bed till another day.

There's always plenty to do:
there's corn to pick,
grain to thresh,
and pumpkins to snip from the vine,

The children were always full of pranks,
always in mischief with their young friends. . . .
One day at the dinner table, after Thomas had gone out,
someone threw water, then someone else. Then the battle was on,
some were running out of doors, out to the pump and commenced to
throw it by the bucket-full. Some ran upstairs for protection, and they
threw water out of the window, nearly drowning the ones under the window.
The battle grew hotter, and they threw the water into the window till
it ran down the back stairs into the dining room. . . . It was a
rollicksome, happy house, and their father would join in
with them, he really was one of them.

just in time—
for Halloween

The very first Thanksgiving I remember
was about the year of 1864. Father was going
to Union Village to buy himself some boots, and he
was to buy me a red dress. I was to be a good girl all day,
in hopes of getting a red dress. I tried to do everything I
was told to do. But when candle-light came, father came
in from the flax mill and said he could not get his boots,
because it was Thanksgiving Day, and the stores
were closed. I was heart-broken, to think I did
not get my red dress! I could not eat my supper.
Mother said it was too bad, as I had been a
good girl that day, but they never thought
of the stores being closed.

and the first snowfall,
when we'll give thanks
for all we have.

We had a very deep snow that year,
and while it was falling, father would hitch up
the horses to the old big red sleigh and break out all of the
roads, as we lived back in the fields, probably half a mile from
the main road, and father had to keep the road open. He would
drive up to the kitchen door, and we would all climb into the sleigh
onto a lot of straw and blankets, and away we would go, out to
the main road, then on through the woods, and oh! that was
grand to drive under the hemlocks and have the snow
fall on us! Then back home and around the barn,
back to the house. Oh, those happy days!

With Christmas around the corner,
we'll have lots of fun outdoors,

Christmas morning . . . Oh! how

good things smelled. The living room and parlor

were all decorated with evergreens around the doors

and windows; everywhere was hemlock, mother's favorite

evergreen. . . . Then breakfast was ready, and while we were

eating, Lester spied a little China dog on the clock shelf. And it was

marked William Lester Robertson, so it was his. Then commenced the

hunt for more toys. We found a small shepherd dog on the reservoir, marked

Horace Greely Robertson. But so far nothing for me. Then I found another little

short-legged dog marked Arthur M. Robertson. Now as you know I

felt pretty bad. And mother said it was too bad, as I had been a

good girl, and for me to keep looking, which I did. When

the men came in for dinner, the hired man said he saw

a lady looking out of the window at him behind the

evergreens. And sure enough, there was

Little Red Riding Hood, for

Anna Mary Robertson.

24

and indoors, too—
opening presents,
playing games,
and feasting on food
we've helped prepare.

Wintertime! . . . [When] the sun came out
and melted the snow on top, and then it froze so hard,
it would almost hold up a horse. It was so cold, my brothers
could not go to school, and we played on the crust of the snow.
We would go up a field above the orchard, get on our sleighs,
and away we would go! Lester had a sleigh with cast iron runners,
Horace had an old wash bench, upside down, but very safe,
Arthur a dust pan, and I an old scoop shovel.
Oh, what fun! We would play out for hours,
and the thermometer at 25 below zero.

But we won't stay inside for long.
When the pond freezes over,
we'll go skating
until our toes tingle with cold.

The snow all went off in February, and
father tapped the maple trees, and we made a lot of
syrup and sugar. We children would have to run to the trees
in the early morning and gather up all the sap that had accumulated
during the night and then again in the afternoon and again just before dark.
Sometimes it would run much faster if it was thawing than at others. Sometimes
it would freeze up, and we would have to wait a day or two before it would start
running again. . . . The sap was boiled down two-thirds away in a large
arch kettle outdoors in the day time, then at night it was finished off
in the house on the cook stove. . . . We all had all the syrup we
wanted to eat on buck-wheat cakes in the morning and
syrup on hot biscuits for supper with butter.

Once they thaw,
we'll go out again—
to help at sugaring time.

Spring came, and I and brothers
would run in the meadows to gather flowers.
The first was the arbutus, that sometimes grows
under the snow, then Indian moccasin, and those starry ones,
we used to call pinks, they were all colors, white, purple, dark blue,
and then there are some that are striped. . . . Oh, those damp, snowy days,
early in spring, when we loved to go to the woods . . . Feeling nearer to
God's intentions, nearer to nature. Where in some respects, we are free,
where there is beauty and tranquillity, where we sometimes long
to be, quiet and undisturbed, free from the hubbub of life.

But it won't stay cold forever:
winter snows will melt,
icy ponds will thaw,
and horses will run wild
as spring comes round again.

ILLUSTRATION CREDITS

Page 4   *Grandma Moses at Her Painting Table, 1952.* Photograph by Ifor Thomas.

Page 7   *Hoosick Valley from the Window.* 1946. Oil on pressed wood. 19½" x 22". K 611. Private Collection, Courtesy Galerie St. Etienne, New York.

Page 9   *Taking in Laundry.* 1951. Oil on pressed wood. 17" x 21¾". K 967. Private Collection, Courtesy Galerie St. Etienne, New York.

Page 11   *Hoosick River, Summer.* 1952. Oil on pressed wood. 18" x 24". K 1032. Private Collection, Courtesy Galerie St. Etienne, New York.

Page 13   *Moving Day on the Farm.* 1951. Oil on pressed wood. 17" x 22". K 965. Private Collection, Courtesy Galerie St. Etienne, New York.

Page 15   *Haying Time.* 1945. Oil on pressed wood. 24" x 30". K 485. Private Collection, Courtesy Galerie St. Etienne, New York.

Page 17   *Pumpkins.* 1959. Oil on pressed wood. 16" x 24". K 1380. Private Collection, Courtesy Galerie St. Etienne, New York.

Page 19   *Halloween.* 1955. Oil on pressed wood. 18" x 24". K 1188. Private Collection, Courtesy Galerie St. Etienne, New York.

Page 21   *Catching the Thanksgiving Turkey.* 1943. Oil on pressed wood. 20" x 24". K 231.

Page 23   *Joy Ride.* 1953. Oil on pressed wood. 18" x 24". K 1079. Private Collection, Courtesy Galerie St. Etienne, New York.

Page 25   *Christmas at Home.* 1946. Oil on pressed wood. 18" x 23". K 586. Private Collection, Courtesy Galerie St. Etienne, New York.

Page 27   *December.* 1943. Oil on pressed wood. 18½" x 21¾". K 287. Private Collection, Courtesy Galerie St. Etienne, New York.

Page 29   *Sugaring Off in Maple Orchard.* Oil on canvas. 18⅛" x 24⅛". K 56. Private Collection, Courtesy Galerie St. Etienne, New York.

Page 31   *A Beautiful World.* 1948. Oil on pressed wood. 20" x 24". K 787. Private Collection, Courtesy Galerie St. Etienne, New York.

BIBLIOGRAPHY

Kallir, Jane. *Grandma Moses: The Artist Behind the Myth.* New York: Clarkson N. Potter, 1982.

——. *Grandma Moses: 25 Masterworks.* New York: Harry N. Abrams, 1997.

Kallir, Otto. *Grandma Moses: American Primitive.* New York: Dryden, 1946.

——. *Grandma Moses.* New York: Harry N. Abrams, 1973.

——, ed. *Art and Life of Grandma Moses.* Cranbury, New Jersey: A. S. Barnes and Co., 1969.

Moses, Grandma. *Christmas.* New York: Galerie St. Etienne, 1952.

——. *My Life's History.* Edited by Otto Kallir. New York: Harper & Brothers, 1952.

Henry Holt and Company, LLC
Publishers since 1866
115 West 18th Street
New York, New York 10011

Henry Holt is a registered trademark of Henry Holt and Company, LLC

Library of Congress Cataloging-in-Publication Data
Nikola-Lisa, W.
The year with Grandma Moses / W. Nikola-Lisa; with selected writings and paintings by Grandma Moses.
Summary: A collection of paintings and memoirs by the American folk artist describing the seasons and their related activities in rural upstate New York.
1. Moses, Grandma, 1860–1961—Juvenile literature. 2. Seasons in art—Juvenile literature. 3. Country life in art—Juvenile literature. 4. Painters—United States—Biography—Juvenile literature. [1. Moses, Grandma, 1860–1961. 2. Artists. 3. Seasons in art. 4. Country life in art.] I. Moses, Grandma, 1860–1961. II. Title.
ND237.M78A4 2000 759.13—dc21 99-40726

ISBN 0-8050-6243-2
First Edition—2000
Printed in the United States of America on acid-free paper. ∞

10 9 8 7 6 5 4 3 2 1